Songs Of Victory

"They that
wait upon the Lord
shall renew their strength:
they shall mount up with wings as eagles;
they shall run and not be weary;
they shall walk
and not faint."

Isaiah 40 : 31

PUBLISHED BY
THE
FAITH
MISSION

Fourth Edition 1998

Published by:
The Faith Mission
Govan House
2 Drum Street
Gilmerton
Edinburgh EH17 8QG

ISBN Words Edition (Hardback)   0 9508058 2 3

ISBN Music Edition   0 9508058 3 1

Printed In Northern Ireland

Printed by J. C. Print Ltd., Belfast.
Telephone (01232) 790420

PREFACE

Singing has always been a part of Christian worship, expressing effectively the aspirations of the soul. The depth of religious experience is revealed in the language and spirit of the songs and hymns.

Previous editions of *Songs of Victory* have made a valuable contribution to the work of Christ's Kingdom. Feeling it was time to include additional hymns and songs, The Faith Mission Council commissioned a new edition. This has been in the hands of a committee which examined numerous recommended songs and compiled this comprehensive selection incorporating some Psalms, Paraphrases, a wide variety of great and well loved hymns of the past and many songs of today which are now popular in Christian worship.

Some new tunes have been composed specifically for this edition together with new arrangements for existing tunes.

We commend this enlarged volume of *Songs of Victory* for use in church services and Christian meetings of all kinds. We believe it will have a wide appeal and dedicate the book to the glory of God.

The Publishers
Edinburgh 1998

WORSHIP

1 Dave Moody
© 1981 Glory Alleluia Music/Admin by Copycare

All hail King Jesus,
all hail Emmanuel;
King of kings,
Lord of lords, bright Morning Star,
every day You give me breath,
I'll sing Your praises
and I'll reign with You throughout eternity.

2 Dave Bilbrough
© 1977 Kingsway's Thankyou Music

Abba Father, let me be
Yours and Yours alone.
May my will for ever be
evermore Your own.
Never let my heart grow cold,
never let me go,
Abba Father, let me be
Yours and Yours alone.

3 © Kay Chance

Ah Lord God,
Thou hast made the heavens and the
earth by Thy great power.
Ah Lord God,
Thou hast made the heavens and the
earth by Thine outstretched arm.

Nothing is too difficult for Thee,
nothing is too difficult for Thee,
O great and mighty God;
great in counsel and mighty in deed,
nothing, nothing, absolutely nothing,
nothing is too difficult for Thee.

4 St Francis of Assisi (1182-1226)
tr. William Henry Draper (1855-1933)
© Chester Music, London

1 All creatures of our God and King,
lift up your voice and with us sing:
Hallelujah, hallelujah!
Thou burning sun with golden beam,
thou silver moon with softer gleam:

*O praise Him, O praise Him,
hallelujah, hallelujah, hallelujah!*

2 Thou rushing wind that art so strong,
ye clouds that sail in heaven along,
O praise Him, hallelujah!
Thou rising morn, in praise rejoice,
ye lights of evening, find a voice:

3 Thou flowing water, pure and clear,
make music for thy Lord to hear,
hallelujah, hallelujah!
Thou fire so masterful and bright,
that givest man both warmth and light:

4 And all ye men of tender heart,
forgiving others, take your part,
O sing ye, hallelujah!
Ye who long pain and sorrow bear,
praise God and on Him cast your care:

5 Let all things their Creator bless,
and worship Him in humbleness,
O praise Him, hallelujah!
Praise, praise the Father, praise the Son,
and praise the Spirit, Three-in-One:

5

Graham Kendrick © 1993 Make Way Music

1 All I once held dear, built my life upon,
all this world reveres and wants to own,
all I once thought gain I have counted
   loss;
spent and worthless now, compared to
this:

   Knowing You, Jesus, knowing You,
   there is no greater thing.
   You're my all, You're the best,
   You're my joy, my righteousness,
   and I love You, Lord.

2 Now my heart's desire is to know You
   more,
to be found in You and known as Yours,
to possess by faith what I could not
   earn,
all-surpassing gift of righteousness.

3 Oh, to know the power of Your risen
   life,
and to know You in Your sufferings,
to become like You in Your death, my
   Lord,
so with You to live and never die.

6

William Kethe (1520-94)
Psalm 100 as in Scottish Psalter

1 All people that on earth do dwell,
sing to the Lord with cheerful voice;
Him serve with mirth, His praise forth
   tell,
come ye before Him and rejoice.

2 Know that the Lord is God indeed,
without our aid He did us make:
we are His flock, He doth us feed
and for His sheep He doth us take.

3 Oh, enter then His gates with praise,
approach with joy His courts unto;
praise, laud, and bless His name always,
for it is seemly so to do.

4 For why? the Lord our God is good,
His mercy is for ever sure;
His truth at all times firmly stood
and shall from age to age endure.

7

© Unidentified

Alleluia, alleluia.
Alleluia, alleluia.
Alleluia, alleluia.
Alleluia, alleluia.

8

Andre Crouch © 1973 Bud John Songs/EMI
Christian Music Publishing/Admin. by Copycare

Bless the Lord, O my soul,
and all that is within me
bless His holy name.
He has done great things,
He has done great things,
He has done great things,
bless His holy name.
Bless the Lord, O my soul,
and all that is within me
bless His holy name.

9

Bob Fitts © 1985 Scripture in Song, a division of
Integrity Music/Adm. By Kingsway's Thankyou
Music

Father in heaven, how we love You,
we lift Your name in all the earth.
May Your kingdom be established in
   our praises
as Your people declare Your mighty works.
Blessed be the Lord God Almighty,
who was and is and is to come,
blessed be the Lord God Almighty,
who reigns for evermore.

10 Gary Sadler and Jamie Harvill © 1992 Integrity's Praise! Music/Adm. By Kingsway's Thankyou Music

Blessing and honour,
glory and power
be unto the Ancient of Days;
from every nation,
all of creation
bow before the Ancient of Days.
Every tongue in heaven and earth shall
declare Your glory,
every knee shall bow at Your throne in
worship;
You will be exalted, O God, and Your
kingdom shall not pass away,
O Ancient of Days.

Blessing and honour ...
Every tongue in heaven and earth ...

Your kingdom shall reign over all the earth,
sing unto the Ancient of Days;
for none can compare to Your matchless
worth,
sing unto the Ancient of Days.
Every tongue in heaven and earth ...

11 From Psalm 37. Phil Potter
Harper Collins Religious/Admin. by Copycare

Delight yourself in the Lord and
He'll give you the desires of your
heart;
delight yourself in the Lord and
He'll give you all you need.

1 Praise Him, thank Him, give Him love;
praise Him, thank Him, give Him love.

2 Seek Him, serve Him, give Him love;
seek Him, serve Him, give Him love.

3 Trust Him, follow Him, give Him love;
trust Him, follow Him, give Him love.

12 © Pete Sanchez Jnr Published by Gabriel Music

For Thou, O Lord,
art high above all the earth;
Thou art exalted far above all gods.
For Thou, O Lord,
art high above all the earth;
Thou art exalted far above all gods.
I exalt Thee, I exalt Thee,
I exalt Thee, O Lord;
I exalt Thee, I exalt Thee,
I exalt Thee, O Lord.

13 Henry Smith © 1978 Integrity's Hosanna! Music/ Adm. By Kingsway's Thankyou Music

Give thanks with a grateful heart,
give thanks to the Holy One;
give thanks because He's given Jesus
Christ, His Son.
Give thanks . . .

And now let the weak say "I am strong",
let the poor say, "I am rich",
because of what the Lord has done for us;
and now let the weak say "I am strong",
let the poor say, "I am rich",
because of what the Lord has done for us.
Give thanks . . .

And now . . .

14 Dale Garratt © 1972 Scripture in Song, a division of Integrity Music/Adm. By Kingsway's Thankyou Music

Hallelujah! for the Lord our God
the Almighty reigns.
Hallelujah! for the Lord our God
the Almighty reigns.
Let us rejoice and be glad and give
the glory unto Him.
Hallelujah! for the Lord our God
the Almighty reigns.

15 Carl Tuttle © 1985 Mercy/Vineyard Publishing/
Music Service/Admin. by Copycare

1 Hosanna, hosanna, hosanna in
   the highest;
   hosanna, hosanna, hosanna in
   the highest:
   Lord, we lift up Your name,
   with hearts full of praise.
   Be exalted, O Lord my God,
   hosanna, in the highest.

2 Glory, glory, glory to the King of
   kings;
   glory, glory, glory to the King of
   kings:
   Lord, we lift up Your name
   with hearts full of praise.
   Be exalted, O Lord my God,
   glory to the King of kings.

16 Leonard E Smith Jnr
© 1974 Kingsway's Thankyou Music

1 How lovely on the mountains are the
   feet of Him
   who brings good news, good news,
   proclaiming peace,
   announcing news of happiness:
   our God reigns, our God reigns!

   Our God reigns, our God reigns!
   Our God reigns, our God reigns!

2 You watchmen lift your voices
   joyfully as one,
   shout for your King, your King.
   See eye to eye the Lord restoring Zion:
   your God reigns, your God reigns!

3 Waste places of Jerusalem break forth
   with joy,
   we are redeemed, redeemed.
   The Lord has saved and comforted His
   people:
   your God reigns, your God reigns!

4 Ends of the earth, see the salvation
   of your God,
   Jesus is Lord, is Lord.
   Before the nations He has bared
   His holy arm:
   your God reigns, your God reigns!

17 Joseph Hart (1712-68)

1 How good is the God we adore!
   Our faithful, unchangeable friend:
   His love is as great as His power
   and knows neither measure nor end.

2 For Christ is the first and the last;
   His Spirit will guide us safe home:
   we'll praise Him for all that is past
   and trust Him for all that's to come.

18 Laurie Klein
© Maranatha! Music!/Admin. by Copycare

I love You, Lord,
and I lift my voice
to worship You,
O my soul rejoice.
Take joy, my King,
in what You hear,
may it be a sweet,
sweet sound in Your ear.

19 Carl Tuttle © 1985 Mercy/Vineyard Publishing/ Music Service/Admin. by Copycare

1 I give You all the honour
 and praise that's due Your name,
 for You are the King of glory,
 the Creator of all things.

> *And I worship You,*
> *I give my life to You,*
> *I fall down on my knees.*
> *Yes, I worship You,*
> *I give my life to You,*
> *I fall down on my knees.*

2 As Your Spirit moves upon me now,
 You meet my deepest need,
 and I lift my hands up to Your throne,
 Your mercy, I've received.

3 You have broken chains that bound me,
 You've set this captive free,
 I will lift my voice to praise Your name
 for all eternity.

20 Andre Kempen © 1989 Kempen Music/ Admin. by Kingsway's Thankyou Music

I lift my hands to the coming King,
to the great 'I AM', to You I sing;
for You're the One
who reigns within my heart.
And I will serve no foreign god
nor any other treasure.
You are my heart's desire,
Spirit without measure;
unto Your name I would raise my sacrifice.

21 Leona van Brethorst © 1976 Maranatha! Music/Admin. by Copycare

I will enter His gates with thanksgiving
 in my heart,
I will enter His courts with praise;
I will say this is the day that the Lord
 has made,
I will rejoice for He has made me glad.
He has made me glad, He has made
 me glad;
I will rejoice for He has made me glad.
He has made me glad, He has made
 me glad;
I will rejoice for He has made me glad.

22 Donya Brockway © His Eye Music/Multisongs/ EMI Christian Music Publishing/Admin. by Copycare

I will sing unto the Lord as long as I
 live,
I will sing praise to my God while I
 have my being,
my meditation of Him shall be sweet,
I will be glad, I will be glad in the Lord.
Bless thou the Lord, O my soul,
praise ye the Lord;
bless thou the Lord, O my soul,
praise ye the Lord;
bless thou the Lord, O my soul,
praise ye the Lord;
bless thou the Lord, O my soul,
praise ye the Lord.

23 Isaac Watts (1674-1748) Ps 146

1 I'll praise my Maker while I've breath,
 and when my voice is lost in death,
 praise shall employ my nobler powers;
 my days of praise shall ne'er be past,
 while life and thought and being last,
 or immortality endures.

2   Happy the man whose hopes rely
on Israel's God! He made the sky
and earth and seas with all their train:
His truth for ever stands secure;
He saves the oppressed, He feeds the
   poor
and none shall find His promise vain.

3   The Lord gives eyesight to the blind;
the Lord supports the fainting mind;
He sends the labouring conscience
   peace;
He helps the stranger in distress,
the widow and the fatherless
and grants the prisoner sweet release.

4   I'll praise Him while He lends me breath
and when my voice is lost in death,
praise shall employ my nobler powers;
my days of praise shall ne'er be past,
while life and thought and being last,
or immortality endures.

24   Sondra Corbett © 1983 Integrity's Hosanna!
      Music/Adm. By Kingsway's Thankyou Music

I worship You, Almighty God,
there is none like You;
I worship You, O Prince of Peace,
that is what I love to do.
I give You praise,
for You are my righteousness;
I worship You, Almighty God,
there is none like You.

25   John Barnett © 1980 Mercy/Vineyard Publishing/
      Music Services/Adm. by Copycare

Jesus, Jesus, holy and anointed One, Jesus.
Jesus, Jesus, risen and exalted One, Jesus.
Your name is like honey on my lips,
Your Spirit like water to my soul;
Your word is a lamp unto my feet -
Jesus, I love You, I love You.

Jesus, Jesus, holy and anointed One, Jesus.
Jesus, Jesus, risen and exalted One, Jesus.

26   J W MacGill
      © Harper Collins Religious/Admin. by Copycare

1   Jesus has loved me, wonderful Saviour!
Jesus has loved me, I cannot tell why,
came He to rescue sinners all worthless,
my heart He conquered, for Him I
would die.

   Glory to Jesus, wonderful Saviour!
   Glory to Jesus, the One I adore.
   Glory to Jesus, wonderful Saviour!
   Glory to Jesus, and praise evermore.

2   Jesus has saved me, wonderful Saviour!
Jesus has saved me, I cannot tell how;
all that I know is He was my ransom,
dying on Calvary with thorns on His
brow.

3   Jesus will lead me, wonderful Saviour!
Jesus will lead me, I cannot tell where;
but I will follow, through joy or sorrow,
sunshine or tempest, sweet peace or
despair.

4   Jesus will crown me, wonderful Saviour!
Jesus will crown me, I cannot tell when;
white throne of splendour hail I with
gladness,
crowned 'mid the plaudits of angels and
men.

27   Chris Bowater
      © 1988 Sovereign Lifestyle Music

Jesus shall take the highest honour,
Jesus shall take the highest praise,
let all earth join heaven in exalting
the name which is above all other names.
Let's bow the knee in humble adoration,

for at His name every knee must bow;
let every tongue confess He is Christ,
   God's only Son.
Sovereign Lord we give You glory now,
for all honour and blessing and power
belongs to You, belongs to You.
All honour and blessing and power
belongs to You, belongs to You,
Lord Jesus Christ, Son of the living God.

28 A Paget Wilkes (d. 1934)
© Japan Evangelistic Band

1 Jesus, Jesus, Jesus,
   sweetest name on earth;
   how can I, a sinner,
   come to know its worth?

2 Oh! the sinful sorrow,
   oh! the strangest shame,
   that I saw no beauty
   in that sacred name.

3 Never felt the sweetness,
   never knew the grace,
   never saw the love-pain
   in that wounded face!

4 Never found the mystery
   in that simple word,
   Jesus, Jesus, Jesus,
   Saviour, Lover, Lord.

5 Now 'tis past and over,
   gone my sin and shame,
   Jesus, Jesus did it,
   glory to His name!

6 I have seen the glory
   of His tender face,
   I have felt with wonder,
   thrills of holy grace.

7 Wonderful compassion
   reaching even me,
   bows my humbled spirit
   in captivity.

8 Jesus, Jesus, Jesus,
   loved me in my shame,
   oh! the joy and rapture
   of that sacred name.

29 Steven L Fry © 1974 Birdwing Music/BMG Songs
Inc./EMI Christian Music Publishing/Admin. by
Copycare

Lift up your heads to the coming King;
bow before Him and adore Him, sing
to His majesty: let your praises be
pure and holy, giving glory to the King
   of kings.

30 Frederick W Faber (1814-63)

1 My God, how wonderful Thou art,
   Thy majesty how bright!
   how beautiful Thy mercy-seat,
   in depths of burning light!

2 How dread are Thine eternal years,
   O everlasting Lord,
   by prostrate spirits day and night
   incessantly adored!

3 How beautiful, how beautiful,
   the sight of Thee must be,
   Thine endless wisdom, boundless power
   and awful purity!

4 O how I fear Thee, living God,
   with deepest, tenderest fears,
   and worship Thee with trembling hope
   and penitential tears!

5 Yet I may love Thee too, O Lord,
   almighty as Thou art,
   for Thou hast stooped to ask of me
   the love of my poor heart.

6 No earthly father loves like Thee;
   no mother, e'er so mild,
   bears and forbears as Thou hast done
   with me, Thy sinful child.

7 Father of Jesus, love's reward,
   what rapture will it be
   prostrate before Thy throne to lie
   and gaze and gaze on Thee!

31 Samuel Medley (1738-99)

1 Now in a song of grateful praise,
   to Thee, O Lord, my voice I'll raise,
   with all Thy saints I'll join to tell,
   my Jesus has done all things well.

   *And above the rest this note shall
      swell, this note shall swell,
      this note shall swell.
   And above the rest this note shall
      swell,
   my Jesus has done all things well.*

2 How sovereign, wonderful and free,
   has been Thy love to sinful me;
   Thou savedst me from the jaws of hell,
   my Jesus has done all things well.

3 Since e'er my soul has known His love,
   what mercies He has made me prove,
   mercies which do all praise excel,
   my Jesus has done all things well.

4 And when to that bright world I rise,
   and join the anthems of the skies,
   above the rest this note shall swell,
   my Jesus has done all things well.

   (When using the tune "Truro" omit chorus)

32 Frederick Whitfield (1829-1904)/ Jim Hill
© Ben Speer Music/Integrated Copyright Group/ Copycare

O, how I love Jesus,
O, how I love Jesus,
O, how I love Jesus,
because He first loved me.

What a day that will be when my Jesus I
   shall see,
when I look upon His face, the One who
   saved me by His grace;
when He takes me by the hand, and leads
   me through the promised land,
what a day, glorious day, that will be.

33 Psalm 103: 1-5 (Scottish Psalter)

1 O Thou my soul, bless God the Lord;
   and all that in me is
   be stirred up, His holy name
   to magnify and bless.

2 Bless, O my soul, the Lord thy God,
   and not forgetful be
   of all His gracious benefits
   He hath bestowed on thee.

3 All thine iniquities who doth
   most graciously forgive:
   who thy diseases all and pains
   doth heal, and thee relieve.

4 Who doth redeem thy life, that thou
   to death may'st not go down;
   who thee with loving-kindness doth
   and tender mercies crown:

5 Who with abundance of good things
   doth satisfy thy mouth;
   so that, e'en as the eagle's age,
   renewed is thy youth.

34 S T Francis (1834-1925)

1 O, the deep, deep love of Jesus,
   vast, unmeasured, boundless, free;
   rolling as a mighty ocean
   in its fullness over me.
   Underneath me, all around me,
   is the current of Thy love;
   leading onward, leading homeward,
   to my glorious rest above.

2 O, the deep, deep love of Jesus,
   spread His praise from shore to shore;
   how He loveth, ever loveth,
   changeth never, nevermore.
   How He watches o'er His loved ones,
   died to call them all His own;
   how for them He intercedeth,
   watches o'er them from the throne.

3 O, the deep, deep love of Jesus,
   love of every love the best
   'tis an ocean vast of blessing,
   'tis a haven sweet of rest.
   O, the deep, deep love of Jesus,
   'tis a heaven of heavens to me;
   and it lifts me up to glory,
   for it lifts me up to Thee.

35 J S B Monsell (1811-75)

1 O worship the Lord in the beauty
      of holiness,
   bow down before Him, His glory
      proclaim;
   with gold of obedience and incense
      of lowliness,
   kneel and adore Him, the Lord is His
      name.

2 Low at His feet lay thy burden of
      carefulness,
   high on His heart He will bear it for thee,
   comfort thy sorrows and answer thy
      prayerfulness,
   guiding thy steps as may best for thee
      be.

3 Fear not to enter His courts in the
      slenderness
   of the poor wealth thou wouldst
      reckon as thine:
   truth in its beauty and love in its
      tenderness,
   these are the offerings to lay on His
      shrine.

4 These, though we bring them in
      trembling and fearfulness,
   He will accept for the name that is dear;
   mornings of joy give for evenings of
      tearfulness,
   trust for our trembling, and hope for
      our fear.

5 O worship the Lord in the beauty
      of holiness,
   bow down before Him, His glory
      proclaim;
   with gold of obedience and incense
      of lowliness,
   kneel and adore Him, the Lord is
      His name.

36 Charles Wesley (1707-88)

1 O for a thousand tongues to sing
   my great Redeemer's praise!
   The glories of my God and King,
   the triumphs of His grace.

2   My gracious Master and my God,
    assist me to proclaim,
    to spread through all the earth abroad,
    the honours of Thy name.

3   Jesus, the name that charms our fears,
    that bids our sorrows cease;
    'tis music in the sinner's ears,
    'tis life, and health, and peace.

4   He breaks the power of cancelled sin,
    He sets the prisoner free;
    His blood can make the foulest clean,
    His blood availed for me.

37   Robert Grant (1779-1838)

1   Oh, worship the King,
    all glorious above!
    Oh, gratefully sing
    His power and His love;
    our Shield and Defender,
    the Ancient of Days,
    pavilioned in splendour
    and girded with praise.

2   Oh, tell of His might,
    oh, sing of His grace!
    whose robe is the light,
    whose canopy space;
    His chariots of wrath
    the deep thunder-clouds form
    and dark is His path
    on the wings of the storm.

3   Thy bountiful care
    what tongue can recite?
    It breathes in the air,
    it shines in the light;
    it streams from the hills,
    it descends to the plain
    and sweetly distils
    in the dew and the rain.

4   Frail children of dust
    and feeble as frail,
    in Thee do we trust,
    nor find Thee to fail;
    Thy mercies how tender,
    how firm to the end,
    our Maker, Defender,
    Redeemer, and Friend.

5   Oh, measureless Might,
    ineffable Love,
    while angels delight
    to hymn Thee above,
    Thy humbler creation,
    though feeble their lays,
    with true adoration
    shall sing to Thy praise.

38   Frances Jane van Alstyne (1820-1915)
       (Fanny J. Crosby)

1   Praise Him, praise Him, Jesus, our
       blessed Redeemer,
    sing, O earth, His wonderful love
       proclaim.
    Hail Him! hail Him! highest archangels
       in glory,
    strength and honour give to His holy
       name.
    Like a shepherd Jesus will guard His
       children,
    in His arms He carries them all day long.
    O ye saints that dwell on the mountain
       of Zion,
    praise Him, praise Him ever in joyful
       song.

2   Praise Him, praise Him, Jesus, our
       blessed Redeemer,
    for our sins He suffered and bled and
       died;
    He, our rock, our hope of eternal
       salvation,

hail Him! hail Him! Jesus, the Crucified.
Loving Saviour, meekly enduring
  sorrow,
crowned with thorns that cruelly pierced
  His brow;
once for us rejected, despised and
  forsaken,
Prince of Glory, ever triumphant now.

3 Praise Him, praise Him, Jesus, our
    blessed Redeemer,
  heavenly portals loud with hosannas
    ring,
  Jesus, Saviour, reigneth for ever and
    ever;
  crown Him, crown Him, Prophet and
    Priest and King!
  Death is vanquished! Tell it with joy
    ye faithful.
  Where is now thy victory boasting
    grave?
  Jesus lives! no longer thy portals are
    cheerless,
  Jesus lives, the mighty and strong to
    save.

39 John Henry Newman (1801-90)

1 Praise to the Holiest in the height,
  and in the depth be praise;
  in all His words most wonderful;
  most sure in all His ways.

2 O loving wisdom of our God,
  when all was sin and shame,
  a second Adam to the fight
  and to the rescue came.

3 O wisest love! that flesh and blood,
  which did in Adam fail,
  should strive afresh against the foe,
  should strive and should prevail.

4 O generous love! that He who smote
  in Man, for man, the foe,
  the double agony in Man,
  for man, should undergo.

5 And in the garden secretly,
  and on the cross on high,
  should teach His brethren, and inspire
  to suffer and to die.

6 Praise to the Holiest in the height,
  and in the depth be praise,
  in all His words most wonderful,
  most sure in all His ways.

40 Joachim Neander (1650-80)
      tr. Catherine Winkworth (1829-78)

1 Praise to the Lord, the Almighty, the
    King of creation;
  O my soul, praise Him, for He is thy
    health and salvation;
  all ye who hear,
  brothers and sisters, draw near,
  praise Him in glad adoration.

2 Praise to the Lord, who o'er all
    things so wondrously reigneth,
  shelters thee under His wings, yea,
    so gently sustaineth:
  hast thou not seen?
  all that is needful hath been
  granted in what He ordaineth.

3 Praise to the Lord, who doth prosper thy
    work and defend thee!
  Surely His goodness and mercy here
  daily attend thee.
  Ponder anew
  what the Almighty can do,
  who with His love doth befriend thee.

4 Praise to the Lord! O let all that is
   in me adore Him!
All that hath life and breath come
   now with praises before Him!
Let the Amen
sound from His people again:
gladly for aye we adore Him.

5 Angels, help us to adore Him;
   ye behold Him face to face;
sun and moon bow down before Him;
dwellers all in time and space.
   Praise Him! Praise Him!
   Praise Him! Praise Him!
   Praise with us the God of grace.

41   Henry Frances Lyte (1793-1847)

1 Praise, my soul, the King of heaven;
to His feet thy tribute bring;
ransomed, healed, restored, forgiven,
who like thee His praise should sing?
   Praise Him! Praise Him!
   Praise Him! Praise Him!
   Praise the everlasting King.

2 Praise Him for His grace and favour
to our fathers in distress;
praise Him, still the same for ever,
slow to chide, and swift to bless.
   Praise Him! Praise Him!
   Praise Him! Praise Him!
   Glorious in His faithfulness.

3 Father-like He tends and spares us;
well our feeble frame He knows;
in His hands He gently bears us,
rescues us from all our foes.
   Praise Him! Praise Him!
   Praise Him! Praise Him!
   Widely as His mercy flows.

4 Frail as summer flowers we flourish;
blows the wind and it is gone;
but while mortals rise and perish,
God endures unchanging on.
   Praise Him! Praise Him!
   Praise Him! Praise Him!
   Praise the high Eternal One.

42   Thomas Ken (1637-1710) (from Ps 100)

Praise God, from whom all blessings
   flow;
praise Him, all creatures here below;
praise Him above, ye heavenly host,
praise Father, Son, and Holy Ghost.

43   James Montgomery (1771 1854)

1 Stand up and bless the Lord,
ye people of His choice:
stand up and bless the Lord your God
with heart and soul and voice.

2 Though high above all praise,
above all blessing high,
who would not fear His holy Name
and laud and magnify?

3 O for the living flame
from His own altar brought,
to touch our lips, our minds inspire
and wing to heaven our thought!

4 God is our strength and song,
and His salvation ours;
then be His love in Christ proclaimed
with all our ransomed powers.

5 Stand up, and bless the Lord,
the Lord your God adore;
stand up, and bless His glorious Name
henceforth for evermore.

44 Les Garrett © 1967 Scripture in Song, a division
of Integrity Music/Adm. by Kingsway's Thankyou
Music

1 This is the day,
this is the day that the Lord has made,
that the Lord has made.
We will rejoice,
we will rejoice and be glad in it,
and be glad in it.
This is the day that the Lord has made,
we will rejoice and be glad in it.
This is the day,
this is the day that the Lord has made.

2 This is the day,
this is the day when He rose again,
when He rose again.
We will rejoice,
we will rejoice and be glad in it,
and be glad in it.
This is the day when He rose again,
we will rejoice and be glad in it.
This is the day,
this is the day when He rose again.

3 This is the day,
this is the day when the Spirit came,
when the Spirit came.
We will rejoice,
we will rejoice and be glad in it,
and be glad in it.
This is the day when the Spirit came,
we will rejoice and be glad in it.
This is the day,
this is the day when the Spirit came.

45 Frances Jan van Alstyne (1820-1915)
(Fanny J. Crosby)

1 To God be the glory, great things He
hath done,
so loved He the world that He gave
us His Son,
who yielded His life an atonement for
sin,
and opened the life gate that all may
go in.

Praise the Lord, praise the Lord,
let the earth hear His voice,
praise the Lord, praise the Lord,
let the people rejoice.
O come to the Father, through
Jesus the Son,
and give Him the glory, great
things He hath done.

2 Oh perfect redemption, the purchase of
blood,
to every believer the promise of God;
the vilest offender who truly believes
that moment from Jesus a pardon
receives.

3 Great things He hath taught us, great
things He hath done
and great our rejoicing through Jesus
the Son;
but purer and higher and greater will be
our wonder, our worship, when Jesus
we see.

46 Graham Kendrick
© 1985 Kingsway's Thankyou Music

We are here to praise You,
lift our hearts and sing;
we are here to give You
the best that we can bring.

And it is our love
rising from our hearts,
everything within us cries:
"Abba Father!"
Help us now to give You
pleasure and delight,
heart and mind and will that say:
"I love You, Lord."

47 Bruce Ballinger
© 1976 Sound III Inc./Admin. by Copycare

1 We have come into His house and
      gathered in His name to worship Him.
   We have come into His house and
      gathered in His name to worship Him.
   We have come into His house and
      gathered in His name
   to worship Christ the Lord,
   worship Him, Christ the Lord.

2 So forget about yourself and concentrate
      on Him and worship Him.
   So forget about yourself and concentrate
      on Him and worship Him.
   So forget about yourself and concentrate
      on Him and worship Christ the Lord,
   worship Him, Christ the Lord.

3 Let us lift up holy hands and magnify
      His name and worship Him.
   Let us lift up holy hands and magnify
      His name and worship Him.
   Let us lift up holy hands and magnify
      His name and worship Christ the Lord,
   worship Him, Christ the Lord.

48 Matthias Claudius (1740-1815)
tr. Jane Montgomery Campbell (1817-78)
altered © 1986 Horrobin/Leavers

1 We plough the fields and scatter
   the good seed on the land,
   but it is fed and watered
   by God's almighty hand;
   He sends the snow in winter,
   the warmth to swell the grain,
   the breezes and the sunshine
   and soft refreshing rain.

   All good gifts around us
   are sent from heaven above,
   then thank the Lord, O thank the Lord,
   for all His love.

2 He only is the Maker
   of all things near and far;
   He paints the wayside flower,
   He lights the evening star;
   the wind and waves obey Him,
   by Him the birds are fed;
   much more to us, His children,
   He gives our daily bread.

3 We thank You then, O Father,
   for all things bright and good,
   the seed-time and the harvest,
   our life, our health, our food.
   Accept the gifts we offer
   for all Your love imparts;
   we come now, Lord, to give You
   our humble, thankful hearts.

49 © Colin N Peckham

1 When the Lord shall come upon us
   and His glory we shall see,
   sense and know His power within us,
   feel His perfect liberty;
   when the Lord our love possesses
   and His love pervades the whole,
   how we easily surrender,
   oh how Jesus fills the soul.

2 When He has our every portion
   and His blood has touched the heart,
   cleansed - we gaze and gaze upon Him,
   can it be! My Lord, my God!
   How I love Him! Oh I love Him!
   How I clasp that matchless Name!
   Jesus, Jesus, Precious Jesus!
   King of kings! To me He came!

3 Oh I bend in adoration,
   Jesus Thou dost flood my soul!
   Jesus fills the very heavens,
   He the Way, the Life, the Goal.
   He the Saviour; His the glory!
   Mortals worship; angels; all!
   Jesus, Jesus only Jesus!
   While eternal ages roll.

50 David Matthews/Kerri Jones
©1978 Word's Spirit of Praise Music/Admin. by
Copycare

When I feel the touch
of Your hand upon my life,
it causes me to sing a song,
that I love You, Lord.
So from deep within
my spirit singeth unto Thee,
You are my King,
You are my God,
and I love You, Lord.

51 Ruth Dryden © 1978 Genesis Music/Admin. by
Kingsway's Thankyou Music

Within the veil I now would come,
into the holy place to look upon Thy face.
I see such beauty there, no other can
        compare,
I worship Thee, my Lord, within the veil.

52 Charles Wesley (1707-88)

1 Ye servants of God,
   your Master proclaim,
   and publish abroad
   His wonderful name:
   the name all-victorious
   of Jesus extol;
   His kingdom is glorious,
   and rules over all.

2 God ruleth on high,
   almighty to save;
   and still He is nigh,
   His presence we have;
   the great congregation
   His triumph shall sing,
   ascribing salvation
   to Jesus our King.

3 "Salvation to God
   who sits on the throne,"
   let all cry aloud
   and honour the Son:
   the praises of Jesus
   all angels proclaim,
   fall down on their faces,
   and worship the Lamb.

4 Then let us adore
   and give Him His right,
   all glory and power,
   all wisdom and might;
   all honour and blessing,
   with angels above;
   and thanks never-ceasing,
   and infinite love.

2.1 THE GODHEAD
Glory and Majesty

53 Austin Martin
© 1983 Kingsway's Thankyou Music

Almighty God, we bring You praise
for Your Son, the Word of God;
by whose power the world was made,
by whose blood we are redeemed.
Morning Star, the Father's glory,
we now worship and adore You;
in our hearts Your light has risen;
Jesus, Lord, we worship You.

54 David J Evans
© 1986 Kingsway's Thankyou Music

1   Be still,
    for the presence of the Lord,
       the Holy One, is here;
    come bow before Him now
    with reverence and fear:
    in Him no sin is found -
    we stand on holy ground.
    Be still,
    for the presence of the Lord,
       the Holy One, is here.

2   Be still,
    for the glory of the Lord
       is shining all around;
    He burns with holy fire,
    with splendour He is crowned:
    how awesome is the sight:
    our radiant King of Light!
    Be still,
    for the glory of the Lord
       is shining all around.

3   Be still,
    for the power of the Lord
       is moving in this place:
    He comes to cleanse and heal,
    to minister His grace -
    no work too hard for Him.
    In faith receive from Him.
    Be still,
    for the power of the Lord
       is moving in this place.

55 Dave Fellingham
© 1983 Kingsway's Thankyou Music

Eternal God, we come to You,
we come before Your throne;
we enter by a new and living way,
with confidence we come.
We declare Your faithfulness,
Your promises are true;
we will now draw near to worship You.

Men
O holy God, we come to You,
O holy God, we see Your faithfulness and
    love,
Your mighty power, Your majesty,
are now revealed to us in Jesus who has
    died,
Jesus who was raised,
Jesus now exalted on high.

Women
O holy God, full of justice,
wisdom and righteousness,
faithfulness and love;
Your mighty power and Your majesty
are now revealed to us
in Jesus who has died for our sin,
Jesus who was raised from the dead,
Jesus now exalted on high.

THE GODHEAD

56 © 1979 Peter West Adm. by Integrity's Hosanna!
Music/Adm. By Kingsway's Thankyou Music

Ascribe greatness to our God the rock,
His work is perfect and all His ways are
just.
Ascribe greatness to our God the rock,
His work is perfect and all His ways are
just.
A God of faithfulness and without injustice;
good and upright is He.
A God of faithfulness and without injustice;
good and upright is He.

57 Psalm 46, verses 1-5 (Scottish Psalter)

1 God is our refuge and our strength,
in straits a present aid;
therefore, although the earth remove,
we will not be afraid.

2 Though hills amidst the seas be cast;
though waters roaring make,
and troubled be; yea, though the hills
by swelling seas do shake.

3 A river is, whose streams make glad
the city of our God,
the holy place, wherein the Lord
most high hath His abode.

4 God in the midst of her doth dwell;
nothing shall her remove:
God unto her an helper will,
and that right early, prove.

5 *To Father, Son, and Holy Ghost,*
the God whom we adore,
be glory, as it was, and is,
and shall be evermore.

58 From Psalm 46
©Richard Bewes/Jubilate Hymns

1 God is our strength and refuge,
our present help in trouble;
and we therefore will not fear,
though the earth should change!
Though mountains shake and
tremble,
though swirling floods are raging,
God the Lord of hosts is with us
evermore!

2 There is a flowing river, within God's
holy city;
God is in the midst of her, she shall
not be moved!
God's help is swiftly given,
thrones vanish at His presence.
God the Lord of hosts is with us
evermore!

3 Come, see the works of our Maker,
learn of His deeds all-powerful;
wars will cease across the world
when He shatters the spear!
Be still and know your Creator,
uplift Him in the nations.
God the Lord of hosts is with us
evermore!

59 Dave Fellingham
© 1982 Kingsway's Thankyou Music

God of glory, we exalt Your name,
You who reign in majesty;
we lift our hearts to You
and we will worship,
praise, and magnify
Your holy name.

In power resplendent
You reign in glory;
eternal King,
You reign for ever:
Your word is mighty,
releasing captives,
Your love is gracious:
You are my God.

60 Thomas O Chisholm (d.1960)
© Hope Publishing/Admin. by Copycare

1   Great is Thy faithfulness, O God my
        Father,
    there is no shadow of turning with Thee;
    Thou changest not, Thy compassions
        they fail not,
    as Thou hast been Thou for ever wilt be.

        Great is Thy faithfulness,
        great is Thy faithfulness;
        morning by morning
        new mercies I see.
        All I have needed
        Thy hand hath provided,
        great is Thy faithfulness,
        Lord, unto me!

2   Summer and winter, and spring-time
        and harvest,
    sun, moon and stars in their courses
        above,
    join with all nature in manifold witness
    to Thy great faithfulness, mercy and
        love.

3   Pardon for sin, and a peace that endureth,
    Thine own dear presence to cheer
        and to guide;
    strength for today and bright hope for
        tomorrow,
    blessings all mine, with ten thousand
        beside!

61 Twila Paris © 1985 Straightway/Mountain Spring/
EMI Christian Music Publishing/Admin. by
Copycare

He is exalted,
the King is exalted on high;
I will praise Him.
He is exalted,
for ever exalted
and I will praise His name!

He is the Lord;
for ever His truth shall reign.
Heaven and earth
rejoice in His holy name.
He is exalted,
the King is exalted on high.

62 Psalm 72 verses 17-19 (Scottish Psalter)

1   His name for ever shall endure;
    last like the sun it shall:
    men shall be blessed in Him, and
        blessed
    all nations shall Him call.

2   Now blessed be the Lord our God,
    the God of Israel,
    for He alone doth wondrous works,
    in glory that excel.

3   And blessed be His glorious name
    to all eternity:
    the whole earth let His glory fill.
    Amen, so let it be.

63 Oliver Wendell Holmes (1809-94)

1   Lord of all being, throned afar,
    Thy glory flames from sun and star;
    centre and soul of every sphere,
    yet to each loving heart how near.

2 Sun of our life, Thy quickening ray
   sheds on our path the glow of day;
   Star of our hope, Thy softened light
   cheers the long watches of the night.

3 Our midnight is Thy smile withdrawn,
   our noontide is Thy gracious dawn,
   our rainbow arch Thy mercy's sign;
   all, save the clouds of sin, are Thine.

4 Lord of all life, below, above,
   whose light is truth, whose warmth is
     love,
   before Thy ever-blazing throne
   we ask no lustre of our own.

5 Grant us Thy truth to make us free,
   and kindling hearts that burn for Thee,
   till all Thy living altars claim
   one holy light, one heavenly flame.

64 (From Isaiah 6) John Chisum & Don Moen
© 1994 Integrity's Hosanna! Music/Adm. by
Kingsway's Thankyou Music

I see the Lord,
I see the Lord exalted high upon the
   worship of the people of the earth;
I see the Lord,
I see the Lord, my eyes have seen the
   King,
the Lamb upon the throne who reigns for
   evermore.

The train of His robe fills the temple,
a cloud of heavenly worshippers
   surrounding His throne;
we join with them now crying,
"Holy, holy is the Lamb, the Lamb
   alone".

I see the Lord,
I see the Lord exalted high upon the
   worship of the people of the earth;
I see the Lord,
I see the Lord, my eyes have seen the King,
the Lamb upon the throne who reigns for
   evermore.

65 Brent Chambers © 1977 Scripture in Song, a
division of Integrity Music/Adm. by Kingsway's
Thankyou Music

I will give thanks to Thee,
O Lord, among the peoples,
I will sing praises to Thee among the
   nations.
For Thy steadfast love is great,
is great to the heavens,
and Thy faithfulness, Thy faithfulness, to
   the clouds.
Be exalted, O God, above the heavens,
let Thy glory be over all the earth!
Be exalted, O God, above the heavens,
let Thy glory, let Thy glory, let Thy glory
   be over all the earth!

66 Walter Chalmers Smith (1824-1908)

1 Immortal, invisible, God only wise,
   in light inaccessible hid from our eyes,
   most blessed, most glorious, the
     Ancient of Days,
   almighty, victorious, Thy great name
     we praise.

2 Unresting, unhasting and silent as light,
   nor wanting, nor wasting, Thou rulest
     in might;
   Thy justice like mountains high soaring
     above
   Thy clouds, which are fountains of
     goodness and love.

3   To all, life Thou givest, to both great
     and small;
    in all life Thou livest, the true life of all;
    we blossom and flourish as leaves on
     the tree,
    and wither and perish, but nought
     changeth Thee.

4   Great Father of glory, pure Father of
     light,
    Thine angels adore Thee, all veiling
     their sight;
    all laud we would render; O help us
     to see
    'tis only the splendour of light hideth
     Thee.

5   Immortal, invisible, God only wise,
    in light inaccessible hid from our eyes,
    most blessed, most glorious, the Ancient
     of Days,
    almighty, victorious, Thy great name
     we praise.

67   Graham Kendrick
       © 1986 Kingsway's Thankyou Music

1   Meekness and majesty,
    manhood and deity,
    in perfect harmony,
    the man who is God:
    Lord of eternity
    dwells in humanity,
    kneels in humility
    and washes our feet.

    Oh, what a mystery,
    meekness and majesty:
    bow down and worship,
    for this is your God,
    this is your God!

2   Father's pure radiance,
    perfect in innocence,
    yet learns obedience
    to death on a cross:
    suffering to give us life,
    conquering through sacrifice;
    and, as they crucify,
    prays "Father, forgive."

3   Wisdom unsearchable,
    God the invisible,
    love indestructable
    in frailty appears.
    Lord of infinity,
    stooping so tenderly,
    lifts our humanity
    to the heights of His throne.

68   Martin Rinkart (1586-1649)
       tr. Catherine Winkworth (1829-78)

1   Now thank we all our God,
    with hearts, and hands, and voices;
    who wondrous things hath done,
    in whom His world rejoices;
    Who, from our mothers' arms,
    hath blessed us on our way
    with countless gifts of love,
    and still is ours today.

2   O may this bounteous God
    through all our life be near us,
    with ever-joyful hearts
    and blessed peace to cheer us;
    and keep us in His grace,
    and guide us when perplexed,
    and free us from all ills
    in this world and the next.

3 All praise and thanks to God
the Father now be given,
the Son, and Him who reigns
with Them in highest heaven;
the one eternal God,
whom heaven and earth adore;
for thus it was, is now,
and shall be evermore.

69 Psalm 95 verses 1-7 (Scottish Psalter)

1 O come, let us sing to the Lord:
come, let us every one
a joyful noise make to the Rock
of our salvation.

2 Let us before His presence come
with praise and thankful voice;
let us sing psalms to Him with grace,
and make a joyful noise.

3 For God, a great God, and great King,
above all gods He is.
Depths of the earth are in His hand,
the strength of hills is His.

4 To Him the spacious sea belongs,
for He the same did make;
the dry land also from His hands
its form at first did take.

5 O come, and let us worship Him,
let us bow withal,
and on our knees before the Lord
our Maker let us fall.

70 Isaac Watts (1674-1748)

1 O God, our help in ages past,
our hope for years to come,
our shelter from the stormy blast
and our eternal home!

2 Beneath the shadow of Thy throne
Thy saints have dwelt secure;
sufficient is Thine arm alone,
and our defence is sure.

3 Before the hills in order stood,
or earth received her frame,
from everlasting Thou art God,
to endless years the same.

4 A thousand ages in Thy sight
are like an evening gone,
short as the watch that ends the night
before the rising sun.

5 Time, like an ever-rolling stream,
bears all its sons away;
they fly forgotten as a dream
dies at the opening day.

6 O God, our help in ages past,
our hope for years to come,
be Thou our guard while troubles last
and our eternal home.

71 Russian hymn, tr. Stuart K Hine (1899-1989)
© 1953 Stuart K. Hine/ Admin. by Kingsway's
Thankyou Music

1 O Lord my God! when I in awesome
wonder
consider all the works Thy hand hath
made,
I see the stars, I hear the mighty
thunder,
Thy power throughout the universe
displayed.

Then sings my soul, my Saviour
  God, to Thee,
how great Thou art, how great
  Thou art!
Then sings my soul, my Saviour
  God, to Thee,
how great Thou art, how great
  Thou art!

2 When through the woods and forest
     glades I wander
   and hear the birds sing sweetly in the
     trees;
   when I look down from lofty mountain
     grandeur,
   and hear the brook, and feel the gentle
     breeze.

3 And when I think that God His Son
     not sparing,
   sent Him to die, I scarce can take it in,
   that on the cross my burden gladly
     bearing,
   He bled and died to take away my sin.

4 When Christ shall come with shouts
     of acclamation
   and take me home, what joy shall
     fill my heart!
   Then shall I bow in humble adoration
   and there proclaim, my God, how great
     Thou art!

2 Among the nations of the earth
   His glory do declare;
   and unto all the people show
   His works that wondrous are.

3 For great's the Lord, and greatly He
     is to be magnified;
   yea, worthy to be feared is He
   above all gods beside.

4 For all the gods are idols dumb,
   which blinded nations fear;
   but our God is the Lord, by whom
   the heavens created were.

5 Great honour is before His face,
   and majesty divine;
   strength is within His holy place,
   and there doth beauty shine.

6 Do ye ascribe unto the Lord,
   of people every tribe,
   glory do ye unto the Lord,
   and mighty power ascribe.

7 Give ye the glory to the Lord
   that to His name is due;
   come ye into His courts, and bring
   an offering with you.

8 In beauty of His holiness,
   do the Lord adore;
   likewise let all the earth throughout
   tremble His face before.

72 Psalm 96 verses 1-9 (Scottish Psalter)

1 O sing a new song to the Lord:
   sing all the earth to God.
   To God sing, bless His name, show still
   His saving health abroad.

73 Psalm 136 (ii) verses 1-5, 23-26 (Scottish Psalter)

1 Praise God, for He is kind:
   His mercy lasts for aye.
   Give thanks with heart and mind
   to God of gods alway:

For certainly
His mercies dure
most firm and sure
eternally.

2 The Lord of lords praise ye,
   whose mercies still endure.
   Great wonders only He
   doth work by His great power:

3 Give praise to His great name,
   who, by His wisdom high,
   the heaven above did frame,
   and built the lofty sky:

4 Who hath remembered us
   when in our low estate;
   and hath delivered us
   from foes who did us hate:

5 Who to all flesh gives food;
   for His grace faileth never.
   Give thanks to God most good,
   the God of heaven, for ever:

74 Horatius Bonar (1809-89)

1 Praise, praise ye the name of Jehovah,
      our God;
   declare, oh, declare ye His glories
      abroad;
   proclaim ye His mercy from nation to
      nation,
   till the uttermost islands have heard
   His salvation.

   For His love floweth on,
   free and full as a river;
   and His mercy endureth
   for ever and ever.

2 Praise, praise ye the Lamb, who for
      sinners was slain,
   who went down to the grave and
      ascended again;
   and who soon shall return when these
      dark days are o'er,
   to set up His kingdom in glory and
      power.

3 Then the heavens and the earth and the
      sea shall rejoice,
   the field and the forest shall lift their
      glad voice;
   the sands of the desert shall flourish in
      green,
   and Lebanon's glory be shed o'er the
      scene.

4 Her bridal attire and her festal array,
   all nature shall wear on that glorious day;
   for her King cometh down with His
      people to reign,
   and His presence shall bless her with
      Eden again.

75 Psalm 65 verses 1-5 (Scottish Psalter)

1 Praise waits for Thee in Sion, Lord
   to Thee vows paid shall be.
   Thou that the hearer art of prayer,
   all flesh shall come to Thee.

2 Iniquities, I must confess,
   prevail against me do:
   but as for our transgressions,
   them purge away shalt Thou.

3 Blessed is the man whom Thou dost
      choose,
   and makest approach to Thee,
   that he within Thy courts, O Lord,
   may still a dweller be.

4 We surely shall be satisfied
with Thy abundant grace,
and with the goodness of Thy house,
even of Thy holy place.

5 O God of our salvation,
Thou, in Thy righteousness,
by fearful works unto our prayers,
Thine answer dost express.

6 Therefore the ends of all the earth,
and those afar that be
upon the sea, their confidence,
O Lord, will place in Thee.

76 © Timothy Dudley-Smith

1 Tell out, my soul, the greatness of the
Lord!
Unnumbered blessings, give my spirit
voice;
tender to me the promise of his word;
in God my Saviour shall my heart
rejoice.

2 Tell out, my soul, the greatness of His
name!
Make known His might, the deeds His
arm has done;
His mercy sure, from age to age the
same;
His holy name - the Lord, the Mighty
One.

3 Tell out, my soul, the greatness of His
might!
Powers and dominions lay their glory by.
Proud hearts and stubborn wills are put
to flight,
the hungry fed, the humble lifted high.

4 Tell out, my soul, the glories of His
word!
Firm is His promise, and His mercy
sure.
Tell out, my soul, the greatness of the
Lord
to children's children and for evermore!

77 Thomas Olivers (1725-99) altd

1 The God of Abraham praise,
who reigns enthroned above,
Ancient of everlasting days,
and God of love.
Jehovah, great I AM!
by earth and heaven confessed;
we bow and bless the sacred name,
for ever blessed.

2 The God of Abraham praise,
at whose supreme command
from earth we rise, and seek the joys
at His right hand;
we all on earth forsake,
its wisdom, fame and power;
and Him our only portion make,
our shield and tower.

3 The God of Abraham praise,
whose all-sufficient grace
shall guide us all our happy days,
in all our ways:
He is our faithful friend;
He is our gracious God;
and He will save us to the end,
through Jesus' blood.

4 He by Himself has sworn,
we on His oath depend,
we shall, on eagles' wings upborne,
to heaven ascend:

we shall behold His face,
we shall His power adore,
and sing the wonders of His grace
for evermore.

5 The whole triumphant host
give thanks to God on high:
"Hail, Father, Son, and Holy Ghost!"
they ever cry.
Hail, Abraham's God and ours!
We join the heavenly lays;
and celebrate with all our powers
His endless praise.

78 Psalm 148 (ii) (Scottish Psalter)

1 The Lord of heaven confess,
on high His glory raise.
Him let all angels bless,
Him all His armies praise.
Him glorify
sun, moon and stars;
ye higher spheres
and cloudy sky.

2 From God your beings are,
Him therefore famous make;
you all created were,
when He the word but spake.
And from that place,
where fixed you be
by His decree,
you cannot pass.

3 Praise God from earth below,
ye dragons, and ye deeps:
fire, hail, clouds, wind, and snow,
whom in command He keeps.
praise ye His name,

hills great and small,
trees low and tall;
beasts wild and tame.

4 O let God's name be praised
above both earth and sky;
for He His saints hath raised
and set their horn on high;
e'en those that be
of Israel's race,
near to His grace.
The Lord praise ye.

79 Psalm 24 (Scottish Psalter)

1 Ye gates, lift up your heads on high;
ye doors that last for aye,
be lifted up, that so the King
of glory enter may.
But who of glory is the King?
The mighty Lord is this;
e'en that same Lord that great in might
and strong in battle is.
E'en that same Lord that great in might
and strong in battle is.

2 Ye gates, lift up your heads; ye doors,
doors that do last for aye,
be lifted up, that so the King
of glory enter may.
But who is He that is the King,
the King of glory? Who is this?
The Lord of hosts, and none but He,
the King of glory is.
The Lord of hosts, and none but He,
the King of glory is.

Alleluia! Alleluia! Alleluia!
Alleluia! Alleluia!
Amen, Amen, Amen.

80 Mark Altrogge
©1987 People of Destiny International/Admin. by
Copycare

You are beautiful beyond description,
too marvellous for words,
too wonderful for comprehension,
like nothing ever seen or heard.
Who can grasp Your infinite wisdom?
Who can fathom the depth of Your love?
You are beautiful beyond description,
Majesty, enthroned above.
And I stand, I stand in awe of You;
I stand, I stand in awe of You.
Holy God, to whom all praise is due,
I stand in awe of You.

81 Adrian Howard and Pat Turner
©1985 Restoration Music Ltd./Sovereign Music UK

Salvation belongs to our God,
who sits upon the throne,
unto the Lamb;
praise and glory, wisdom and thanks,
honour and power and strength
be to our God forever and ever,
be to our God forever and ever,
be to our God forever and ever, amen!

And we, the redeemed shall be strong
in purpose and unity,
declaring aloud:
praise and glory, wisdom and thanks,
honour and power and strength
be to our God ...

2.2 THE GODHEAD
The Trinity

82 Reginald Heber (1783-1826)

1   Holy, holy, holy! Lord God Almighty,
    early in the morning our song shall rise
      to Thee!
    Holy, holy, holy! Merciful and
    Mighty!
    God in Three Persons, blessed Trinity!

2   Holy, holy, holy! all the saints adore
      Thee,
    casting down their golden crowns
      around the glassy sea;
    cherubim and seraphim falling down
      before Thee
    which wert and art, and evermore shalt
    be.

3   Holy, holy, holy! though the darkness
      hide Thee,
    though the eye of sinful man Thy glory
      may not see:
    only Thou art holy, there is none beside
      Thee,
    perfect in power, in love, and purity.

4   Holy, holy, holy! Lord God Almighty,
    all Thy works shall praise Thy name
      in earth, and sky, and sea;
    holy, holy, holy! Merciful and
      Mighty!
    God in three Persons, blessed Trinity.

83 John Marriott (1780-1825)

1   Thou, whose almighty word
    chaos and darkness heard
    and took their flight;

hear us, we humbly pray,
and where the gospel day
sheds not its glorious ray,
let there be light!

2   Thou, who didst come to bring,
on Thy redeeming wing,
healing and sight;
health to the sick in mind,
sight to the inly blind,
O now to all mankind
let there be light!

3   Spirit of truth and love,
life-giving, holy Dove,
speed forth Thy flight;
move on the water's face,
bearing the lamp of grace,
and in earth's darkest place
let there be light!

4   Blessed and holy Three,
glorious Trinity,
wisdom, love, might;
boundless as ocean's tide,
rolling in fullest pride,
through the earth, far and wide
let there be light!

2.3   THE GODHEAD
Love

84   Graham Kendrick
© 1988 Make Way Music

1   Such love, pure as the whitest snow;
such love weeps for the shame I know;
such love, paying the debt I owe;
O Jesus, such love.

2   Such love, stilling my restlessness;
such love, filling my emptiness;
such love, showing me holiness;
O Jesus, such love.

3   Such love, springs from eternity;
such love, streaming through history;
such love, fountain of life to me;
O Jesus, such love.

85   F M Lehman
© 1945 Nazarene Publishing/Admin. by Copycare

1   The love of God is greater far
than tongue or pen can ever tell,
it goes beyond the highest star,
and reaches to the lowest hell.
The guilty pair, bowed down with care,
God gave His Son to win;
His erring child He reconciled,
and pardoned from his sin.

Oh, love of God, how rich and pure!
How measureless and strong!
It shall for evermore endure,
the saints' and angels' song.

2   When hoary time shall pass away
and earthly thrones and kingdoms fall;
when men who here refuse to pray,
on rocks and hills and mountains call;
God's love, so sure, shall still endure,
all measureless and strong;
redeeming grace to Adam's race
the saints' and angels' song.

3   Could we with ink the ocean fill,
and were the skies of parchment made;
were every stalk on earth a quill,
and every man a scribe by trade;
to write the love of God above
would drain the ocean dry;
nor could the scroll contain the whole,
though stretched from sky to sky.

3.1 THE LORD JESUS CHRIST
His Glory, Name and Praise

86 Dave Bilbrough
© 1988 Kingsway's Thankyou Music

All hail the Lamb
enthroned on high,
His praise shall be
our battle cry.
He reigns victorious,
for ever glorious,
His name is Jesus,
He is the Lord.

87 Edward Perronet (1726-92) and
John Rippon (1751-1836)

1 All hail the power of Jesus' name!
let angels prostrate fall;
bring forth the royal diadem,
and crown Him Lord of all!

2 Crown Him, ye martyrs of our God,
who from His altar call;
extol the stem of Jesse's rod,
and crown Him Lord of all!

3 Let every kindred, every tribe,
on this terrestrial ball,
to Him all majesty ascribe,
and crown Him Lord of all!

4 Oh, that with yonder sacred throng
we at His feet may fall;
join in the everlasting song,
and crown Him Lord of all!

88 Caroline Maria Noel (1817-77)

1 At the name of Jesus
every knee shall bow,
every tongue confess Him
King of glory now.
'Tis the Father's pleasure
we should call Him Lord,
who from the beginning
was the mighty Word.

2 Mighty and mysterious
in the highest height,
God from everlasting,
very Light of light.
In the Father's bosom,
with the Spirit's blest
love, in love eternal,
rest, in perfect rest.

3 Humbled for a season,
to receive a name
from the lips of sinners
unto whom He came;
faithfully He bore it
spotless to the last,
brought it back victorious,
when from death He passed.

4 Bore it up triumphant
with its human light,
through all ranks of creatures,
to the central height;
to the throne of Godhead,
to the Father's breast,
filled it with the glory
of that perfect rest.

5 In your hearts enthrone Him;
there let Him subdue
all that is not holy,
all that is not true;
crown Him as your Captain
in temptation's hour,
let His will enfold you
in its light and power.

6 Brothers, this Lord Jesus
shall return again,
with His Father's glory,
with His angel-train;
for all wreaths of empire
meet upon His brow,
and our hearts confess Him
King of glory now.

89 Isaac Watts (1674-1748)

1 Come, let us join our cheerful songs
with angels round the throne;
ten thousand thousand are their tongues,
but all their joys are one.

2 "Worthy the Lamb that died!" they cry,
"to be exalted thus;"
"Worthy the Lamb!" our lips reply,
"for He was slain for us."

3 Jesus is worthy to receive
honour and power divine;
and blessings more than we can give
be, Lord, for ever Thine.

4 The whole creation join in one,
to bless the sacred name
of Him that sits upon the throne,
and to adore the Lamb.

90 Matthew Bridges (1800-94)

1 Crown Him with many crowns,
the Lamb upon His throne!
Hark! how the heavenly anthem drowns
all music but its own.
Awake, my soul, and sing
of Him who died for thee,
and hail Him as thy matchless King
through all eternity.

2 Crown Him the Lord of love!
Behold His hands and side,
His wounds yet visible above,
in beauty glorified.
No angel in the sky
can fully bear that sight,
but downward bends his burning eye
at mysteries so bright.

3 Crown Him the Lord of peace!
Whose power a sceptre sways
from pole to pole, that wars may cease,
absorbed in prayer and praise.
His reign shall know no end;
and round His pierced feet
fair flowers of Paradise extend
their fragrance ever sweet.

4 Crown Him the Lord of years!
The Potentate of time,
Creator of the rolling spheres,
ineffably sublime!
All hail! Redeemer, hail!
For Thou hast died for me:
Thy praise shall never, never fail
throughout eternity.

91 Paul S Deming (from Ps 113) © 1976 Integrity's Hosanna! Music/Adm. by Kingsway's Thankyou Music

From the rising of the sun
to the going down of the same,
the Lord's name is to be praised.
From the rising of the sun
to the going down of the same,
the Lord's name is to be praised.
Praise ye the Lord,
praise Him O ye servants of the Lord,
praise the name of the Lord;
blessed be the name of the Lord
from this time forth,
and for evermore.

92
Steve McEwan
©1985 Body Songs/Admin. by Copycare

Great is the Lord and most worthy of
  praise,
the city of our God, the holy place,
the joy of the whole earth.
Great is the Lord in whom we have the
  victory,
He aids us against the enemy,
we bow down on our knees.

And Lord, we want to lift Your name
  on high,
and Lord, we want to thank You,
for the works You've done in our lives;
and Lord, we trust in Your unfailing love,
for You alone are God eternal,
throughout earth and heaven above.

93
Anon © Unidentified

His name is higher than any other,
His name is Jesus, His name is Lord.
His name is Wonderful,
His name is Counsellor,
His name is Prince of Peace,
the Mighty God.
His name is higher than any other,
His name is Jesus, His name is Lord.

94
John Bakewell (1721-1819)

1 Hail, Thou once despised Jesus,
   hail, Thou Galilean King!
   Thou didst suffer to release us,
   Thou didst free salvation bring.
   Hail, Thou agonising Saviour,
   bearer of our sin and shame;
   by Thy merits we find favour;
   life is given through Thy name.

2 Paschal Lamb, by God appointed,
   all our sins on Thee were laid;
   by almighty love anointed,
   Thou hast full atonement made.
   All Thy people are forgiven
   through the virtue of Thy blood;
   opened is the gate of heaven,
   peace is made 'twixt man and God.

3 Jesus, hail! enthroned in glory,
   there for ever to abide;
   all the heavenly hosts adore Thee,
   seated at Thy Father's side:
   there for sinners Thou art pleading,
   there Thou dost our place prepare;
   ever for us interceding,
   till in glory we appear.

4 Worship, honour, power and blessing,
   Thou art worthy to receive;
   loudest praises, without ceasing,
   meet it is for us to give:
   Help, ye bright angelic spirits!
   bring your sweetest, noblest lays;
   help to sing our Saviour's merits,
   help to chant Immanuel's praise.

95
Tim Cullen © 1975 Celebration/ Admin. by
Kingsway's Thankyou Music

Hallelujah, my Father,
for giving us Your Son,
sending Him into the world
to be given up for men,
knowing we would bruise Him
and smite Him from the earth.
Hallelujah, my Father,
in His death is my birth;
Hallelujah, my Father,
in His life is my life.

96 Audrey Mieir © 1959 Manna Music/ Admin. by Kingsway's Thankyou Music

His name is wonderful,
His name is wonderful,
His name is wonderful,
Jesus my Lord.

He is the mighty king,
Master of everything,
His name is wonderful,
Jesus my Lord.

He's the great Shepherd,
the rock of all ages,
Almighty God is He;
bow down before Him.
love and adore Him,
His name is wonderful,
Jesus my Lord!

97 John Newton (1725-1807) altd

1 How sweet the name of Jesus sounds
  in a believer's ear!
  It soothes his sorrows, heals his wounds
  and drives away his fear.

2 It makes the wounded spirit whole
  and calms the troubled breast;
  'tis manna to the hungry soul
  and to the weary rest.

3 Dear Name! the Rock on which I
  build,
  my Shield and Hiding place,
  my never-failing Treasury, filled
  with boundless stores of grace!

4 Jesus, my Shepherd, Saviour, Friend,
  my Prophet, Priest, and King,
  my Lord, my Life, my Way, my End,
  accept the praise I bring.

5 Weak is the effort of my heart,
  and cold my warmest thought;
  but when I see You as You are
  I'll praise You as I ought.

6 I would Your boundless love proclaim
  with every fleeting breath;
  so shall the music of Your name
  refresh my soul in death.

  (When using the tune "Rachel", repeat last line
  of every second verse)

98 Joe Parks
© 1983 Tennessee Music Publishing Co./
Admin. by Copycare

It's a lovely, lovely name, the name of
  Jesus.
It's a lovely, lovely name, from heaven
  above,
dispelling the clouds of doubt and fear,
  filling the saddened heart with cheer;
it's a lovely, lovely name, the name I love.

99 © William Vernon Higham

1 I saw a new vision of Jesus,
  a view I'd not seen here before,
  beholding in glory so wondrous
  with beauty I had to adore.
  I stood on the shores of my weakness,
  and gazed at the brink of such fear;
  'twas then that I saw Him in newness,
  regarding Him fair and so dear.

2 My Saviour will never forsake me,
  unveiling His merciful face,
  His presence and promise almighty,
  redeeming His loved ones by grace.
  In shades of the valley's dark terror,
  where hell and its horror hold sway,
  my Jesus will reach out in power,
  and save me by His only way.

3   For yonder a light shines eternal,
     which spreads through the valley of
        gloom;
     Lord Jesus, resplendent and regal,
     drives fear far away from the tomb.
     Our God is the end of the journey,
     His pleasant and glorious domain;
     for there are the children of mercy,
     who praise Him for Calvary's pain.

100   Mary Shekleton (1827-83)

1   It passeth knowledge, that dear love of
        Thine,
     my Saviour, Jesus! yet this soul of mine
     would of Thy love, in all its breadth and
        length,
     its height and depth, and everlasting
        strength,
     know more and more.

2   It passeth telling, that dear love of
        Thine,
     my Saviour, Jesus! yet this heart of mine
     would fain proclaim to sinners, far and
        near,
     a love which can remove all guilty fear,
     and love beget.

3   It passeth praises, that dear love of
        Thine,
     my Saviour, Jesus! yet this heart of mine
     would sing that love, so full, so rich, so
        free,
     which brings a rebel sinner, such as me,
     nigh unto God.

4   O fill me, Saviour, Jesus, with Thy love;
     lead, lead me to the living fount above;
     thither may I, in simple faith, draw nigh,
     and never to another fountain fly,
     but unto Thee.

5   And then, when Jesus face to face I see,
     when at His lofty throne I bow the knee,
     then of His love, in all its breadth and
        length,
     its height and depth, its everlasting
        strength,
     my soul shall sing.

101   David Bolton
         © 1975 Kingsway's Thankyou Music

Jesus, how lovely You are!
You are so gentle, so pure and kind,
You shine like the morning star:
Jesus, how lovely You are.

1   Alleluia, Jesus is my Lord and King;
     Alleluia, Jesus is my everything.
     Jesus, how lovely You are ...

2   Alleluia, Jesus died and rose again;
     Alleluia, Jesus forgave all my sin.
     Jesus, how lovely You are ...

3   Alleluia, Jesus is meek and lowly;
     Alleluia, Jesus is pure and holy.
     Jesus, how lovely You are ...

4   Alleluia, Jesus is the bridegroom;
     Alleluia, Jesus will take His bride soon.
     Jesus, how lovely You are ...

102   Wendy Churchill
         ©1982 Word's Spirit of Praise Music/Admin.
         by Copycare

1   Jesus is King
     and I will extol Him,
     give Him the glory,
     and honour His name;
     He reigns on high,
     enthroned in the heavens,
     Word of the Father,
     exalted for us.

2 We have a hope
   that is steadfast and certain,
   gone through the curtain
   and touching the throne;
   we have a Priest
   who is there interceding,
   pouring His grace
   on our lives day by day.

3 We come to Him,
   our Priest and Apostle,
   clothed in His glory
   and bearing His name,
   laying our lives
   with gladness before Him -
   filled with His Spirit
   we worship the King:

4 "O Holy One,
   our hearts do adore You;
   thrilled with Your goodness
   we give You our praise!"
   Angels in light
   with worship surround Him,
   Jesus, our Saviour,
   for ever the same.

103 David Mansell
         ©1982 Word's Spirit of Praise Music/Admin.
         by Copycare

1 Jesus is Lord! Creation's voice
      proclaims it,
   for by His power each tree and
      flower was planned and made.
   Jesus is Lord! The universe declares it;
   sun, moon and stars in heaven cry:
   Jesus is Lord!

   Jesus is Lord! Jesus is Lord!
   Praise Him with 'Hallelujahs',
   for Jesus is Lord!

2 Jesus is Lord! Yet from His throne
      eternal
   in flesh He came to die in pain on
      Calvary's tree.
   Jesus is Lord! From Him all life
      proceeding,
   yet gave His life a ransom thus setting
      us free.

3 Jesus is Lord! O'er sin the mighty
      conqueror,
   from death He rose and all His foes
      shall own His name.
   Jesus is Lord! God sends His Holy Spirit
   to show by works of power that Jesus is
      Lord.

104 Phil Lawson-Johnston
         © 1991 Kingsway's Thankyou Music

1 Jesus is the name we honour,
   Jesus is the name we praise.
   Majestic name above all other names;
   the highest heaven and earth proclaim
   that Jesus is our God.

   We will glorify,
   we will lift Him high,
   we will give Him honour and praise.
   We will glorify,
   we will lift Him high,
   we will give Him honour and praise.

2 Jesus is the name we worship,
   Jesus is the name we trust.
   He is the King above all other kings;
   let all creation stand and sing
   that Jesus is our God.

3 Jesus is the Father's splendour,
   Jesus is the Father's joy.
   He will return to reign in majesty,
   and every eye at last shall see
   that Jesus is our God.

105 Naida Hearn © 1974 Scripture in Song, a division of Integrity Music/Adm. by Kingsway's Thankyou Music

Jesus, name above all names,
beautiful Saviour, glorious Lord;
Emmanuel, God is with us,
blessed Redeemer, living Word.

106 Isaac Watts (1674-1748)

1 Jesus shall reign where'er the sun
doth his successive journeys run,
His kingdom stretch from shore to shore,
till moons shall wax and wane no more.

2 To Him shall endless prayer be made,
and praises throng to crown His head:
His name like sweet perfume shall rise
with every morning sacrifice.

3 Peoples and realms of every tongue
dwell on His love with sweetest song,
and infant voices shall proclaim
their early blessings on His name.

4 Blessings abound where'er He reigns:
the prisoner leaps to lose his chains;
the weary find eternal rest;
and all the sons of want are blest.

5 Let every creature rise and bring
peculiar honours to our King;
angels descend with songs again
and earth repeat the loud "Amen".

107 Nikolaus Ludwig von Zinzendorf (1700-60); tr John Wesley

1 Jesus, Thy blood and righteousness
my beauty are, my glorious dress;
'midst flaming worlds, in these arrayed,
with joy shall I lift up my head.

2 Bold shall I stand in that great day,
for who aught to my charge shall lay?
Fully absolved through these I am,
from sin and fear, from guilt and shame.

3 When from the dust of death I rise,
to claim my mansion in the skies,
e'en then shall this be all my plea,
"Jesus hath lived and died, for me."

4 This spotless robe the same appears,
when ruined nature sinks in years;
no age can change its glorious hue,
the robe of Christ is ever new.

5 Oh, let the dead now hear Thy voice,
bid, Lord, Thy banished ones rejoice;
their beauty this, their glorious dress,
Jesus, the Lord our Righteousness!

108 Isaac Watts (1674-1748)

1 Join all the glorious names
of wisdom, love and power,
that mortals ever knew,
that angels ever bore:
all are too mean to speak His worth,
too mean to set my Saviour forth.

2 Great Prophet of my God,
my tongue would bless Thy name;
by Thee the joyful news
of our salvation came;
the joyful news of sins forgiven,
of hell subdued, and peace with heaven.

3 Jesus, my great High Priest,
offered His blood and died;
my guilty conscience seeks
no sacrifice beside:
His powerful blood did once atone
and now it pleads before the throne.

4 My dear Almighty Lord
   my Conqueror and my King!
   Thy matchless power and love,
   Thy saving grace, I sing:
   Thine is the power, oh, may I sit
   in willing bonds beneath Thy feet.

5 Then let my soul arise
   and tread the tempter down;
   my Captain leads me forth
   to conquest and a crown.
   The feeblest saint shall win the day,
   though death and hell obstruct the way.

109 Charles Wesley (1707-88)

1 Jesus! the name high over all,
   in hell, or earth, or sky;
   angels and men before it fall,
   and devils fear and fly.

2 Jesus, the name to sinners dear,
   the name to sinners given;
   it scatters all their guilty fear;
   it turns their hell to heaven.

3 Jesus the prisoner's fetters breaks,
   and bruises Satan's head;
   power into strengthless souls it speaks,
   and life into the dead.

4 O that the world might taste and see
   the riches of His grace;
   The arms of love that compass me
   would all mankind embrace.

5 His only righteousness I show,
   His saving grace proclaim;
   'tis all my business here below:
   to cry: "Behold the Lamb!"

6 Happy, if with my latest breath
   I might but gasp His name;
   preach Him to all, and cry in death:
   "Behold, behold the Lamb!"
   (When using the tune "Scottish Air",
   repeat last line of each verse)

110 © Unidentified

Lift Jesus higher, lift Jesus higher,
lift Him up for the world to see.
He said if I be lifted up from the earth
I will draw all men unto Me.

111 Jack Hayford © 1981 Pub. Rocksmith Music Adm. by Leosong CS Ltd. UK & Eire

Majesty, worship His Majesty;
unto Jesus be glory, honour and praise.
Majesty, kingdom authority,
flows from His throne unto His own,
His anthem raise.
So exalt,
lift up on high the name of Jesus,
magnify, come glorify,
Christ Jesus the King.
Majesty, worship His Majesty,
Jesus who died, now glorified,
King of all kings.

112 Darlene Zschech © 1993 Darlene Zschech/ Hillsongs Australia/Admin. by Kingsway's Thankyou Music

My Jesus, my Saviour, Lord, there is none
   like You;
all of my days I want to praise the wonders
   of Your mighty love.
My comfort, my shelter, tower of refuge
   and strength,
let every breath, all that I am,
never cease to worship You.

Shout to the Lord all the earth, let us sing
power and majesty, praise to the
   King:
mountains bow down and the seas will roar
   at the sound of Your name.
I sing for joy at the work of Your hands,
forever I'll love You, for ever I'll stand:
nothing compares to the promise I have in
   You.

113 Gerhard Tersteegen (1697-1769)
tr. Emma F Bevan (1827-1909)

1 Name of Jesus! highest name!
Name that earth and heaven adore!
From the heart of God it came,
leads me to God's heart once more.

2 Name of Jesus! living tide!
Days of drought for me are past;
how much more than satisfied
are the thirsty lips at last!

3 Name of Jesus! dearest name!
Bread of heaven, and balm of love:
oil of gladness, surest claim
to the treasures stored above.

4 Jesus gives forgiveness free,
Jesus cleanses all my stains;
Jesus gives His life to me,
Jesus always He remains.

5 Only Jesus! fairest name!
Life and rest and peace and bliss;
Jesus, evermore the same,
He is mine and I am His.

114 Michael Perry
© Mrs B. Perry/Jubilate Hymns

1 Not the grandeur of the mountains,
nor the splendour of the sea,
can excel the ceaseless wonder
of my Saviour's love to me:

For His love to me is faithful,
and His mercy is divine:
and His truth is everlasting,
and His perfect peace is mine.

2 Not the streams that fill the valleys,
nor the clouds that drift along,
can delight me more than Jesus
or replace my grateful song:

3 Yet these all convey His beauty
and proclaim His power and grace,
for they are among the tokens
of the love upon His face:

115 © Timothy Dudley-Smith

1 Name of all majesty,
fathomless mystery,
King of the ages
by angels adored;
  power and authority,
  splendour and dignity,
  bow to his mastery -
Jesus is Lord!

2 Child of our destiny,
God from eternity,
love of the Father
on sinners outpoured;
  see now what God has done
  sending His only Son,
  Christ the beloved One -
Jesus is Lord!

3 Saviour of Calvary,
costliest victory,
darkness defeated
and Eden restored;
  born as a man to die,
  nailed to a cross on high,
  cold in the grave to lie -
Jesus is Lord!

4 Source of all sovereignty,
   light, immortality,
   life everlasting
   and heaven assured;
      so with the ransomed, we
      praise Him eternally,
      Christ in His majesty -
   Jesus is Lord!

116 Roy Hicks Jnr © 1976 Latter Rain Music/
EMI Christian Music Publishing/Admin. by
Copycare

Praise the name of Jesus,
praise the name of Jesus,
He's my rock, He's my fortress,
He's my deliverer, in Him will I trust;
praise the name of Jesus.

117 Charles Wesley (1707-88)

1 Rejoice, the Lord is King!
   Your Lord and King adore;
   mortals, give thanks and sing
   and triumph evermore.

   Lift up your heart, lift up your voice;
   Rejoice, again I say, rejoice.

2 Jesus the Saviour reigns,
   the God of truth and love:
   when He had purged our stains,
   He took His seat above.

3 His kingdom cannot fail;
   He rules o'er earth and heaven;
   the keys of death and hell
   are to our Jesus given.

4 He sits at God's right hand
   till all His foes submit,
   and bow to His command,
   and fall beneath His feet.

5 He all His foes shall quell,
   shall all our sins destroy,
   and every bosom swell
   with pure seraphic joy.

6 Rejoice in glorious hope;
   Jesus the Judge shall come
   and take His servants up
   to their eternal home.

   We soon shall hear the
   archangel's voice;
   the trump of God shall sound,
   rejoice!

118 Thomas Kelly (1769-1854)

1 Praise the Saviour, ye who know Him;
   who can tell how much we owe Him?
   Gladly let us render to Him
   all we have and are.

2 "Jesus" is the name that charms us;
   He for conflicts fits and arms us;
   nothing moves and nothing harms us
   when we trust in Him.

3 Trust in Him, ye saints, for ever;
   He is faithful, changing never;
   neither force nor guile can sever
   those He loves from Him.

4 Keep us, Lord, oh, keep us cleaving
   to Thyself and still believing,
   till the hour of our receiving
   promised joys in heaven.

119 Copyright Control

Thank You God, for sending Jesus;
thank You Jesus, that You came;
Holy Spirit, won't You teach us
more about His wondrous name?

120 Mrs L. Baxter (1809-74)

1 Take the name of Jesus with you,
child of sorrow and of woe;
it will joy and comfort give you,
take it then where'er you go.

Precious name, oh, how sweet!
hope of earth and joy of heaven;
precious name, oh, how sweet!
hope of earth and joy of heaven.

2 Take the name of Jesus ever,
as a shield from every snare;
if temptations round you gather,
breathe that holy name in prayer.

3 Oh, the precious name of Jesus!
How it thrills our souls with joy,
when His loving arms receive us,
and His songs our tongues employ!

4 At the name of Jesus bowing,
falling prostrate at His feet;
King of kings in heaven we'll crown
Him,
when our journey is complete.

121 F Whitfield (1829-1904)

1 There is a name I love to hear,
I love to speak its worth;
it sounds like music in my ear,
the sweetest name on earth.

O how I love the Saviour's name,
O how I love the Saviour's name,
O how I love the Saviour's name,
the sweetest name on earth.

2 It tells me of a Saviour's love,
who died to set me free;
it tells me of His precious blood,
the sinner's perfect plea.

3 It tells of one whose loving heart
can feel my deepest woe,
who in my sorrow bears a part
that none can bear below.

4 It bids my trembling heart rejoice,
it dries each rising tear;
it tells me in a 'still, small voice'
to trust and never fear.

5 Jesus, the name I love so well,
the name I love to hear!
No saints on earth its worth can tell,
no heart conceive how dear!

122 Michael Baughen
© Michael Baughen/Jubilee Hymns

1 There's no greater name than Jesus,
name of Him who came to save us;
in that saving name so gracious
every knee shall bow.

2 Let everything that's beneath the ground,
   let everything in the world around,
   let everything exalted on high
   bow at Jesus' name.

3 In our minds, by faith professing,
   in our hearts, by inward blessing,
   on our tongues, by words confessing,
   Jesus Christ is Lord.

123 Josiah Conder (1789-1855)

1 Thou art the everlasting Word,
   the Father's only Son;
   God manifestly seen and heard,
   and heaven's Beloved One.
   Worthy, O Lamb of God, art Thou,
   that every knee to Thee should bow.
   (Repeat last line)

2 In Thee most perfectly expressed
   the Father's glories shine,
   of the full deity possessed,
   eternally divine!
   Worthy, O Lamb of God, art Thou,
   that every knee to Thee should bow.

3 True image of the infinite,
   whose essence is concealed;
   brightness of uncreated light,
   the heart of God revealed.
   Worthy, O Lamb of God, art Thou,
   that every knee to Thee should bow.

4 But the high mysteries of Thy name
   an angel's grasp transcend;
   the Father only, glorious claim!
   the Son can comprehend.
   Worthy, O Lamb of God, art Thou,
   that every knee to Thee should bow.

5 Yet loving Thee, on whom His love
   ineffable doth rest,
   Thy glorious worshippers above,
   as one with Thee are blest!
   Worthy, O Lamb of God, art Thou,
   that every knee to Thee should bow.

124 Pauline Michael Mills © 1963 Fred Bock
Music Company/Admin. by Kingsway's
Thankyou Music

1 Thou art worthy, Thou art worthy,
   Thou art worthy, O Lord.
   Thou art worthy, to receive glory,
   glory and honour and power.
   For Thou hast created,
   hast all things created,
   for Thou hast created all things;
   and for Thy pleasure
   they are created:
   Thou art worthy, O Lord.

2 Thou art worthy, Thou art worthy,
   Thou art worthy, O Lamb.
   Thou art worthy, to receive glory
   and power at the Father's right hand.
   For Thou hast redeemed us;
   hast ransomed and cleaned us,
   by Thy blood setting us free.
   In white robes arrayed us,
   kings and priests made us, and
   we are reigning in Thee.

125 J Kent (1766-1843)

1 'Tis the Church triumphant singing,
   worthy the Lamb;
   heaven throughout with praises ringing,
   worthy the Lamb;
   thrones and powers before Him
   bending,

odours sweet with voice ascending,
swell the chorus never ending,
worthy the Lamb.

2 Every kindred, tongue and nation,
worthy the Lamb;
join to sing the great salvation,
worthy the Lamb.;
loud as mighty thunders roaring,
floods of mighty waters pouring,
prostrate at His feet adoring,
worthy the Lamb.

3 Harps and songs for ever sounding
worthy the Lamb;
mighty grace o'er sin abounding,
worthy the Lamb.
By His blood He dearly bought us;
wandering from the fold He sought us,
and to glory safely brought us,
worthy the Lamb.

4 Sing with blest anticipation,
worthy the Lamb;
through the vale of tribulation,
worthy the Lamb.
Sweetest notes, all notes excelling,
on the theme for ever dwelling,
still untold, though ever telling,
worthy the Lamb.

126 Noel Richards
© 1989 Kingsway's Thankyou Music

1 There is power in the name of Jesus:
we believe in His name.
We have called on the name of Jesus:
we are saved, we are saved!
At His name the demons flee,
at His name captives are freed;
for there is no other name that is higher
than Jesus.

2 There is power in the name of Jesus,
like a sword in our hands.
We declare in the name of Jesus:
we shall stand, we shall stand!
At His name, God's enemies
shall be crushed beneath our feet;
for there is no other name that is higher
than Jesus.

127 Anon. Copyright Control

Wherever I am I'll praise Him,
whenever I can I'll praise Him;
for His love surrounds me like a sea;
I'll praise the name of Jesus,
lift up the name of Jesus,
for the name of Jesus lifted me.

128 W J Stuart
© Unidentified

1 Wonderful love does Jesus show,
wonderful grace He does bestow,
wonderful peace in Him I know,
bless His holy name!

Wonderful, wonderful Jesus!
Wonderful, wonderful Jesus!
Oh! He's a wonderful Saviour!
Bless His holy name!

2 Wonderful! He is always near,
wonderful! I have naught to fear,
wonderful is His voice so dear,
bless His holy name!

3 Wonderful help does Jesus send,
wonderful keeping to the end,
wonderful is this constant Friend,
bless His holy name!

4 Wonderful day, so pure, so bright,
wonderful living in His sight,
wonderful, 'round me all is light,
bless His holy name!

129 Copyright Control

1 Worthy is the Lamb;
worthy is the Lamb;
worthy is the Lamb;
worthy is the Lamb.

2 Holy is the Lamb ...

3 Precious is the Lamb ...

4 Praises to the Lamb ...

5 Glory to the Lamb ...

6 Jesus is our Lamb; ...

130 Bob Fitts © 1993 Integrity's Hosanna! Music/
Adm. by Kingsway's Thankyou Music

I will praise Your name,
I will praise Your name,
I will praise Your name,
and extol You;
I will praise Your name,
I will praise Your name,
I will praise Your name,
as I behold You.

I will magnify,
I will glorify,
I will lift on high.
Your name, Lord Jesus.
I will magnify,
I will glorify,
I will lift on high,
Your name, Lord Jesus.

*For Your love is never ending
and Your mercy ever true;
I will bless Your name, Lord Jesus,
for my heart belongs to You.*

I will praise Your name,
I will praise Your name,
I will praise Your name,
as I behold You.
I will magnify,
I will glorify,
I will lift on high,
Your name, Lord Jesus.

131 Mark S Kinzer
© 1976 Word of God Music/Admin. by
Copycare

Worthy, O worthy are You Lord,
worthy to be thanked and praised and
     worshipped and adored;
worthy, O worthy are You Lord,
worthy to be thanked and praised and
     worshipped and adored.
Singing hallelujah,
Lamb upon the throne,
we worship and adore You,
make Your glory known.
Hallelujah, glory to the King:
You're more than a conqueror,
You're Lord of everything!

132 Mavis Ford © 1978 Word's Spirit of Praise
Music/Admin. by Copycare

You are the King of glory,
You are the Prince of Peace,
You are the Lord of heaven and earth,
You're the Son of righteousness.
Angels bow down before You,
worship and adore,
for You have the words of eternal life,
You are Jesus Christ the Lord.
Hosanna to the Son of David!
Hosanna to the King of kings!
Glory in the highest heaven,
for Jesus the Messiah reigns!

133 Noel Richards
© 1985 Kingsway's Thankyou Music

You laid aside Your majesty,
gave up everything for me,
suffered at the hands of those You had
    created;
You took all my guilt and shame,
when You died and rose again;
now today You reign in heaven and earth
    exalted.
I really want to worship You, my Lord,
You have won my heart and I am Yours
    for ever and ever:
I will love You.
You are the only one who died for me,
gave Your life to set me free,
so I lift my voice to You in adoration.

3.2   THE LORD JESUS CHRIST
His Incarnation

134 J Montgomery (1771-1854)
© in this version Jubilate Hymns

1   Angels from the realms of glory,
    wing your flight through all the earth;
    heralds of creation's story
    now proclaim Messiah's birth!

    Come and worship
    Christ, the new-born King;
    come and worship,
    worship Christ the new-born King.

2   Shepherds in the fields abiding,
    watching by your flocks at night,
    God with man is now residing:
    see, there shines the infant light!

3   Wise men, leave your contemplations,
    brighter visions shine afar;
    seek in Him the hope of nations,
    you have seen His rising star:

4   Though an infant now we view Him,
    He will share His Father's throne,
    gather all the nations to Him;
    every knee shall then bow down:

135 W C Dix (1837-98)
altered © 1986 Horrobin/Leavers

1   As with gladness men of old
    did the guiding star behold;
    as with joy they hailed its light,
    leading onward, beaming bright,
    so, most gracious God, may we
    led by You for ever be.

2 As with joyful steps they sped,
Saviour, to Your lowly bed,
there to bend the knee before
You whom heaven and earth adore,
so may we with one accord,
seek forgiveness from our Lord.

3 As they offered gifts most rare,
gold and frankincense and myrrh,
so may we, cleansed from our sin,
lives of service now begin,
as in love our treasures bring,
Christ, to You our heavenly King.

4 Holy Jesus, every day
keep us in the narrow way;
and when earthly things are past,
bring our ransomed souls at last
where they need no star to guide,
where no clouds Your glory hide.

5 In the heavenly country bright
need they no created light;
You its light, its joy, its crown,
You its sun which goes not down.
There for ever may we sing
hallelujahs to our King.

136 v1 & 2 Unidentified, v3 J T McFarland (c1906)

1 Away in a manger, no crib for a bed,
the little Lord Jesus laid down His
sweet head.
The stars in the bright sky looked
down where He lay,
the little Lord Jesus asleep on the hay.

2 The cattle are lowing, the Baby
awakes,
but little Lord Jesus no crying He
makes.
I love Thee, Lord Jesus! Look down
from the sky,
and stay by my side until morning is
nigh.

3 Be near me, Lord Jesus; I ask Thee
to stay
close by me for ever and love me,
I pray.
Bless all the dear children in Thy
tender care,
and fit us for heaven, to live with
Thee there.

137 John Byrom (1692-1763) altd.

1 Christians awake! salute the happy
morn,
whereon the Saviour of mankind was
born;
rise to adore the mystery of love
which hosts of angels chanted from
above;
with them the joyful tidings first begun
of God incarnate, and the Virgin's Son.

2 Then to the watchful shepherds it was
told,
who heard the angelic herald's voice
"Behold, I bring good tidings of a
Saviour's birth
to you and all the nations upon earth:
this day hath God fulfilled His promised
word,
this day is born a Saviour, Christ the
Lord."

3 He spake; and straightway the celestial
    choir,
  in hymns of joy unknown before
    conspire;
  the praises of redeeming love they sang,
  and heaven's whole orb with hallelujahs
    rang:
  God's highest glory was their anthem
    still,
  "On earth be peace, and unto men
    goodwill."

4 To Bethlehem straight the enlightened
    shepherds ran,
  to see the wonder God had wrought for
    man;
  then to their flocks, still praising God,
    return,
  and their glad hearts with holy rapture
    burn;
  amazed, the wondrous tidings they
    proclaim,
  the first apostles of His infant fame.

5 Then may we hope, the angelic hosts
    among,
  to sing, redeemed, a glad triumphal song:
  He that was born upon this joyful day
  around us all His glory shall display;
  saved by His love, incessant we shall
    sing
  eternal praise to heaven's almighty King.

Valerie Collison
© 1970 High-Fye Music Ltd.
Used by permission of Music Sales
Limited. All Rights reserved.
International Copyright Secured.

138

*Come and join the celebration,
it's a very special day;
come and share our jubilation,
there's a new King born today!*

1 See the shepherds
  hurry down to Bethlehem;
  gaze in wonder at the Son of God
  who lay before them.

2 Wise men journey,
  led to worship by a star,
  kneel in homage,
  bringing precious gifts from lands
    afar, so

3 "God is with us,"
  round the world the message bring;
  He is with us,
  "Welcome!" all the bells on earth are
    pealing.

139 after M MacDonald (1789-1872)
L Macbean (1853-1931)

1 Child in the manger, infant of Mary,
  outcast and stranger, Lord of all!
  Child who inherits all our transgressions,
  all our demerits on Him fall.

2 Once the most holy child of salvation
  gentle and lowly lived below:
  now as our glorious mighty Redeemer,
  see Him victorious over each foe.

3 Prophets foretold Him, infant of wonder;
  angels behold Him on His throne:
  worthy our Saviour of all their praises;
  happy for ever are His own.

140 from Isaiah 9

For unto us a child is born,
unto us a Son is given;
and the government shall be upon
    His shoulders.
And His name shall be called Wonderful,
    Counsellor,
the Mighty God, the everlasting Father
and the Prince of Peace is He.

141 William E Booth-Clibborn (1893-1969)
© 1921 Zondervan Corporation/Benson Music
Publishing Inc./Admin. by Copycare

1 Down from His glory, ever-living story,
   my God and Saviour came, and Jesus
       was His name;
   born in a manger, to His own a stranger,
   a man of sorrows, tears and agony!

   O how I love Him! how I adore Him!
   My breath, my sunshine, my all-in-all!
   The great Creator became my Saviour,
   and all God's fullness dwelleth in Him!

2 What condescension, bringing us
       redemption,
   that in the dead of night, not one faint
       hope in sight;
   God, gracious, tender, laid aside His
       splendour,
   stooping to woo, to win, to save my soul.

3 Without reluctance, flesh and blood,
       His substance,
   He took the form of man, revealed the
       hidden plan;
   O glorious mystery, sacrifice of Calvary!
   And now I know He is the great 'I AM'!

142 Charles Wesley (1707-88) and others

1 Hark! the herald angels sing,
   "Glory to the new-born King!
   Peace on earth, and mercy mild,
   God and sinners reconciled!"
   Joyful, all ye nations, rise,
   join the triumph of the skies,
   with the angelic host proclaim:
   "Christ is born in Bethlehem."

       Hark! the herald angels sing
       "Glory to the new-born King!"

2 Christ, by highest heaven adored!
   Christ, the everlasting Lord!
   Late in time behold Him come,
   offspring of a Virgin's womb:
   veiled in flesh the Godhead see;
   hail the Incarnate Deity,
   pleased as Man with man to dwell,
   Jesus, our Emmanuel.

3 Hail, the heaven-born Prince of Peace!
   Hail, the Sun of righteousness!
   Light and life to all He brings,
   risen with healing in His wings.
   Mild, He lays His glory by,
   born that man no more may die,
   born to raise the sons of earth,
   born to give them second birth.

143 © Timothy Dudley-Smith

1 Holy child, how still You lie!
   safe the manger, soft the hay;
   faint upon the eastern sky
   breaks the dawn of Christmas Day.

2 Holy child, whose birthday brings
shepherds from their field and fold,
angel choirs and eastern kings,
myrrh and frankincense and gold:

3 Holy child, what gift of grace
from the Father freely willed!
In Your infant form we trace
all God's promises fulfilled.

4 Holy child, whose human years
span like ours delight and pain;
one in human joys and tears,
one in all but sin and stain:

5 Holy child, so far from home,
sons of men to seek and save:
to what dreadful death You come,
to what dark and silent grave!

6 Holy child, before whose name
powers of darkness faint and fall;
conquered death and sin and shame -
Jesus Christ is Lord of all!

7 Holy child, how still You lie!
safe the manger, soft the hay;
clear upon the eastern sky
breaks the dawn of Christmas Day.

2 Our God, heaven cannot hold Him,
nor earth sustain,
heaven and earth shall flee away
when He comes to reign;
in the bleak mid-winter
a stable-place sufficed
the Lord God Almighty,
Jesus Christ.

3 Angels and archangels
may have gathered there,
cherubim and seraphim
thronged the air;
but His mother only,
in her maiden bliss,
worshipped the Beloved
with a kiss.

4 What can I give Him,
poor as I am?
If I were a shepherd,
I would bring a lamb;
if I were a wise man,
I would do my part;
yet what I can I give Him -
give my heart.

144 Christina Georgina Rossetti (1830-94)

1 In the bleak mid-winter,
frosty wind made moan,
earth stood hard as iron,
water like a stone;
snow had fallen, snow on snow,
snow on snow,
in the bleak mid-winter,
long ago.

145 Edmund Hamilton Sears (1810-76)
© in this version Jubilate Hymns

1 It came upon the midnight clear,
that glorious song of old,
from angels bending near the earth
to touch their harps of gold:
"Peace on the earth, goodwill to men
from heaven's all-gracious king!"
The world in solemn stillness lay
to hear the angels sing.

2 With sorrow brought by sin and strife
the world has suffered long,
and, since the angels sang, have passed
two thousand years of wrong;
for man at war with man hears not
the love-song which they bring:
O hush the noise, you men of strife,
and hear the angels sing!

3 And those whose journey now is hard,
whose hope is burning low,
who tread the rocky path of life
with painful steps and slow:
O listen to the news of love
which makes the heavens ring!
O rest beside the weary road
and hear the angels sing!

4 And still the days are hastening on -
by prophets seen of old -
towards the fullness of the time
when comes the age foretold:
then earth and heaven renewed shall see
the Prince of Peace, their King;
and all the world repeat the song
which now the angels sing.

146 Isaac Watts (1674-1748)

1 Joy to the world, the Lord has come!
let earth receive her King;
let every heart prepare Him room
and heaven and nature sing,
and heaven and nature sing,
and heaven, and heaven and nature
sing!

2 Joy to the earth, the Saviour reigns!
your sweetest songs employ
while fields and streams and hills
and plains
repeat the sounding joy,
repeat the sounding joy,
repeat, repeat the sounding joy.

3 He rules the world with truth and grace,
and makes the nations prove
the glories of His righteousness,
the wonders of His love,
the wonders of His love,
the wonders, wonders of His love.

147 Charles Wesley (1707-88)

1 Let earth and heaven combine,
angels and men agree,
to praise in songs divine,
the incarnate Deity,
our God contracted to a span,
incomprehensibly made man.

2 He laid His glory by,
He wrapped Him in our clay;
unmarked by human eye,
the latent Godhead lay;
infant of days He here became,
and bore the mild Immanuel's Name.

3 Unsearchable the love
that hath the Saviour brought;
the grace is far above
or man or angel's thought:
suffice for us that God, we know,
our God, is manifest below.

4 He deigns in flesh to appear,
  widest extremes to join;
  to bring our vileness near,
  and make us all divine:
  and we the life of God shall know,
  for God is manifest below.

5 Made perfect by His love,
  and sanctified by grace,
  we shall from earth remove,
  and see His glorious face:
  then shall His love be fully showed,
  and man shall then be lost in God.

148 Nahum Tate (1652-1715)

1 While shepherds watched their flocks by
    night
  all seated on the ground;
  the angel of the Lord came down,
  and glory shone around.

2 "Fear not!" said he - for mighty dread
  had seized their troubled mind -
  "Glad tidings of great joy I bring
  to you and all mankind.

3 "To you, in David's town, this day,
  is born of David's line
  a Saviour, who is Christ the Lord
  and this shall be the sign:

4 "The heavenly Babe you there shall find
  to human view displayed,
  all meanly wrapped in swaddling bands,
  and in a manger laid."

5 Thus spake the seraph, and forthwith
  appeared a shining throng
  of angels, praising God, who thus
  addressed their joyful song:

6 "All glory be to God on high,
  and on the earth be peace;
  goodwill henceforth from heaven to
    men
  begin and never cease."

149 Latin, 18th century
tr. Frederick Oakley (1802-80)

1 O come, all ye faithful,
  joyful and triumphant,
  O come ye, O come ye to Bethlehem;
  come and behold Him,
  born the King of angels:

    O come, let us adore Him,
    O come, let us adore Him,
    O come, let us adore Him,
    Christ the Lord!

2 God of God,
  Light of light, eternal,
  Lo, He abhors not the virgin's womb;
  Very God,
  begotten not created:

3 Sing choirs of angels,
  sing in exultation,
  sing all ye citizens of heaven above,
  "Glory to God,
  glory in the highest:"

4 Yea, Lord, we greet Thee,
  born this happy morning,
  Jesus, to Thee be glory given!
  Word of the Father,
  now in flesh appearing:

150 Latin, 12th century
tr. John Mason Neale (1818-66)

1 O come, O come, Emmanuel,
and ransom captive Israel,
that mourns in lonely exile here
until the Son of God appear.

*Rejoice, rejoice! Emmanuel
shall come to thee, O Israel.*

2 O come, O come, Thou Lord of might,
who to Thy tribes, on Sinai's height
in ancient times didst give the law
in cloud and majesty and awe.

3 O come, Thou rod of Jesse, free
Thine own from Satan's tyranny;
from depths of hell Thy people save,
and give them victory o'er the grave.

4 O come, Thou day-spring, come and
cheer
our spirits by Thine advent here;
disperse the gloomy clouds of night,
and death's dark shadows put to flight.

5 O come, Thou key of David, come
and open wide our heavenly home;
make safe the way that leads on high,
and close the path to misery.

151 Phillips Brooks (1835-93)

1 O little town of Bethlehem,
how still we see you lie!
Above your deep and dreamless sleep
the silent stars go by:
yet in your dark streets shining
is everlasting Light;
the hopes and fears of all the years
are met in you tonight.

2 For Christ is born of Mary;
and, gathered all above,
while mortals sleep, the angels keep
their watch of wondering love.
O morning stars, together
proclaim the holy birth,
and praises sing to God the King,
and peace to men on earth.

3 How silently, how silently,
the wondrous gift is given!
So God imparts to human hearts
the blessings of His heaven.
No ear may hear His coming;
but in this world of sin,
where meek souls will receive Him, still
the dear Christ enters in.

4 O holy child of Bethlehem,
descend to us, we pray;
cast out our sin, and enter in;
be born in us today.
We hear the Christmas angels
the great glad tidings tell;
O come to us, abide with us,
our Lord Immanuel.

152 Cecil Frances Alexander (1823-95)

1 Once in royal David's city
stood a lowly cattle-shed,
where a mother laid her Baby
in a manger for His bed.
Mary was that mother mild,
Jesus Christ her little child.

2 He came down to earth from heaven
who is God and Lord of all,
and His shelter was a stable,
and His cradle was a stall.

With the poor and mean and lowly
lived on earth our Saviour holy.

3   And through all His wondrous
      childhood
    He would honour and obey,
    love, and watch the lowly maiden
    in whose gentle arms He lay.
    Christian children all must be
    mild, obedient, good as He.

4   For He is our childhood's pattern:
    day by day like us He grew;
    He was little, weak, and helpless;
    tears and smiles like us He knew;
    and He feeleth for our sadness,
    and He shareth in our gladness.

5   And our eyes at last shall see Him
    through His own redeeming love;
    for that Child so dear and gentle
    is our Lord in heaven above;
    and He leads His children on
    to the place where He is gone.

6   Not in that poor lowly stable,
    With the oxen standing by,
    We shall see Him, but in heaven,
    set at God's right hand on high,
    when, like stars, His children crowned
    all in white shall wait around.

153   Edward Caswall (1814-78)

1   See, amid the winter's snow,
    born for us on earth below,
    see, the Lamb of God appears,
    promised from eternal years.

    Hail, thou ever-blessed morn!
    Hail, redemption's happy dawn!
    Sing through all Jerusalem,
    Christ is born in Bethlehem!

2   Lo, within a manger lies
    He who built the starry skies,
    He who, throned in height sublime,
    sits amid the cherubim.

3   Say, ye holy shepherds, say,
    what your joyful news today;
    wherefore have ye left your sheep
    on the lonely mountain steep?

4   As we watched at dead of night,
    lo, we saw a wondrous light:
    angels singing, "Peace on earth"
    told us of the Saviour's birth.

5   Sacred infant, all divine,
    what a tender love was Thine,
    thus to come from highest bliss
    down to such a world as this!

6   Teach, O teach us, holy child,
    by Thy face so meek and mild,
    teach us to resemble Thee
    in Thy sweet humility.

154   Michael Perry
        © Mrs B Perry/Jubilate Hymns

1   See Him lying on a bed of straw:
    a draughty stable with an open door;
    Mary cradling the babe she bore,
    the Prince of glory is His name.

    O now carry me to Bethlehem
    to see the Lord appear to men,
    just as poor as was the stable then,
    the Prince of glory when He came.

2   Star of silver, sweep across the skies,
    show where Jesus in the manger lies;
    shepherds, swiftly from your stupor rise
    to see the Saviour of the world!

3 Angels, sing the song that you began,
  bring God's glory to the heart of man;
  sing that Bethlehem's little baby can
  be salvation to the soul.

4 Mine are riches, from Your poverty,
  from Your innocence, eternity;
  mine forgiveness by Your death for me,
  child of sorrow for my joy.

155 Author unknon (c 17th Century)
© in this version Jubilate Hymns

1 The first nowell the angel did say,
  was to Bethlehem's shepherds in fields
  as they lay;
  in fields where they lay keeping their
  sheep
  on a cold winter's night that was so
  deep:

  Nowell, nowell, nowell, nowell,
  born is the King of Israel!

2 Then wise men from a country far
  looked up and saw a guiding star;
  they travelled on by night and day
  to reach the place where Jesus lay:

3 At Bethlehem they entered in,
  on bended knee they worshipped Him;
  they offered there in His presence
  their gold and myrrh and frankincense:

4 Then let us all with one accord
  sing praises to our heavenly Lord;
  for Christ has our salvation wrought
  and with His blood mankind has
  bought:

156 Frank Houghton © OMF International

1 Thou who wast rich beyond all
    splendour,
  all for love's sake becamest poor,
  thrones for a manger didst surrender
  sapphire-paved courts for stable floor.
  Thou who wast rich beyond all
    splendour,
  all for love's sake becamest poor.

2 Thou who art God beyond all praising,
  all for love's sake becamest man;
  stooping so low, but sinners raising
  heavenwards by Thine eternal plan.
  Thou who art God beyond all praising,
  all for love's sake becamest man.

3 Thou who art love beyond all telling,
  Saviour and King, we worship Thee.
  Immanuel, within us dwelling,
  make us what Thou wouldst have us be.
  Thou who art love beyond all telling,
  Saviour and King, we worship Thee.

3.3 THE LORD JESUS CHRIST
His Life and Work

157 Graham Kendrick
© 1985 Kingsway's Thankyou Music

1 For this purpose Christ was revealed
  to destroy all the works of the evil one.
  Christ in us has overcome,
  so with gladness we sing
  and welcome His kingdom in.

Men   *Over sin He has conquered:*
Women *Hallelujah! He has conquered.*
Men   *Over death victorious:*
Women *Hallelujah! victorious.*
Men   *Over sickness He has triumphed*
Women *Hallelujah! He has triumphed.*
ALL   *Jesus reigns over all!*

2 In the name of Jesus we stand;
    by the power of His blood
    we now claim this ground:
    Satan has no authority here,
    powers of darkness must flee,
    for Christ has the victory.

158 Alison Revell
      © 1978 Kingsway's Thankyou Music

1 Thank You Jesus, thank You Jesus,
    thank You Lord for loving me.
    Thank You Jesus, thank You Jesus,
    thank You Lord for loving me.

2 You went to Calvary, there You died
      for me,
    thank You Lord for loving me.
    You went to Calvary, there You died
      for me,
    thank You Lord for loving me.

3 You rose up from the grave, to me new
      life You gave,
    thank You Lord for loving me.
    You rose up from the grave, to me new
      life You gave,
    thank You Lord for loving me.

4 You're coming back again, and we with
      You shall reign,
    thank You Lord for loving me.
    You're coming back again, and we with
      You shall reign,
    thank You Lord for loving me.

159 William Young Fullerton (1857-1932)
      © Unidentified

1 I cannot tell why He, whom angels
      worship,
    should set His love upon the sons
      of men,
    or why, as Shepherd, He should
      seek the wanderers,
    to bring them back, they know
      not how or when.
    but this I know, that He was born
      of Mary,
    when Bethlehem's manger was His
      only home,
    and that He lived at Nazareth and
      laboured,
    and so the Saviour, Saviour of the
      world, is come.

2 I cannot tell how silently He suffered,
    as with His peace He graced this
      place of tears,
    or how His heart upon the Cross was
      broken,
    the crown of pain to three and thirty
      years.
    But this I know, He heals the broken-
      hearted,
    and stays our sin. and calms our
      lurking fear,
    and lifts the burden from the heavy
      laden,
    for yet the Saviour, Saviour of the
      world is here.

3 I cannot tell how He will win the
      nations;
    how He will claim His earthly heritage,
    how satisfy the needs and aspirations
    of east and west, of sinner and of sage.
    But this I know, all flesh shall see His
      glory,

and He shall reap the harvest He has
 sown,
and some glad day His sun shall shine
 in splendour
when He the Saviour, Saviour of the
 world is known.

4 I cannot tell how all the lands shall
  worship
 when, at His bidding, every storm is
  stilled,
 or who can say how great the jubilation
 when all the hearts of men with love are
  filled.
 But this I know, the skies will thrill with
  rapture,
 and myriad, myriad human voices sing,
 and earth to heaven, and heaven to earth,
  will answer:
 at last the Saviour, Saviour of the world,
  is King.

160 Samuel Crossman (1624-83)

1 My song is love unknown;
 my Saviour's love to me;
 love to the loveless shown,
 that they might lovely be.
 O who am I,
 that for my sake,
 my Lord should take
 frail flesh, and die?

2 He came from His blest throne,
 salvation to bestow;
 but men made strange, and none
 the longed-for Christ would know.
 But O my friend,
 my friend indeed,
 who at my need
 His life did spend.

3 Sometimes they strew His way
 and His sweet praises sing;
 resounding all the day
 hosannas to their King.
 Then: "Crucify!"
 is all their breath,
 and for His death
 they thirst and cry.

4 Why, what hath my Lord done?
 What makes this rage and spite?
 He made the lame to run,
 He gave the blind their sight.
 Sweet injuries!
 yet they at these
 themselves displease,
 and 'gainst Him rise.

5 They rise and needs will have
 my dear Lord made away:
 a murderer they save,
 the Prince of Life they slay.
 Yet cheerful He
 to suffering goes,
 that He His foes
 from thence might free.

6 In life, no house, no home
 my Lord on earth might have;
 in death, no friendly tomb,
 but what a stranger gave.
 What may I say?
 Heaven was His home;
 but mine the tomb
 wherein He lay.

7 Here might I stay and sing,
 no story so divine;
 never was love, dear King,
 never was grief like Thine.
 This is my friend,
 in whose sweet praise
 I all my days
 could gladly spend.

161 A B Simpson (1843-1919)

1 Oh, how sweet the glorious message
simple faith may claim;
yesterday, today, forever,
Jesus is the same.
Still He loves to save the sinful,
heal the sick and lame;
cheer the mourner, still the tempest;
glory to His name!

Yesterday, today, forever,
Jesus is the same.
All may change, but Jesus never!
Glory to His name.
Glory to His name, glory to His name.
All may change, but Jesus never!
Glory to His name.

2 He who was the Friend of sinners
seeks you, lost one, now;
sinner come, and at His footstool
penitently bow.
He who said, "I'll not condemn you,
go and sin no more,"
speaks to you that word of pardon,
as in days of yore.

3 He who pardoned erring Peter,
never need you fear;
He that came to faithless Thomas,
all your doubt will clear.
He who let the loved disciple
on His bosom rest,
bids you still, with love as tender,
lean upon His breast.

4 He who, 'mid the raging billows,
walked upon the sea,
still can hush our wildest tempest,
as on Galilee.

He who wept and prayed in anguish
in Gethsemane,
drinks with us each cup of trembling
in our agony.

5 As of old He walked to Emmaus,
with them to abide;
so through all life's way He walketh
ever near our side.
Soon again shall we behold Him,
hasten, Lord, the day!
But 'twill still be "this same Jesus,"
as He went away.

162 J Wilbur Chapman (1859-1918)

1 One day when heaven was filled with
His praises,
one day when sin was as black as could
be,
Jesus came forth to be born of a virgin,
dwelt amongst men, my example is
He!

Living, He loved me; dying He saved
me;
buried, He carried my sins far away,
rising, He justified freely for ever:
one day He's coming: O glorious day.

2 One day they led Him up Calvary's
mountain,
one day they nailed Him to die on the
tree;
suffering anguish, despised and rejected;
bearing our sins, my Redeemer is He!

3 One day they left Him alone in the
garden,
one day He rested, from suffering free;
angels came down o'er His tomb to
keep vigil;
hope of the hopeless, my Saviour is He!

4 One day the grave could conceal Him
      no longer,
   one day the stone rolled away from the
      door;
   then He arose, over death He had
      conquered;
   now is ascended, my Lord evermore!

5 One day the trumpet will sound for His
      coming,
   one day the skies with His glory will
      shine;
   wonderful day, my beloved ones
      bringing;
   glorious Saviour, this Jesus is mine!

163 Melody Green © 1982 Birdwing Music/BMG
         Songs Inc./Ears to Hear Music/EMI Christian
         Music Publishing/Admin. by Copycare

1 There is a Redeemer,
   Jesus, God's own Son,
   precious Lamb of God, Messiah,
   Holy One.

      Thank You, O my Father,
      for giving us Your Son,
      and leaving Your Spirit
      till the work on earth is done.

2 Jesus my Redeemer,
   name above all names,
   precious Lamb of God, Messiah,
   O for sinners slain:

3 When I stand in glory
   I will see His face,
   and there I'll serve my King for ever
   in that holy place.

164 E E S Elliott (1836-1897)

1 Thou did'st leave Thy throne and Thy
      Kingly crown,
   when Thou camest to earth for me:
   but in Bethlehem's home was there
      found no room
   for Thy holy nativity.
   Oh, come to my heart, Lord Jesus!
   There is room in my heart for Thee.

2 Heaven's arches rang when the angels
      sang,
   proclaiming Thy royal degree;
   but of lowly birth camest Thou, Lord,
      on earth,
   and in great humility.
   Oh, come to my heart, Lord Jesus!
   There is room in my heart for Thee.

3 The foxes found rest, and the birds
      had their nest
   in the shade of the forest tree;
   but Thy couch was the sod, O Thou
      Son of God,
   in the deserts of Galilee.
   Oh, come to my heart, Lord Jesus!
   There is room in my heart for Thee.

4 Thou camest, O Lord, with the living
      Word
   that should set Thy people free;
   but with mocking scorn, and with
      crown of thorn,
   they bore Thee to Calvary.
   Oh, come to my heart, Lord Jesus!
   Thy cross is my only plea.

5 When heaven's arches shall ring, and
      her choirs shall sing
   at Thy coming to victory,

let Thy voice call me home, saying,
  "Yet there is room,
there is room at My side for thee!"
And my heart shall rejoice, Lord
Jesus!
When Thou comest and callest for
  me.

165 Benjamin Russell Hanby (1833-67)

1 Who is He in yonder stall,
  at whose feet the shepherds fall?

  'Tis the Lord, O wondrous story,
  'tis the Lord, the King of Glory!
  At His feet we humbly fall -
  crown Him, crown Him Lord of all!

2 Who is He in deep distress,
  fasting in the wilderness?

3 Who is He who stands and weeps
  at the grave where Lazarus sleeps?

4 Lo, at midnight, who is He
  prays in dark Gethsemane?

5 Who is He on Calvary's tree
  dies in grief and agony?

6 Who is He who from the grave
  comes to heal, to help and save?

7 Who is He who from His throne
  rules through all the worlds alone?

166 A H Ackley
© The Rodeheaver Co./ Word Music/Admin.
by Copycare

1 Wonderful birth, to a manger He came,
  made in the likeness of man, to proclaim
  God's boundless love for a world sick
    with sin,
  pleading with sinners to let Him come
    in.

  Wonderful name He bears,
  wonderful crown He wears,
  wonderful blessings His triumphs
    afford;
  wonderful Calvary,
  wonderful grace for me,
  wonderful love of my wonderful Lord!

2 Wonderful life, full of service so free,
  friend to the poor and the needy was He;
  unfailing goodness on all He bestowed,
  undying faith in the vilest He showed.

3 Wonderful death, for it meant not defeat,
  Calvary made His great mission
    complete,
  wrought our redemption, and when He
    arose,
  banished for ever the last of our foes.

4 Wonderful hope, He is coming again,
  coming as King o'er the nations to
    reign;
  glorious promise, His word cannot fail,
  His righteous kingdom at last must
    prevail!

167 W G Ovens (1870-1945) v1
Mrs G W Roberts (b. 1888) vs 2-4
© Unidentified

1 Wounded for me, wounded for me,
  there on the Cross He was wounded
    for me;

gone my transgressions and now I
  am free,
all because Jesus was wounded for me.

2 Risen for me, risen for me,
up from the grave He has risen for me;
now evermore from death's sting I
  am free,
all because Jesus has risen for me.

3 Living for me, living for me,
there on the throne He is living for me;
saved to the uttermost now I shall be,
all because Jesus is living for me.

4 Coming for me, coming for me,
one day to earth He is coming for me;
then with what joy His dear face I shall
  see,
  oh, how I praise Him - He's coming
  for me.

3.4 THE LORD JESUS CHRIST
His Sufferings and Death

168 James Montgomery (1771-1854)

1 According to Thy gracious word,
in meek humility,
this will I do, my dying Lord:
I will remember Thee.

2 Thy body, broken for my sake,
my bread from heaven shall be;
Thy testamental cup I take,
and thus remember Thee.

3 Gethsemane can I forget?
Or there Thy conflict see,
Thine agony and bloody sweat,
and not remember Thee?

4 When to the cross I turn my eyes
and rest on Calvary,
O Lamb of God, my sacrifice,
I must remember Thee.

5 Remember Thee and all Thy pains,
and all Thy love to me;
yea, while a breath, a pulse remains,
will I remember Thee.

6 And when these failing lips grow dumb,
and mind and memory flee,
when Thou shalt in Thy kingdom come
then, Lord, remember me.

169 Charles Wesley (1707-88)

1 All you that pass by,
to Jesus draw nigh:
to you is it nothing that Jesus should die?
Your ransom and peace,
your surety He is:
come, see if there ever was sorrow like
  His.

2 For what you have done
His blood must atone:
the Father hath stricken for you His
  dear Son.
The Lord, in the day
of His anger, did lay
your sins on the Lamb, and He bore
  them away.

3 He answered for all:
O come at His call,
and low at His cross with astonishment
  fall!
But lift up your eyes
at Jesus' cries:
impassive, He suffers; immortal, He
  dies.

4   He dies to atone
    for sins not His own;
    your debt He hath paid, and your work
      He hath done.
    You all may receive
    the peace He did leave,
    who made intercession - "My Father,
      forgive!"

5   For you and for me
    He prayed on the tree:
    the prayer is accepted, the sinner is free.
    That sinner am I,
    who on Jesus rely,
    and come for the pardon God will not
      deny.

6   My pardon I claim;
    for a sinner I am,
    a sinner believing in Jesus' name.
    He purchased the grace
    which now I embrace:
    Father, Thou know'st He hath died in
      my place.

7   His death is my plea;
    my Advocate see,
    and hear the blood speak that hath
      answered for me.
    My ransom He was
    when He bled on the cross;
    and by losing His life He hath carried
      my cause.

170   Isaac Watts (1674-1748)

1   Alas! and did my Saviour bleed,
    and did my Sovereign die?
    Would He devote that sacred head
    for such a worm as I?

2   Was it for crimes that I had done,
    He groaned upon the tree?
    Amazing pity, grace unknown,
    and love beyond degree!

3   Well might the sun in darkness hide,
    and shut his glories in,
    when Christ, the great Creator, died
    for man the creature's sin.

4   Thus might I hide my blushing face
    while His dear cross appears,
    dissolve my heart in thankfulness,
    and melt mine eyes to tears.

5   But drops of grief can ne'er repay
    the debt of love I owe;
    here, Lord, I give myself away,
    'tis all that I can do!

171   Graham Kendrick
© 1983 Kingsway's Thankyou Music

1   From heaven You came, helpless Babe,
    entered our world, Your glory veiled,
    not to be served but to serve,
    and give Your life that we might live.

    This is our God, the Servant King,
    He calls us now to follow Him,
    to bring our lives as a daily offering
    of worship to the Servant King.

2   There in the garden of tears
    my heavy load He chose to bear;
    His heart with sorrow was torn,
    "Yet not My will but Yours," He said.

3   Come see His hands and His feet,
    the scars that speak of sacrifice,
    hands that flung stars into space
    to cruel nails surrendered.

4 So let us learn how to serve
and in our lives enthrone Him,
each other's needs to prefer,
for it is Christ we're serving.

172 Elizabeth Clephane (1830-69)

1 Beneath the Cross of Jesus
I fain would take my stand,
the shadow of a mighty Rock,
within a weary land;
a home within the wilderness,
a rest upon the way,
from the burning of the noon-tide heat,
and the burden of the day.

2 O safe and happy shelter,
O refuge tried and sweet,
O trysting-place, where Heaven's love
and Heaven's justice meet!
As to the holy patriarch
that wondrous dream was given,
so seems my Saviour's Cross to me,
a ladder up to heaven.

3 There lies beneath its shadow,
but on the farther side,
the darkness of an awful grave
that gapes both deep and wide:
and there between us stands the Cross,
two arms outstretched to save,
like a watchman set to guard the way
from that eternal grave.

4 Upon that Cross of Jesus
mine eye at times can see
the very dying form of One
who suffered there for me;
and from my smitten heart, with tears,
two wonders I confess,
the wonder of His glorious love,
and my own worthlessness.

5 I take, O Cross, thy shadow
for my abiding place;
I ask no other sunshine than
the sunshine of His face;
content to let the world go by,
to know no gain nor loss,
my sinful self my only shame,
my glory all the Cross.

173 Graham Kendrick
© 1989 Make Way Music

1 Come and see, come and see,
come and see the King of love;
see the purple robe and crown of
thorns He wears.
Soldiers mock, rulers sneer
as He lifts the cruel cross;
lone and friendless now,
He climbs towards the hill.

We worship at Your feet,
where wrath and mercy meet,
and a guilty world is washed by
love's pure stream.
For us He was made sin -
oh, help me take it in.
Deep wounds of love cry out
"Father, forgive".
I worship,
I worship the Lamb who was slain.

2 Come and weep, come and mourn
for your sin that pierced Him there;
so much deeper than the wounds of
thorn and nail.
All our pride, all our greed,
all our fallenness and shame;
and the Lord has laid the
punishment on Him.

3   Man of heaven, born to earth
    to restore us to Your heaven.
    Here we bow in awe beneath Your
        searching eyes.
    From Your tears comes our joy,
    from Your death our life shall spring;
    by Your resurrection power we shall
        rise.

174 Graham Kendrick
         © 1985 Kingsway's Thankyou Music

Come see the beauty of the Lord,
come see the beauty of His face.
See the Lamb that once was slain,
see on His palms is carved your name.
See how our pain has pierced His heart,
and on His brow He bears our pride;
a crown of thorns.
Come see the beauty of the Lord,
come see the beauty of His face.

But only love pours from His heart,
as silently He takes the blame.
He has my name upon His lips,
my condemnation falls on Him.
This love is marvellous to me,
His sacrifice has set me free,
and now I live.
Come see the beauty of the Lord,
come see the beauty of His face.

175 Katherine A M Kelly (1869-1942)
         © Young Life

1   Give me a sight, O Saviour,
    of Thy wondrous love to me,
    of the love that brought Thee down
        to earth,
    to die on Calvary.

Oh, make me understand it,
help me to take it in,
what it meant to Thee, the Holy One,
to bear away my sin.

2   Was it the nails, O Saviour,
    that bound Thee to the tree?
    Nay, 'twas Thine everlasting love,
    Thy love for me, for me.

3   Oh, wonder of all wonders,
    that through Thy death for me,
    my open sins, my secret sins,
    can all forgiven be.

4   Then melt my heart, O Saviour,
    bend me, yea, break me down,
    until I own Thee Conqueror,
    and Lord and Sovereign crown.

176 John Newton (1725-1807)

1   Glory to Thee, Thou Son of God most
        High,
    all praise to Thee!
    Glory to Thee, enthroned above the sky,
    who died for me;
    high on Thy throne, Thine ear, Lord
        Jesus bend
    as grateful hearts now to Thyself
    ascend.

2   Deep were Thy sorrows, Lord, when
        heaven frowned -
    Gethsemane!
    Bloodlike Thy sweat, Lord, falling to
        the ground
    so heavily;
    dark was the night, but heaven was
        darker still,
    O Christ my God! - is this the Father's
        will?

3 Thorns wreathed Thy brow when
   hanging on the tree,
   man's cruelty!
   Why lavish love like this, O Lord, on
   me?
   Thou lovest me!
   Would that my soul could understand
   its length,
   its breadth, depth, height and
   everlasting strength!

4 Thy precious blood was freely shed
   for me
   on Calvary
   to save me from a lost eternity;
   glory to Thee!
   Nor death, nor hell, nor things below,
   above
   can sever me from Thy eternal love.

5 Like shoreless seas, Thy love can
   know no bound;
   Thou lovest me!
   Deep, vast, immense, unfathomed,
   Lord, profound,
   Lord, I love Thee!
   And when above, my crown is at Thy
   feet,
   I'll praise Thee still for Calvary's
   mercy seat.

177 Joseph Shabalala
© 1996 Empire Music Ltd./Polygram
Music Ltd. Used by permission of Music Sales
Limited. All rights reserved. International
Copyright Secured.

He showed me His hands that were marred
   for my sinning,
He showed me His feet that were nailed to
   the tree.
I then saw His brow, and His side deeply
   wounded,
and now I love Jesus, and Jesus loves me.

178 Maggi Dawn
© 1987 Kingsway's Thankyou Music

1 He was pierced for our transgressions,
   and bruised for our iniquities;
   and to bring us peace He was punished,
   and by His stripes we are healed.

2 He was led like a lamb to the slaughter,
   although He was innocent of crime;
   and cut off from the land of the living,
   He paid for the guilt that was mine.

   We like sheep have gone astray,
   turned each one to his own way,
   and the Lord has laid on Him
   the iniquity of us all.

   We like sheep . . .

179 William Rees (1802-83),
tr. William Edwards (1848-1929)
Copyright control

1 Here is love, vast as the ocean,
   lovingkindness as the flood,
   when the Prince of life, our ransom,
   shed for us His precious blood.
   Who His love will not remember?
   Who can cease to sing His praise?
   He can never be forgotten
   throughout heaven's eternal days.

2 On the Mount of Crucifixion
   fountains opened deep and wide;
   through the floodgates of God's mercy
   flowed a vast and gracious tide.
   Grace and love, like mighty rivers,
   poured incessant from above,
   and heaven's peace and perfect justice
   kissed a guilty world in love.

180 Stuart Townend
© 1995 Kingsway's Thankyou Music

1 How deep the Father's love for us,
   how vast beyond all measure,
   that He should give His only Son
   to make a wretch His treasure.
   How great the pain of searing loss,
   the Father turns His face away,
   as wounds which mar the Chosen One
   bring many sons to glory.

2 Behold the Man upon a cross,
   my sin upon His shoulders;
   ashamed, I hear my mocking voice
   call out among the scoffers.
   It was my sin that held Him there
   until it was accomplished;
   His dying breath has brought me life,
   I know that it is finished.

3 I will not boast in anything,
   no gifts, no power, no wisdom;
   but I will boast in Jesus Christ,
   His death and resurrection.
   Why should I gain from His reward?
   I cannot give an answer,
   but this I know with all my heart,
   His wounds have paid my ransom.

181 Charles H Gabriel (1856-1932)
© Unidentified

1 I stand amazed in the presence
   of Jesus the Nazarene,
   and wonder how He could love me,
   a sinner, condemned, unclean.

   How marvellous! how wonderful!
   and my song shall ever be:
   How marvellous! how wonderful!
   is my Saviour's love for me!

2 For me it was in the garden
   He prayed - "Not My will, but Thine;"
   He had no tears for His own griefs,
   but sweat drops of blood for mine.

3 In pity angels beheld Him
   and came from the world of light,
   to comfort Him in the sorrows
   He bore for my soul that night.

4 He took my sins and my sorrows,
   He made them His very own;
   He bore the burden to Calvary
   and suffered and died alone.

5 When with the ransomed in glory
   His face I at last shall see,
   'twill be my joy through the ages
   to sing of His love for me.

182 D Woods
Copyright Control

1 His hands were pierced, the hands
      that made
   the mountain range and everglade;
   that washed the stains of sin away
   and changed earth's darkness into day.

2 His feet were pierced, the feet that trod
   the furthest shining star of God;
   and left their imprint deep and clear
   on every winding pathway here.

3 His heart was pierced, the heart that
      burned
   to comfort every heart that yearned;
   and from it came a cleansing flood,
   the river of redeeming blood.

4   His hands and feet and heart, all three
    were pierced for me on Calvary;
    and here and now, to Him I bring
    my hands, feet, heart, an offering.

183   Philip Paul Bliss (1838-76)

1   "Man of Sorrows," what a name
    for the Son of God, who came,
    ruined sinners to reclaim!
    Hallelujah, what a Saviour!

2   Bearing shame and scoffing rude,
    in my place condemned He stood:
    sealed my pardon with His blood.
    Hallelujah, what a Saviour!

3   Guilty, vile, and helpless, we;
    spotless Lamb of God was He;
    "Full atonement," can it be?
    Hallelujah, what a Saviour!

4   Lifted up was He to die,
    "It is finished," was His cry,
    now in heaven exalted high:
    Hallelujah, what a Saviour!

5   When He comes, our glorious King,
    all His ransomed home to bring,
    then anew this song we'll sing:
    Hallelujah, what a Saviour!

184   Isaac Watts (1674-1748)

1   Not all the blood of beasts
    on Jewish altars slain,
    could give the guilty conscience peace,
    or wash away the stain.

2   But Christ, the heavenly Lamb,
    takes all our sins away;
    a sacrifice of nobler name
    and richer blood than they.

3   My faith would lay her hand
    on that dear head of Thine,
    while like a penitent I stand
    and there confess my sin.

4   My soul looks back to see
    the burdens Thou didst bear,
    when hanging on the cursed tree,
    and knows her guilt was there.

5   Believing, we rejoice
    to see the curse remove;
    we bless the Lamb with cheerful voice
    and sing His bleeding love.

185   Charles Wesley (1707-88)

1   O Love Divine! what hast Thou done?
    The immortal God hath died for me!
    The Father's co-eternal Son
    bore all my sins upon the tree;
    the immortal God for me hath died!
    my Lord, my Love is crucified.

2   Behold Him, ye that pass Him by,
    the bleeding Prince of life and peace!
    Come sinners, see your Maker die
    and say, was ever grief like His?
    Come, feel with me His blood applied:
    my Lord, my Love is crucified:

3   Is crucified for me and you,
    to bring us rebels back to God:
    believe, believe the record true,
    ye now are bought with Jesus' blood,
    pardon for sin flows from His side:
    my Lord, my Love is crucified.

4   Then let us sit beneath His cross,
    and gladly catch the healing stream,
    all things for Him account but loss,
    and give up all our hearts to Him;
    of nothing think or speak beside:
    my Lord, my Love is crucified.

186   George Bennard (d. 1958)
© The Rodeheaver Co./ Word Music/Admin.
by Copycare

1   On a hill far away stood an old rugged
        cross,
    the emblem of suffering and shame;
    and I love that old cross where the
        dearest and best
    for a world of lost sinners was slain.

    So I'll cherish the old rugged cross
    till my trophies at last I lay down;
    I will cling to the old rugged cross
    and exchange it some day for a
    crown.

2   O, the old rugged cross, so despised by
        the world,
    has a wondrous attraction for me;
    for the dear Lamb of God left His glory
        above
    to bear it to dark Calvary.

3   In the old rugged cross, stained with
        blood so divine,
    a wondrous beauty I see;
    for 'twas on that old cross Jesus suffered
        and died
    to pardon and sanctify me.

4   To the old rugged cross I will ever be
        true,
    its shame and reproach gladly bear;
    then He'll call me some day to my home
        far away,
    when His glory for ever I'll share.

187   J C Bateman (1854-88)

1   On the cross of Calvary,
    Jesus died for you and me,
    there He shed His precious blood,
    that from sin we might be free.
    Oh, the cleansing stream doth flow,
    and it washes white as snow;
    it was for me that Jesus died,
    on the cross of Calvary.

2   Clouds and darkness veiled the sky
    when the Lord was crucified,
    "It is finished," was His cry,
    when He bowed His head and died.
    It is finished! yes, indeed,
    all the world may now go free.
    It was for this that Jesus died,
    on the cross of Calvary.

3   Oh, what wondrous, wondrous love,
    brought me down at Jesus' feet!
    Oh, such wondrous dying love,
    asks a sacrifice complete.
    Here I give myself to Thee,
    soul and body, Thine to be,
    it was for me Thy blood was shed,
    on the cross of Calvary.

4   Take me, Lord, and seal me Thine,
    wholly Thine, for evermore,
    sweet assurance, Thou art mine,
    and the night of death is o'er.
    Cleanse, oh, cleanse my heart from sin,
    make and keep me pure within!
    It was for this Thy blood was shed,
    on the cross of Calvary.

188 N B Herrell
© Nazarene Publishing/Admin. by Copycare

1 Once our blessed Christ of beauty
was veiled off from human view;
but through suffering death and sorrow
He has rent the veil in two.

   O behold the Man of Sorrows,
   O behold Him in plain view,
   lo! He is the mighty conqueror,
   since He rent the veil in two,
   lo! He is the mighty conqueror,
   since He rent the veil in two.

2 Yes, He is with God the Father,
interceding there for you;
for He is the mighty conqueror,
since He rent the veil in two.

3 Holy angels bow before Him,
men of earth give praises due;
for He is the well beloved,
since He rent the veil in two.

4 Throughout time and endless ages,
heights and depths of love so true;
He alone can be the giver,
since He rent the veil in two.

189 A R Consin (1824-1906)

1 O Christ, what burdens bowed Thy
head!
Our load was laid on Thee;
Thou stoodest in the sinner's stead,
didst bear all ill for me.
A victim led, Thy blood was shed;
now there's no load for me.

2 Death and the curse were in our cup:
O Christ, 'twas full for Thee!
But Thou hast drained the last dark
drop,
'tis empty now for me:
that bitter cup, love drank it up:
now blessing's draught for me.

3 The tempest's awful voice was heard,
O Christ, it broke on Thee!
Thy open bosom was my ward,
it braved the storm for me.
Thy form was scarred, Thy visage
marred,
now cloudless peace for me.

4 For me, Lord Jesus, Thou hast died,
and I have died in Thee:
Thou'rt risen, my bands are all untied,
and now Thou livest in me:
when purified, made white and tried,
Thy glory then for me!

190 Cecil Francis Alexander (1818-95)

1 There is a green hill far away,
outside a city wall,
where the dear Lord was crucified,
who died to save us all.

2 We may not know, we cannot tell
what pains He had to bear;
but we believe it was for us
He hung and suffered there.

3 He died that we might be forgiven,
He died to make us good,
that we might go at last to heaven,
saved by His precious blood.

4 There was no other good enough
  to pay the price of sin;
  He only could unlock the gate
  of heaven, and let us in.

5 Oh, dearly, dearly has He loved
  and we must love Him too,
  and trust in His redeeming blood,
  and try His works to do.

191 Graham Kendrick
        © 1983 Kingsway's Thankyou Music

1 The price is paid:
  come, let us enter in
  to all that Jesus died
  to make our own.
  For every sin
  more than enough He gave,
  and bought our freedom
  from each guilty stain.

  The price is paid, alleluia,
  amazing grace,
  so strong and sure!
  And so with all my heart,
  my life in every part,
  I live to thank You
  for the price You paid.

2 The price is paid:
  see Satan flee away,
  for Jesus, crucified,
  destroys his power.
  No more to pay!
  Let accusation cease:
  in Christ there is
  no condemnation now!

3 The price is paid:
  and by that scourging cruel,
  He took our sicknesses
  as if His own.
  And by His wounds,
  His body broken there,
  His healing touch may now
  by faith be known.

4 The price is paid:
  "Worthy the Lamb!" we cry,
  eternity shall never
  cease His praise.
  The Church of Christ
  shall rule upon the earth:
  in Jesus' name
  we have authority!

192 Charles Wesley (1707-88)

1 'Tis finished! the Messiah dies,
  cut off for sin, but not His own;
  accomplished is the sacrifice,
  the great redeeming work is done.
  'Tis finished! all the debt is paid,
  justice divine is satisfied,
  the grand and full atonement made;
  God for a guilty world hath died.

2 The veil is rent in Christ alone;
  the living way to heaven is seen;
  the middle wall is broken down
  and all mankind may enter in.
  The types and figures are fulfilled,
  exacted is the legal pain,
  the precious promises are sealed;
  the spotless Lamb of God is slain.

3 The reign of sin and death is o'er
and all may live from sin set free;
Satan has lost his mortal power;
'tis swallowed up in victory.
Saved from the legal curse I am,
my Saviour hangs on yonder tree:
see there the meek, expiring Lamb!
'Tis finished, He expires for me.

4 Accepted in the well-beloved
and clothed in righteousness divine,
I see the bar to heaven removed
and all Thy merits, Lord, are mine.
Death, hell, and sin are now subdued,
all grace is now to sinners given,
and lo, I plead the atoning blood,
and in Thy right I claim Thy heaven.

193
Avis Christiansen (d. 1985)
© 1949 Singspiration Music/Brentwood
Benson Music Publishing Inc./Admin. by
Copycare

1 Up Calvary's mountain, one dreadful
morn,
walked Christ my Saviour, weary and
worn;
facing for sinners death on the cross,
that He might save them from endless
loss.

*Blessed Redeemer, precious
Redeemer!
Seems now I see Him on Calvary's tree
wounded and bleeding, for sinners
pleading,
blind and unheeding, dying for me!*

2 "Father forgive them!" thus did He pray,
e'en while His life-blood flowed fast
away;
praying for sinners while in such woe,
no one but Jesus ever loved so.

3 O how I love Him, Saviour and
Friend!
How can my praises ever find end!
Through years unnumbered on heaven's
shore,
my tongue shall praise Him for
evermore.

194 Traditional

1 Were you there when they crucified my
Lord?
Were you there when they crucified my
Lord?
Oh! Sometimes it causes me to tremble,
tremble, tremble!
Were you there when they crucified my
Lord?

2 Were you there when they nailed Him
to the tree?
Were you there when they nailed Him
to the tree?
Oh! Sometimes it causes me to tremble,
tremble, tremble!
Were you there when they nailed Him
to the tree?

3 Were you there when they laid Him in
the tomb?
Were you there when they laid Him in
the tomb?
Oh! Sometimes it causes me to tremble,
tremble, tremble!
Were you there when they laid Him in
the tomb?

4 Were you there when He rose up from
the dead?
Were you there when He rose up from
the dead?
Oh! Sometimes I feel like shouting
glory, glory, glory!
Were you there when He rose up from
the dead?

195 Isaac Watts (1674-1748)

1 When I survey the wondrous cross
on which the Prince of glory died,
my richest gain I count but loss,
and pour contempt on all my pride.

2 Forbid it, Lord, that I should boast,
save in the death of Christ, my God;
all the vain things that charm me most,
I sacrifice them to His blood.

3 See, from His head, His hands, His feet,
sorrow and love flow mingled down!
Did e'er such love and sorrow meet,
or thorns compose so rich a crown?

4 Were the whole realm of nature mine,
that were an offering far too small;
love so amazing, so divine,
demands my soul, my life, my all.

196 Thomas Kelly (1769-1855)

1 We sing the praise of Him who died,
of Him who died upon the cross;
the sinner's hope let men deride,
for this we count the world but lost.

2 Inscribed upon the cross we see,
in shining letters, "God is love;"
He bears our sins upon the tree,
He brings us mercy from above.

3 The cross! it takes our guilt away,
it holds the fainting spirit up;
it cheers with hope the gloomy day
and sweetens every bitter cup.

4 It makes the coward spirit brave
and nerves the feeble arm for fight;
it takes the terror from the grave
and gilds the bed of death with light.

5 The balm of life, the cure of woe,
the measure and the pledge of love;
the sinner's refuge here below,
the angels' theme in heaven above.

3.5 THE LORD JESUS CHRIST
His Resurrection

197 Philip Dodderidge (1702-51)
altered © Horrobin/Leavers

1 Hark, the glad sound! the Saviour
comes,
the Saviour promised long;
let every heart prepare a throne
and every voice a song.

2 He comes, the prisoners to release
in Satan's bondage held;
the chains of sin before Him break,
the iron fetters yield.

3 He comes to free the captive mind
where evil thoughts control;
and for the darkness of the blind,
gives light that makes them whole.

4 He comes the broken heart to bind,
the wounded soul to cure;
and with the treasures of His grace
to enrich the humble poor.

5 Our glad hosannas, Prince of Peace,
   Your welcome shall proclaim;
   and heaven's eternal arches ring
   with Your beloved name.

198 Noel & Tricia Richards
© 1987 Kingsway's Thankyou Music

1 All heaven declares
   the glory of the risen Lord;
   who can compare
   with the beauty of the Lord?
   For ever He will be
   the Lamb upon the throne;
   I gladly bow the knee,
   and worship Him alone.

2 I will proclaim
   the glory of the risen Lord,
   who once was slain
   to reconcile man to God.
   For ever You will be
   the Lamb upon the throne;
   I gladly bow the knee,
   and worship You alone.

199 Dave Fellingham
© 1982 Kingsway's Thankyou Music

1 At Your feet we fall, mighty risen Lord,
   as we come before Your throne to
      worship You.
   By Your Spirit's power You now draw
      our hearts,
   and we hear Your voice in triumph
      ringing clear:

   "I am He that liveth,
   that liveth and was dead.
   Behold, I am alive for evermore."

2 There we see You stand, mighty risen
      Lord,
   clothed in garments pure and holy,
      shining bright;
   eyes of flashing fire, feet like burnished
      bronze,
   and the sound of many waters is Your
      voice.

3 Like the shining sun in its noon-day
      strength,
   we now see the glory of Your wondrous
      face:
   once that face was marred, but now
      You're glorified;
   and Your words, like a two-edged
      sword have mighty power.

200 John Samuel Bewley Monsell (1811-75)

1 Christ is risen! hallelujah!
   risen our victorious Head;
   sing His praises; hallelujah!
   Christ is risen from the dead.
   Gratefully our hearts adore Him,
   as His light once more appears;
   bowing down in joy before Him,
   rising up from grief and tears.

   Christ is risen! hallelujah!
   risen our victorious Head;
   sing His praises; hallelujah!
   Christ is risen from the dead.

2 Christ is risen! all the sadness
   of His earthly life is o'er;
   through the open gates of gladness
   He returns to life once more.
   Death and hell before Him bending,
   He doth rise the Victor now,
   angels on His steps attending,
   glory round His wounded brow.

3   Christ is risen! henceforth never
    death or hell shall us enthral;
    we are Christ's, in Him for ever
    we have triumphed over all;
    all the doubting and dejection
    of our trembling hearts have ceased.
    'Tis His day of resurrection;
    let us rise and keep the feast.

201   Chris Rolinson
          © 1989 Kingsway's Thankyou Music

   *Christ is risen -
      hallelujah, hallelujah!
   Christ is risen indeed -
      hallelujah!*

1   Love's work is done, the battle is won.
    Where now, O death, is your sting?
    He rose again to rule and to reign,
    Jesus our conquering King.

2   Lord over sin, Lord over death,
    at His feet Satan must fall!
    Every knee, bow! All will confess
    Jesus is Lord over all!

3   Tell it abroad, 'Jesus is Lord!'
    shout it and let your praise ring!
    Gladly we raise our songs of praise,
    worship is our offering.

202   Charles Wesley (1707-88)

1   "Christ the Lord is risen today!"
    Hallelujah!
    sons of men and angels say:
    Hallelujah!
    raise your joy and triumph high,
    Hallelujah!
    sing, ye heavens, and earth reply.
    Hallelujah!

2   Love's redeeming work is done:
    fought the fight, the battle won:
    lo! our Sun's eclipse is o'er;
    lo! He sets in blood no more.

3   Vain the stone, the watch, the seal,
    Christ hath burst the gates of hell;
    death in vain forbids His rise,
    Christ hath opened Paradise.

4   Lives again our glorious King:
    where, O death, is now thy sting;
    once He died our souls to save;
    where's thy victory, boasting grave?

5   King of glory, soul of bliss,
    everlasting life is this:
    Thee to know, Thy power to prove
    thus to sing, and thus to love.

203   William J Gaither
          © 1971 Gaither Music Company/WJG Inc./
          Admin. by Kingsway's Thankyou Music

1   God sent His Son, they called Him Je-
    sus;
    He came to love, heal, and forgive;
    He lived and died to buy my pardon,
    an empty grave is there to prove my
      Saviour lives.

   *Because He lives I can face tomorrow;
   because He lives all fear is gone;
   because I know He holds the future,
   and life is worth the living
   just because He lives.*

2   How sweet to hold a new-born baby,
    and feel the pride and joy he gives;
    but greater still the calm assurance,
    this child can face uncertain days
      because He lives.

3   And then one day I'll cross the river;
    I'll fight life's final war with pain;
    and then as death gives way to victory,
    I'll see the lights of glory and I'll know
        He lives.

204   Graham Kendrick
          © 1986 Kingsway's Thankyou Music

1   In the tomb so cold they laid Him,
    death its victim claimed;
    powers of hell, they could not hold
        Him,
    back to life He came!

    Christ is risen,
    (Christ is risen),
    death has been conquered,
    (death has been conquered),
    Christ is risen,
    (Christ is risen):
    He shall reign for ever!

2   Hell had spent its fury on Him,
    left Him crucified;
    yet by blood He boldly conquered,
    sin and death defied.

3   Now the fear of death is broken,
    Love has won the crown.
    Prisoners of the darkness - listen,
    walls are tumbling down!

4   Raised from death, to heaven ascending,
    Love's exalted King:
    let His song of joy unending
    through the nations ring!

205   A H Ackley © 1961 The Rodeheaver Co./
          Word Music/Admin. by Copycare

1   I serve a risen Saviour,
    He's in the world today;
    I know that He is living,
    whatever men may say.
    I see His hand of mercy,
    I hear His voice of cheer;
    and just the time I need Him,
    He's always near.

    He lives, He lives,
    Christ Jesus lives today!
    He walks with me and talks with me
    along life's narrow way.
    He lives, He lives,
    Salvation to impart!
    You ask me how I know He lives?
    He lives within my heart.

2   In all the world around me
    I see His loving care,
    and though my heart grows weary
    I never will despair;
    I know that He is leading,
    through all the stormy blast,
    the day of His appearing
    will come at last.

3   Rejoice, rejoice, O Christian,
    lift up your voice and sing
    eternal hallelujahs
    to Jesus Christ the King!
    The hope of all who seek Him,
    The help of all who find,
    none other is so loving,
    so good and kind.

206

Scottish Paraphrase 1781 from Romans 8: 34-39

1 The Saviour died, but rose again
triumphant from the grave
and pleads our cause at God's right
    hand,
omnipotent to save.

2 Who then can e'er divide us more
from Jesus and His love,
or break the sacred chain that binds
the earth to heaven above?

3 Let troubles rise and terrors frown
and days of darkness fall;
through Him all dangers we'll defy
and more than conquer all.

4 Nor death nor life, nor earth nor hell,
nor time's destroying sway,
can e'er efface us from His heart,
or make His love decay.

5 Each future period that will bless,
as it has blessed the past;
He loved us from the first of time,
He loves us to the last.

207

© Timothy Dudley-Smith

1 Jesus, Prince and Saviour,
Lord of life who died;
Christ, the friend of sinners,
mocked and crucified;
for a world's salvation
he his body gave,
lay at last death's victim,
lifeless in the grave.

Lord of life triumphant,
risen now to reign!
King of endless ages,
Jesus lives again!

2 In his power and Godhead
every victory won,
pain and passion ended,
all his purpose done:
Christ the Lord is risen!
sighs and sorrows past,
death's dark night is over,
morning comes at last!

3 Resurrection morning!
sinners' bondage freed.
Christ the Lord is risen -
He is risen indeed!
Jesus, Prince and Saviour,
Lord of life who died,
Christ the King of glory
now is glorified!

208

Robert Lowry (1826-99)

1 Low in the grave He lay,
Jesus, my Saviour;
waiting the coming day,
Jesus, my Lord!

Up from the grave He arose,
with a mighty triumph o'er His foes:
He arose a victor from the dark
*   domain*
and He lives forever with His saints
*   to reign.*
He arose! He arose!
Hallelujah! Christ arose!

2 Vainly they watch His bed,
  Jesus, my Saviour;
  vainly they seal the dead,
  Jesus, my Lord.

3 Death cannot keep his prey,
  Jesus, my Saviour;
  He tore the bars away,
  Jesus, my Lord.

3.6 THE LORD JESUS CHRIST
His Ascension and Exaltation

209 Charles Wesley (1707-88)

1 Arise, my soul, arise,
  shake off thy guilty fears,
  the bleeding Sacrifice
  in my behalf appears;
  before the throne my Surety stands,
  my name is written on His Hands.

2 He ever lives above,
  for me to intercede,
  His all redeeming love,
  His precious blood to plead;
  His blood atoned for all our race,
  and sprinkles now the throne of grace.

3 Five bleeding wounds He bears,
  received on Calvary:
  they pour effectual prayers,
  they strongly speak for me.
  "Forgive him, oh, forgive," they cry,
  "Nor let that ransomed sinner die."

4 My God is reconciled;
  His pardoning voice I hear;
  He owns me for His child;
  I can no longer fear:
  with confidence I now draw nigh,
  and "Father, Abba Father!" cry.

210 © Michael Saward/Jubilate Hymns

1 Christ triumphant, ever reigning,
  Saviour, Master, King,
  Lord of heaven, our lives sustaining,
  hear us as we sing:

  Yours the glory and the crown,
  the high renown, the eternal name.

2 Word incarnate, truth revealing,
  Son of Man on earth!
  power and majesty concealing
  by Your humble birth:

3 Suffering servant, scorned, ill-treated,
  victim crucified!
  death is through the cross defeated,
  sinners justified:

4 Priestly King, enthroned for ever
  high in heaven above!
  sin and death and hell shall never
  stifle hymns of love:

5 So, our hearts and voices raising
  through the ages long,
  ceaselessly upon You gazing,
  this shall be our song:

211 M P Ferguson © Unidentified

1 Fairest of all the earth beside,
  chiefest of all unto Thy bride,
  fullness divine in Thee I see,
  wonderful Man of Calvary.

  That Man of Calvary
  has won my heart from me,
  and died to set me free,
  blest Man of Calvary!

2   Granting the sinner life and peace,
    granting the captive sweet release,
    shedding His blood to make us free,
    merciful Man of Calvary!

3   Giving the gifts obtained for men,
    pouring out love beyond our ken,
    giving us spotless purity,
    bountiful Man of Calvary!

4   Comfort of all my earthly way,
    Jesus, I'll meet Thee some sweet day;
    centre of glory Thee I'll see,
    wonderful Man of Calvary!

212   H E Govan
          © The Faith Mission (1866-1932)

1   "Far above all" is our Saviour
        enthroned;
    crowned is the Lamb who for sinners
        atoned,
    living for ever, to list to our call,
    God hath exalted Him "far above all."

    Far above all, far above all!
    Jesus the Crucified, "far above all!"
    Low at His footstool adoring we fall,
    God hath exalted Him "far above all."

2   When the fierce tempest, uplifting its
        waves,
    seeks to engulf us, we cry and He saves;
    looking to Jesus, upheld by His hand,
    tread we the billows as safe as on land.

3   High are the cities that dare our assault,
    strong are the barriers that call us to halt;
    march we on fearless and down they
        must fall,
    vanquished by faith in Him "far above
        all."

4   His is the kingdom from pole unto pole,
    "Far above all" while the ages shall roll.
    With Him the victors, who followed His
        call,
    share in His royalty "far above all."

213   Author Unknown © Unidentified

He is Lord, He is Lord,
He is risen from the dead
and He is Lord!
Every knee shall bow,
every tongue confess
that Jesus Christ is Lord.

214   Larry Dempsey
          © 1983 Zionsong Music/Admin. by Copycare

Glory, glory, glory to the Lamb.
Glory, glory, glory to the Lamb.
For He is glorious and worthy to be
        praised,
the Lamb upon the throne:
and unto Him we lift our voice in praise,
the Lamb upon the throne.

215   Graham Kendrick
          © 1986 Kingsway's Thankyou Music

    He that is in us is greater
    than he that is in the world;
    He that is in us is greater
    than he that is in the world.

1   Therefore I will sing and I will rejoice,
    for His Spirit lives in me.
    Christ the living One has overcome,
    and we share in His victory.

2 All the powers of death and hell and sin
   lic crushed beneath His feet.
   Jesus owns the name above all names,
   crowned with honour and majesty.

216 © Unidentified

Jesus Christ is alive today,
I know, I know it's true.
Sovereign of the universe,
I give Him homage due.
Seated there at God's right hand,
I am with Him in the promised land.
Jesus lives and reigns in me,
that's how I know it's true.

217 Thomas Kelly (1769-1855)

1 Look, ye saints, the sight is glorious;
   see the "Man of Sorrows" now
   from the fight returned victorious:
   every knee to Him shall bow!
   Crown Him! crown Him!
   crown Him! crown Him!
   Crowns become the Victor's brow.

2 Crown the Saviour! angels, crown Him!
   Rich the trophies Jesus brings:
   in the seat of power enthrone Him,
   while the vault of heaven rings!
   Crown Him! crown Him!
   crown Him! crown Him!
   Crown the Saviour King of kings!

3 Sinners in derision crowned Him,
   mocking thus the Saviour's claim;
   saints and angels crowd around Him,
   own His title, praise His name.
   Crown Him! crown Him!
   crown Him! crown Him!
   Spread abroad the Victor's fame.

4 Hark those bursts of acclamation!
   Hark those loud triumphant chords!
   Jesus takes the highest station,
   oh, what joy the sight affords!
   Crown Him! crown Him!
   crown Him! crown Him!
   King of kings and Lord of lords!

218 Thomas Kelly (1769-1855)

1 The head that once was crowned with
      thorns,
   is crowned with glory now:
   a royal diadem adorns
   the mighty Victor's brow.

2 The highest place that heaven affords
   is His, is His by right:
   the King of kings and Lord of lords,
   and heaven's eternal light.

3 The joy of all who dwell above,
   the joy of all below,
   to whom He manifests His love
   and grants His name to know.

4 To them the cross, with all its shame,
   with all its grace, is given:
   their name, an everlasting name:
   their joy, the joy of heaven.

5 They suffer with their Lord below,
   they reign with Him above,
   their profit and their joy to know
   the mystery of His love.

(When sung to 218a repeat lines 2 & 4 of
each verse and add chorus)

He lives, He lives.
I know that my Redeemer lives.
He lives, He lives.
I know that my Redeemer lives.

219

Josiah Conder (1789-1855)

1 The Lord is King! lift up thy voice,
   O earth, and all ye heavens rejoice;
   from world to world the joy shall ring,
   "The Lord omnipotent is King!"

2 The Lord is King! who then shall dare
   resist His will, distrust His care,
   or murmur at His wise decrees,
   or doubt His royal promises?

3 The Lord is King! Child of the dust,
   the Judge of all the earth is just;
   holy and true are all His ways:
   let every creature speak His praise.

4 He reigns! ye saints, exalt your strains;
   your God is King, your Father reigns;
   and He is at the Father's side,
   the Man of love, the crucified.

5 One Lord, one empire, all secures;
   He reigns, and life and death are yours.
   Through earth and heaven one song
     shall ring,
   "The Lord omnipotent is King!"

220

Edmond Budry (1854-1932)
tr R. Birch Hoyle (1875-1939)
Copyright Control

1 Thine be the glory, risen, conquering
     Son,
   endless is the victory Thou o'er death
     hast won;
   angels in bright raiment rolled the
     stone away,
   kept the folded grave-clothes where
     Thy body lay.

Thine be the glory, risen, conquering
  Son,
endless is the victory Thou o'er death
  hast won.

2 Lo! Jesus meets us, risen from the tomb;
   lovingly He greets us, scatters fear and
     gloom.
   Let the Church with gladness hymns of
     triumph sing,
   for her Lord now liveth; death hath
     lost its sting.

3 No more we doubt Thee, glorious Prince
     of life;
   life is nought without Thee: aid us in
     our strife.
   Make us more than conquerors,
     through Thy deathless love:
   bring us safe through Jordan to Thy
     home above.

3.7 **THE LORD JESUS CHRIST**
     His Second Advent

221

Scottish Paraphrases, 1781 from Isaiah 2:2-5

1 Behold! the mountain of the Lord
   in latter days shall rise
   on mountain tops above the hills,
   and draw the wondering eyes.

2 To this the joyful nations round,
   all tribes and tongues, shall flow;
   up to the hill of God, they'll say,
   and to His house we'll go.

3 The beam that shines from Zion hill
   shall lighten every land;
   the King who reigns in Salem's towers
   shall all the world command.

4 Among the nations He shall judge;
   His judgements truth shall guide;
   His sceptre shall protect the just,
   and quell the sinner's pride.

5 No strife shall rage, nor hostile feuds
   disturb those peaceful years;
   to ploughshares men shall beat their
      swords,
   to pruning-hooks their spears.

6 No longer hosts encountering hosts
   shall crowds of slain deplore:
   they hang the trumpet in the hall,
   and study war no more.

7 Come then, O house of Jacob! come
   to worship at His shrine;
   and, walking in the light of God,
   with holy beauties shine.

222 Unidentified

By-and-by we'll see the King,
by-and-by we'll see the King,
by-and-by we'll see the King,
and crown Him Lord of all.

(repeat last line four times)

223 H Alford (1810-71)
© in this version Jubilate Hymns

1 Come, you thankful people, come,
   raise the song of harvest home,
   fruit and crops are gathered in
   safe before the storms begin:
   God our maker will provide
   for our needs to be supplied;
   come, with all His people, come,
   raise the song of harvest home!

2 All the world is God's own field,
   harvests for His praise to yield;
   wheat and weeds together sown
   here for joy or sorrow grown:
   first the blade and then the ear,
   then the full corn shall appear,
   Lord of harvest, grant that we
   wholesome grain and pure may be.

3 For the Lord our God shall come
   and shall bring His harvest home.
   He Himself on that great day,
   worthless things shall take away,
   give His angels charge at last
   in the fire the weeds to cast,
   but the fruitful ears to store
   in His care for evermore.

4 Even so, Lord, quickly come,
   bring Your final harvest home,
   gather all Your people in
   free from sorrow, free from sin,
   there together purified,
   ever thankful at Your side,
   come, with all Your angels, come,
   bring that glorious harvest home!

224
James Montgomery (1771-1854)

1 Hail to the Lord's Anointed,
   great David's greater Son!
   Hail, in the time appointed,
   His reign on earth begun!
   He comes to break oppression,
   to set the captive free,
   to take away transgression,
   and rule in equity.

2 He shall come down like showers
   upon the fruitful earth,
   and love, joy, hope, like flowers,
   spring in His path to birth.
   Before Him, on the mountains,
   shall peace the herald go;
   and righteousness in fountains
   from hill to valley flow.

3 Kings shall fall down before Him,
   and gold and incense bring:
   all nations shall adore Him,
   His praise all people sing;
   for He shall have dominion
   o'er river, sea and shore,
   far as the eagle's pinion
   or dove's light wing can soar.

4 O'er every foe victorious,
   He on His throne shall rest,
   from age to age more glorious,
   all blessing and all-blest.
   The tide of time shall never
   His covenant remove;
   His name shall stand for ever;
   that name to us is Love.

225
H L Turner (b. 19th c.)

1 It may be at morn, when the day is
   awaking,
   when sunlight through darkness and
   shadow is breaking,
   that Jesus will come in the fullness of
   glory,
   to receive from the world "His own."

   O Lord Jesus, how long?
   How long ere we shout the glad song?
   Christ returneth! Hallelujah!
   Hallelujah! Amen!
   Hallelujah! Amen!

2 It may be at midday, it may be at
   twilight,
   it may be, perchance, that the black-
   ness of midnight
   will burst into light in the blaze of His
   glory,
   when Jesus receives "His own."

3 While hosts cry "Hosanna!" from
   heaven descending,
   with glorified saints and the angels
   attending,
   with grace on His brow, like a halo of
   glory,
   will Jesus receive "His own."

4 Oh, joy! oh, delight! should we go
   without dying!
   No sickness, no sadness, no dread,
   and no crying;
   caught up through the clouds with
   our Lord into glory,
   when Jesus receives "His own."

226 Daniel W Whittle (1840-1901)

1 Jesus is coming, sing the glad word,
  coming for those He redeemed by His
    blood,
  coming to reign as the glorified Lord:
  Jesus is coming again!

  Jesus is coming, is coming again,
    Jesus is coming again.
  Shout the glad tidings o'er mountain
    and plain
  Jesus is coming again!

2 Jesus is coming! The dead shall arise;
  loved ones shall meet in a joyful
    surprise,
  caught up together to Him in the skies:
  Jesus is coming again!

3 Jesus is coming, His saints to release,
  coming to give to the warring earth
    peace!
  Sinning, and sighing, and sorrow shall
    cease:
  Jesus is coming again!

4 Jesus is coming! The promise is true!
  Who are the chosen, the faithful, the few,
    waiting and watching, prepared for
    review?
  Jesus is coming again!

227 Charles Wesley (1707-88)

1 Lo! He comes, with clouds descending,
  once for favoured sinners slain:
  thousand thousand saints attending
  swell the triumph of His train.
  Hallelujah!, hallelujah, hallelujah!
  God appears on earth to reign.

2 Every eye shall now behold Him
  robed in dreadful majesty.
  Those who set at nought and sold Him,
  pierced and nailed Him to the tree,
  deeply wailing, deeply wailing,
    deeply wailing,
  shall the true Messiah see.

3 Now redemption, long expected,
  see in solemn pomp appear.
  All His saints, by man rejected,
  now shall meet Him in the air.
  Hallelujah, hallelujah, hallelujah!
  see the day of God appear.

4 Yea, Amen! let all adore Thee
  high on Thy eternal throne.
  Saviour, take the power and glory,
  claim the kingdom of Thine own.
  Hallelujah, hallelujah, hallelujah!
  everlasting God, come down!

228 Daniel W Whittle (1840-1901)

1 Our Lord is now rejected
  and by the world disowned;
  by the many still neglected
  and by the few enthroned.
  But soon He'll come in glory;
  the hour is drawing nigh
  for the crowning day is coming
  by and by.

  Oh, the crowning day is coming!
  is coming by and by,
  when our Lord shall come in
  power
  and glory from on high.
  Oh, the glorious sight will gladden
  each waiting, watchful eye,
  in the crowning day that's coming
  by and by.

2 The heavens shall glow with splendour,
   but brighter far than they,
   the saints shall shine in glory
   as Christ shall them array.
   The beauty of the Saviour
   shall dazzle every eye,
   in the crowning day that's coming
   by and by.

3 Let all that look for, hasten
   the coming joyful day
   by earnest consecration,
   to walk the narrow way;
   by gathering in the lost ones
   for whom our Lord did die,
   for the crowing day that's coming
   by and by.

3 There'll be crowns for the conquerors
   and white robes to wear,
   there will be no more sorrow or pain;
   and the battles of earth shall be lost in
   the sight,
   of the glorious Lamb that was slain.

4 Now the King of the ages approaches
   the earth,
   He will burst through the gates of the
   sky;
   and all men shall bow down to His
   beautiful name;
   we shall rise with a shout, we shall fly!

   Come on heaven's children,
   the city is in sight.
   There will be no sadness
   on the other side.
   (repeat verse 4)

229 Graham Kendrick
© 1978 Kingsway's Thankyou Music

1 There's a sound on the wind like a
   victory song;
   listen now, let it rest on your soul.
   It's a song that I learned from a
   heavenly King,
   it's a song of a battle royal.

2 There's a loud shout of victory that
   leaps from our hearts,
   as we wait for our conquering King.
   There's a triumph resounding from
   dark ages past,
   to the victory song we now sing.

   Come on heaven's children,
   the city is in sight.
   There will be no sadness
   on the other side.

230 Charles Silvester Horne (1865-1914)

1 Sing we the King who is coming to
   reign;
   glory to Jesus the Lamb that was slain;
   life and salvation His empire shall bring,
   joy to the nations, when Jesus is King.

   Come, let us sing praise to our King,
   Jesus, our King, Jesus our King;
   this is our song, who to Jesus belong
   glory to Jesus, to Jesus our King.

2 Souls shall be saved from the burden
   of sin,
   doubts shall not darken His witness
   within,
   hell hath no terror, and death hath no
   sting,
   love is victorious when Jesus is King.

3 All men shall dwell in His marvellous
    light,
   races long severed His love shall unite,
   justice and truth from His sceptre shall
    spring,
   wrong shall be ended when Jesus is
    King.

4 Kingdom of Christ, for Thy coming we
    pray;
   hasten, O Father, the dawn of the day,
   when this new song Thy creation shall
    sing
   Satan is vanquished, and Jesus is King.

---

231 James M Black (1856-1938)
© Hope Publishing/Admin. by Copycare

1 When the trumpet of the Lord shall
    sound and time shall be no more,
   and the morning breaks, eternal, bright
    and fair;
   when the saved of earth shall gather over
    on the other shore,
   and the roll is called up yonder, I'll be
    there.

   When the roll is called up yonder,
   when the roll is called up yonder,
   when the roll is called up yonder,
   when the roll is called up yonder,
   I'll be there.

2 On that bright and cloudless morning
    when the dead in Christ shall rise,
   and the glory of His resurrection share;
   when His chosen ones shall gather to
    their home beyond the skies,
   and the roll is called up yonder, I'll be
    there.

---

3 Let us labour for the Master from the
    dawn till setting sun,
   let us tell of all His wondrous love and
    care;
   then when all of life is over and our
    work on earth is done,
   and the roll is called up yonder, we'll
    be there.

---

232 Francis Jane van Alstyne (1820-1915)
(Fanny J Crosby)

1 When Jesus comes to reward His
    servants,
   whether it be noon or night,
   faithful to Him will He find us
    watching,
   with our lamps all trimmed and bright?

   Oh, can we say we are ready, brother,
   ready for the soul's bright home?
   Say, will He find you and me still
    watching,
   waiting, waiting when the Lord shall
    come?

2 If at the dawn of the early morning,
   He shall call us one by one,
   when to the Lord we restore our talents,
   will He answer thee, "Well done"?

3 Have we been true to the trust He left
    us?
   Do we seek to do our best?
   If, in our hearts, there is nought
    condemns us,
   we shall have a glorious rest.

4 Blessed are those whom the Lord finds watching;
   in His glory they shall share.
   If He should come at the dawn or midnight
   will He find us watching there?

233 Robin Mark
© Daybreak Music Ltd.

1 You're the Lion of Judah, the Lamb that was slain,
   You ascended to heaven and evermore will reign;
   at the end of the age when the earth You reclaim,
   You will gather the nations before You.
   And the eyes of all men will be fixed on the Lamb who was crucified,
   for with wisdom and mercy and justice He reigns at the Father's side.

   And the angels will cry:
   "Hail the Lamb who was slain for the world - rule in power."
   And the earth will reply:
   "You shall reign as the King of all kings and the Lord of all lords."

2 There's a shield in our hand and a sword at our side,
   there's a fire in our spirit that cannot be denied;
   as the Father has told us: for these You have died,
   for the nations that gather before You.
   And the ears of all men need to hear of the Lamb who was crucified,
   who descended to hell yet was raised up
   to reign at the Father's side.

4.1 THE HOLY SPIRIT
His Person and Work

234 James Montgomery (1771-1854)

1 O Spirit of the living God,
   in all Thy plentitude of grace,
   where'er the foot of man hath trod,
   descend on our apostate race.

2 Give tongues of fire and hearts of love
   to preach the reconciling word;
   give power and unction from above,
   whene'er the joyful sound is heard.

3 Be darkness, at Thy coming, light;
   confusion, order in Thy path;
   souls without strength inspire with might
   bid mercy triumph over wrath.

4 O Spirit of the Lord, prepare
   all the round earth her God to meet;
   breathe Thou abroad like morning air,
   till hearts of stone begin to beat.

5 Baptize the nations; far and nigh
   the triumphs of the cross record;
   the Name of Jesus glorify
   till every kindred call Him Lord.

6 God from eternity hath willed
   all flesh shall His salvation see;
   so be the Father's love fulfilled,
   the Saviour's sufferings crowned
   through Thee.

235 William and Gloria Gaither
© Gaither Music Company/WJG Inc./Admin. by
Kingsway's Thankyou Music

1 Come, as a wisdom to children,
come, as new sight to the blind,
come, Lord, as strength to my weakness;
take me; soul, body and mind.

Come, Holy Spirit, I need Thee,
come, sweet Spirit, I pray;
come, in Thy strength and Thy power,
come in Thine own gentle way.

2 Come as a rest to the weary,
come as a balm for the sore,
come, as a dew to my dryness;
fill me with joy evermore.

3 Come, like a spring in the desert,
come to the withered of soul;
oh, let Thy sweet healing power
touch me and make me whole.

236 Charles Wesley (1707-88) and
Horatius Bonar (1808-89)

1 Come, Thou everlasting Spirit,
bring to every thankful mind
all the Saviour's dying merit,
all His sufferings for mankind:
true Recorder of His passion,
now the living faith impart;
now reveal His great salvation
unto every faithful heart.

2 Come, Thou witness of His dying;
come, Remembrancer divine;
let us feel Thy power applying
Christ to every soul, and mine.

Let us groan Thine inward groaning,
look on Him we pierced, and grieve;
all partake the grace atoning,
all the sprinkled blood receive.

3 Yes, in me, in me He dwelleth;
I in Him, and He in me!
And my empty soul He filleth,
here and through eternity.
Thus I wait for His returning,
singing all the way to heaven;
such the joyous song of morning,
such the banquet song of even.

237 Thomas T Lynch (1818-1871)

1 Gracious Spirit, dwell with me,
I myself would gracious be,
and, with words that help and heal,
would Thy life in mine reveal;
and with actions bold and meek,
would for Christ my Saviour speak.

2 Holy Spirit, dwell with me,
I myself would holy be.
Separate from sin, I would
choose and cherish all things good,
and whatever I can be
give to Him who gave me Thee.

3 Mighty Spirit, dwell with me,
I myself would mighty be;
mighty so as to prevail
where unaided man must fail:
ever, by a mighty hope,
pressing on and bearing up.

4   Tender Spirit, dwell with me,
    I myself would tender be.
    Shut my heart up like a flower
    at temptation's darksome hour;
    open it, when shines the sun,
    and His love by fragrance own.

4   Inspire the living faith,
    which whosoe'er receives,
    the witness in himself he hath,
    and consciously believes;
    the faith that conquers all,
    and doth the mountain move,
    and saves whoe'er on Jesus call,
    and perfects them in love.

238   Charles Wesley (1707-88)

1   Spirit of faith, come down,
    reveal the things of God;
    and make to us the Godhead known,
    and witness with the blood.
    'Tis thine the blood to apply,
    and give us eyes to see
    who did for guilty sinners die
    hath surely died for me.

2   No man can truly say
    that Jesus is the Lord,
    unless Thou take the veil away,
    and breathe the living word;
    then, only then, we feel
    our interest in His blood,
    and cry, with joy unspeakable:
    "Thou art my Lord, my God!"

3   O that the world might know
    the all-atoning Lamb!
    Spirit of faith, descend, and show
    the virtue of His Name;
    the grace which all may find,
    the saving power impart;
    and testify to all mankind,
    and speak in every heart.

239   H Auber (1773-1862)

1   Our blest Redeemer, ere He breathed
    His tender, last farewell,
    a Guide, a Comforter, bequeathed
    with us to dwell.

2   He came sweet influence to impart,
    a gracious, willing guest,
    where He can find one humble heart
    wherein to rest.

3   And His that gentle voice we hear,
    soft as the breath of even,
    that checks each thought, that calms
       each fear
    and speaks of heaven.

4   And every virtue we possess,
    and every conquest won,
    and every thought of holiness,
    are His alone.

5   Spirit of purity and grace,
    our weakness, pitying, see;
    oh, make our hearts Thy dwelling
       place
    and worthier Thee!

6 Oh, praise the Father, praise the Son:
blest Spirit, praise to Thee!
All praise to God, the Three in One,
the One in Three.

4.2 THE HOLY SPIRIT
His Manifestation and Power

240 Roy Turner
© 1984 Kingsway's Thankyou Music

1 All over the world the Spirit is moving,
all over the world as the prophet said
it would be;
all over the world there's a mighty
revelation of the glory of the Lord,
as the waters cover the sea.

2 All over His church God's Spirit is
moving,
all over His church as the prophet
said it would be;
all over His church there's a mighty
revelation of the glory of the Lord,
as the waters cover the sea.

3 Right here in this place the Spirit is
moving,
right here in this place as the prophet
said it would be;
right here in this place there's a
mighty revelation of the glory of the
Lord,
as the waters cover the sea.

241 Andrew Reed (1787-1862)

1 Spirit divine, attend our prayers,
and make this house Thy home;
descend with all Thy gracious powers,
O come, great Spirit, come!

2 Come as the light; to us reveal
our emptiness and woe,
and lead us in those paths of life
where all the righteous go.

3 Come as the fire, and purge our hearts
like sacrificial flame;
let our whole soul an offering be
to our Redeemer's name.

4 Come as the Dove, and spread Thy
wings,
the wings of perfect love;
and let Thy Church on earth become
blest as the Church above.

5 Spirit divine, attend our prayers,
make a lost world Thy home;
descend with all Thy gracious powers,
O come, great Spirit, come!

242 Paul Armstrong
© 1984 Restoration Music Ltd., admin. by
Sovereign Music UK

Spirit of the living God fall afresh on me;
Spirit of the living God fall afresh on me;
fill me anew, fill me anew;
Spirit of the Lord fall afresh on me.

243 Daniel Iverson
© 1963 Birdwing Music/EMI Christian Music
Publishing/Admin. by Copycare

Spirit of the living God, fall afresh on me;
Spirit of the living God, fall afresh on me;
break me, melt me, mould me, fill me;
Spirit of the living God, fall afresh on me.

244 William Booth (d.1912)
© Salvationist Publishing & Supplies/
Admin. by Copycare

1 Thou Christ of burning, cleansing flame,
 send the fire, send the fire!
 Thy blood-bought gift today we claim,
 send the fire, send the fire!
 Look down and see this waiting host,
 give us the promised Holy Ghost;
 we want another Pentecost,
 send the fire, send the fire!

2 God of Elijah, hear our cry!
 Oh, make us fit to live or die!
 To burn up every trace of sin,
 to bring the light and glory in,
 the revolution now begin.

3 'Tis fire we want, for fire we plead,
 the fire will meet our every need;
 for strength to ever do the right,
 for grace to conquer in the fight,
 for power to walk the world in white.

4 To make our weak hearts strong and
 brave,
 to live a dying world to save;
 oh, see us on Thy altar lay
 our lives, our all, this very day;
 to crown the offering now, we pray

245 Henrietta E Blair
© Unidentified

1 Thy Holy Spirit, Lord alone
 can turn our hearts from sin;
 His power alone can sanctify
 and keep us pure within.

 O Spirit of faith and love,
 come in our midst, we pray,
 and purify each waiting heart;
 baptise us with power today.

2 Thy Holy Spirit, Lord, alone
 can deeper love inspire;
 His power alone within our souls
 can light the sacred fire.

3 Thy Holy Spirit, Lord, can bring
 the gifts we seek in prayer;
 His voice can words of comfort speak
 and still each wave of care.

4 Thy Holy Spirit, Lord, can give
 the grace we need this hour;
 and while we wait, O Spirit, come
 in sanctifying power.

 O Spirit of love, descend,
 come in our midst, we pray,
 and like a rushing, mighty wind
 sweep over our souls today.

5 THE WORD OF GOD

246 Mary A Lathbury (1841-1913) and
Alexander Groves (1843-1909)

1 Break Thou the Bread of Life,
 dear Lord, to me,
 as Thou didst break the loaves
 beside the sea;
 beyond the sacred page
 I seek Thee, Lord;
 my spirit pants for Thee,
 O living Word.

2 Thou art the Bread of Life,
 O Lord, to me,
 Thy Holy Word the truth
 that saveth me;
 give me to eat and live
 with Thee above;
 teach me to love Thy truth,
 for Thou art Love.

3 Oh, send Thy Spirit, Lord,
      now unto me,
   that He may touch my eyes,
   and make me see;
   show me the truth concealed
   within Thy Word,
   and in Thy Book revealed
   I see the Lord.

4 Bless Thou the truth, dear Lord,
      to me, to me,
   as Thou didst bless the bread
   by Galilee;
   then shall all bondage cease,
   all fetters fall,
   and I shall find my peace,
   my all in all.

247 Charles Wesley (1707-88)

1 Come, Holy Ghost, our hearts inspire,
   let us Thine influence prove:
   source of the old prophetic fire,
   fountain of life and love.

2 Come, Holy Ghost, for moved by Thee
   the prophets wrote and spoke;
   unlock the truth, Thyself the key,
   unseal the sacred book.

3 Expand Thy wings, celestial Dove,
   brood o'er our nature's night;
   on our disordered spirits move,
   and let there now be light.

4 God, through Himself, we then shall
      know
   if Thou within us shine,
   and sound with all Thy saints below,
   the depths of love divine.

248 'K' in Rippon's Selection, 1787 alt.

1 How firm a foundation, ye saints of
      the Lord,
   is laid for your faith in His excellent
      word;
   what more can He say than to you He
      hath said,
   you who unto Jesus for refuge have fled?

2 Fear not, He is with thee, O be not
      dismayed;
   for He is thy God, and will still give
      thee aid:
   He'll strengthen thee, help thee, and
      cause thee to stand,
   upheld by His righteous, omnipotent
      hand.

3 In every condition, in sickness, in health,
   in poverty's vale, or abounding in
      wealth,
   at home and abroad, on the land, on the
      sea,
   as thy days may demand shall thy
      strength ever be.

4 When through the deep waters He calls
      thee to go,
   the rivers of grief shall not thee
      overflow;
   for He will be with thee in trouble to
      bless,
   and sanctify to thee thy deepest distress.

5 When through fiery trials thy pathway
      shall lie,
   His grace all-sufficient shall be thy
      supply;
   the flame shall not hurt thee, His only
      design
   thy dross to consume and thy gold to
      refine.

6   The soul that on Jesus has leaned for
    repose
    He will not, He will not, desert to its
    foes;
    that soul, though all hell should
    endeavour to shake,
    He'll never, no never, no never
    forsake.

249   Graham Kendrick
         © 1993 Make Way Music

1   Now in reverence and awe
    we gather round Your word;
    in wonder we draw near
    to mysteries that angels strain to hear,
    that prophets dimly saw:
    so let Your Spirit shine upon the page
    and teach me;

    open up my eyes with truth to free me,
    light to chase the lies.
    Lord Jesus, let me meet You in Your
    word;
    Lord Jesus, let me meet You in Your
    word.

2   Lord, Your truth cannot be chained;
    it searches everything,
    my secrets, my desires.
    Your word is like a hammer and a fire
    it breaks, it purifies:
    so let Your Spirit shine into my heart
    and teach me;

250   R Kelso Carter (1849-1928)
         © Unidentified

1   Standing on the promises of Christ our
    King,
    through eternal ages let His praises
    ring:
    glory in the highest I will shout and
    sing,
    standing on the promises of God.

    Standing, standing,
    standing on the promises of God,
    my Saviour.
    Standing, standing,
    I'm standing on the promises of God.

2   Standing on the promises that cannot
    fail
    when the howling storms of doubt and
    fear assail;
    by the living word of God I shall
    prevail,
    standing on the promises of God.

3   Standing on the promises I now can see
    perfect, present cleansing in the blood
    for me;
    standing in the liberty where Christ
    makes free,
    standing on the promises of God.

4   Standing on the promises of Christ
    the Lord,
    bound to Him eternally by love's strong
    cord,
    overcoming daily with the Spirit's
    sword,
    standing on the promises of God.

251 Psalm 1 (Scottish Psalter)

1 That man hath perfect blessedness
who walketh not astray
in counsel of ungodly men,
nor stands in sinners' way,

2 nor sitteth in the scorner's chair:
but placeth his delight
upon God's law, and meditates
on His law day and night.

3 He shall be like a tree that grows
near planted by a river,
which in his season yields his fruit,
and his leaf fadeth never:

4 and all he doth shall prosper well.
The wicked are not so;
but like they are unto the chaff,
which wind drives to and fro.

5 In judgement therefore shall not stand
such as ungodly are;
nor in the assembly of the just
shall wicked men appear.

6 For why? The way of godly men
unto the Lord is known:
whereas the way of wicked men
shall quite be overthrown.

252 Psalm 119:105-112 (Scottish Psalter)

1 Thy word is to my feet a lamp,
and to my path a light.
I sworn have, and I will perform,
to keep Thy judgements right.

2 I am with sore affliction
even overwhelmed, O Lord:
In mercy raise and quicken me,
according to Thy word.

3 The freewill-offerings of my mouth
accept, I Thee beseech:
and unto me Thy servant, Lord,
Thy judgements clearly teach.

4 Though still my soul be in my hand,
Thy laws I'll not forget.
I erred not from them, though for me
the wicked snares did set.

5 I of Thy testimonies have
above all things made choice,
to be my heritage for aye;
for they my heart rejoice.

6 I carefully inclined have
my heart still to attend;
that I Thy statutes may perform
alway unto the end.

6   THE CHURCH

253 Henry March (1791-1869)

1 Arm of the Lord, awake, awake!
Thy power unconquerable take;
Thy strength put on, assert Thy might,
and triumph in the dreadful fight.

2 Why dost Thou tarry, mighty Lord?
Why slumbers in its sheath Thy sword?
O rouse Thee, for Thine honour's sake;
arm of the Lord, awake, awake!

3 Behold, what numbers still withstand
Thy sovereign rule and just command,
reject Thy grace, Thy threats despise,
and hurl defiance at the skies.

4 Haste then, but come not to destroy;
mercy is Thine, Thy crown, Thy joy:
their hatred quell, their pride remove,
but melt with grace, subdue with love.

5 Why dost Thou from the conquest stay?
Why do Thy chariot wheels delay?
Lift up Thyself, hell's kingdom shake;
arm of the Lord, awake, awake!

254 Psalm 133 (Scottish Psalter)

1 Behold, how good a thing it is,
and how becoming well.
Together such as brethren are
in unity to dwell!

2 Like precious ointment on the head,
that down the beard did flow,
even Aaron's beard, and to the skirts
did of his garments go.

3 As Hermon's dew, the dew that doth
on Sion's hills descend:
for there the blessing God commands,
life that shall never end.

255 from Latin, J M Neale (1818-66)
© in this version Jubilate Hymns

1 Christ is made the sure foundation,
Christ the head and corner-stone,
chosen of the Lord and precious,
binding all the Church in one;
holy Zion's help for ever,
and her confidence alone.

2 All within that holy city
dearly loved of God on high,
in exultant jubilation
sing, in perfect harmony;
God the One-in-Three adoring
in glad hymns eternally.

3 We as living stones invoke You:
come among us, Lord, today!
With Your gracious loving-kindness
hear Your children as we pray;
and the fullness of Your blessing
in our fellowship display.

4 Here entrust to all Your servants
what we long from You to gain,
that on earth and in the heavens
we one people shall remain,
till united in Your glory
evermore with You we reign.

5 Praise and honour to the Father,
praise and honour to the Son,
praise and honour to the Spirit,
ever Three and ever One:
one in power and one in glory
while eternal ages run.

256 Dave Richards
© 1977 Kingsway's Thankyou Music

For I'm building a people of power
and I'm making a people of praise,
that will move through this land by
My Spirit,
and will glorify My precious name.
Build Your Church, Lord,
make us strong, Lord,
join our hearts, Lord,
through Your Son;
make us one, Lord,
in Your Body,
in the Kingdom of Your Son.
Build Your Church, Lord,
make us strong, Lord,
join our hearts, Lord,
through Your Son;
make us one, Lord,
in Your Body,
in the Kingdom of Your Son.

257 John Newton (1725-1807)

1 Glorious things of Thee are spoken,
Zion, city of our God!
He, whose word cannot be broken,
formed thee for His own abode.
On the Rock of Ages founded
what can shake thy sure repose?
With salvation's walls surrounded
thou may'st smile at all thy foes.

2 See, the streams of living waters,
springing from eternal love,
well supply thy sons and daughters,
and all fear of want remove:
who can faint, while such a river
ever flows their thirst to assuage?
Grace, which like the Lord, the Giver,
never fails from age to age.

3 Round each habitation hovering,
see the cloud and fire appear
for a glory and a covering,
showing that the Lord is near.
He who gives them daily manna,
He who listens when they cry,
let Him hear the loud hosanna,
rising to His throne on high.

2 Elect from every nation,
yet one o'er all the earth;
her charter of salvation
one Lord, one faith, one birth,
one holy name she blesses,
partakes one holy food;
and to one hope she presses,
with every grace endued.

3 Though with a scornful wonder
men see her sore oppressed,
by schisms rent asunder,
by heresies distressed;
yet saints their watch are keeping,
their cry goes up: "How long?"
and soon the night of weeping
shall be the morn of song.

4 Mid toil and tribulation
and tumult of her war,
she waits the consummation
of peace for evermore,
till with the vision glorious
her longing eyes are blest,
and the great Church victorious
shall be the Church at rest.

258 Samuel John Stone (1839-1900)

1 The Church's one foundation
is Jesus Christ our Lord:
she is His new creation
by water and the word.
From heaven He came and sought her
to be His holy bride;
with His own blood He bought her,
and for her life He died.

259 (Psalm 84:1-5) (Scottish Psalter)

1 How lovely is Thy dwelling-place,
O Lord of hosts, to me;
the tabernacles of Thy grace
how pleasant, Lord, they be!

2 My thirsty soul longs vehemently,
yea faints, Thy courts to see:
my very heart and flesh cry out,
O living God, for Thee.

3   Behold, the sparrow findeth out
an house wherein to rest;
the swallow also for herself
hath purchased a nest;

4   E'en Thine own altars, where she safe
her young ones forth may bring,
O Thou almighty Lord of hosts,
who art my God and King.

5   Blest are they in Thy house that dwell,
they ever give Thee praise.
Blest is the man whose strength Thou
art,
in whose heart are Thy ways.

6   *To Father, Son, and Holy Ghost,*
the God whom we adore,
be glory, as it was, and is,
and shall be evermore.

7.1   THE GOSPEL
Proclamation

260   <small>Unidentified</small>

1   I have decided to follow Jesus,
(3 times)
no turning back, no turning back.

2   The world behind me, the cross
before me,   *(3 times)*
no turning back, no turning back.

3   Though none go with me, I still will
follow,   *(3 times)*
no turning back, no turning back.

4   Will you decide now to follow Jesus?
(3 times)
no turning back, no turning back

261   <small>W T Sleeper (1840-1904)</small>

1   A ruler once came to Jesus by night,
to ask Him the way of salvation and
light;
the Master made answer in words true
and plain:
"Ye must be born again!"

   "Ye must be born again!"
   "Ye must be born again!"
   I verily, verily, say unto you,
   "Ye must be born again!"

2   Ye children of men, attend to the word
so solemnly uttered by Jesus, the Lord;
and let not this message to you be in
vain,
"Ye must be born again!"

3   O ye who would enter that glorious rest
and sing with the ransomed the song of
the blest,
the life everlasting if ye would obtain,
"Ye must be born again!"

4   A dear one in heaven thy heart yearns to
see,
at the beautiful gates may be watching
for thee;
then list to the note of this solemn
refrain:
"Ye must be born again!"

262   <small>John M Moore
© 1954 Singspiration Music/Brentwood Benson
Music Publishing Inc./Admin. by Copycare</small>

1   Days are filled with sorrow and care,
hearts are lonely and drear;
burdens are lifted at Calvary,
Jesus is very near.

Burdens are lifted at Calvary,
Calvary, Calvary,
burdens are lifted at Calvary,
Jesus is very near.

2 Cast your care on Jesus today,
   leave your worry and fear;
   burdens are lifted at Calvary,
   Jesus is very near.

3 Troubled soul, the Saviour can see
   every heartache and tear;
   burdens are lifted at Calvary,
   Jesus is very near.

263 Philip Paul Bliss (1838-76)

1 Free from the law, oh, happy condition,
   Jesus hath bled, and there is remission,
   cursed by the law and bruised by the fall,
   grace hath redeemed us once for all.

   Once for all, oh sinner receive it,
   once for all, oh, brother believe it;
   cling to the Cross, the burden will fall,
   Christ hath redeemed us once for all.

2 Now are we free, there's no
      condemnation,
   Jesus provides a perfect salvation;
   "Come unto Me," oh, hear His sweet
      call,
   come, and He saves us once for all.

3 "Children of God," oh, glorious calling,
   surely His grace will keep us from
      falling;
   passing from death to life at His call,
   blessed salvation once for all.

264 Mrs M M Stockton (1821-1885)

1 God loved the world of sinners, lost
   and ruined by the Fall;
   salvation full, at highest cost,
   He offers free to all.

   Oh, 'twas love, 'twas wondrous love,
   the love of God to me;
   it brought my Saviour from above,
   to die on Calvary.

2 E'en now, by faith, I claim Him mine,
   the risen Son of God!
   Redemption by His death I find,
   and cleansing through the blood.

3 Love brings the glorious fullness in,
   and to His saints makes known
   the blessed rest from inbred sin,
   through faith in Christ alone.

4 Believing souls, rejoicing go!
   There shall to you be given
   a glorious foretaste, here below,
   of endless rest in heaven.

5 Of victory now o'er Satan's power
   let all the ransomed sing,
   and triumph in the dying hour,
   through Christ the Lord, our King.

265 Samuel Davies (1723-61) altd.

1 Great God of wonders, all Thy ways
   are matchless, God-like and divine;
   but the fair glories of Thy grace
   more God-like and unrivalled shine:

Who is a pardoning God like Thee?
Or who has grace so rich and free?

2 Such dire offences to forgive,
  such guilty daring souls to spare;
  this is Thy grand prerogative,
  and none shall in the honour share:

3 In wonder lost, with trembling joy,
  we take the pardon of our God,
  pardon for sins of deepest dye,
  a pardon sealed with Jesus' blood:

4 O may this glorious matchless love,
  this God-like miracle of grace,
  teach mortal tongues, like those above,
  to raise this song of lofty praise:

266 © William Vernon Higham

1 Great is the gospel of our glorious God,
  where mercy met the anger of God's rod;
  a penalty was paid and pardon bought,
  and sinners lost at last to Him were
    brought:

  O let the praises of my heart be Thine,
  for Christ has died that I may call Him
    mine,
  that I may sing with those who dwell
    above,
  adoring, praising Jesus, King of love.

2 Great is the mystery of godliness,
  great is the work of God's own holiness;
  it moves my soul, and causes me to long
  for greater joys than to the earth belong:

3 The Spirit vindicated Christ our Lord,
  and angels sang with joy and sweet
    accord;
  the nations heard, a dark world flamed
    with light
  when Jesus rose in glory and in might:

267 Elisha A Hoffman (1839-1929) © Unidentified

1 Have you been to Jesus for the
    cleansing power?
  Are you washed in the blood of the
    Lamb?
  Are you fully trusting in His grace this
    hour?
  Are you washed in the blood of the
    Lamb?

  Are you washed in the blood,
  in the soul-cleansing blood of the
    Lamb?
  Are your garments spotless? Are
    they white as snow?
  Are you washed in the blood of the
    Lamb?

2 Are you walking daily by the Saviour's
    side?
  Are you washed in the blood of the
    Lamb?
  Do you rest each moment in the
    Crucified?
  Are you washed in the blood of the
    Lamb?

3 When the Bridegroom cometh, will
    your robes be white,
  pure and white in the blood of the Lamb?
  Will your soul be ready for the
    mansions bright
  and be washed in the blood of the Lamb?

4 Lay aside the garments that are
        stained by sin,
    and be washed in the blood of the
        Lamb!
    There's a fountain flowing for the soul
        unclean -
    oh, be washed in the blood of the
        Lamb!

268 Randy and Terry Butler
© 1993 Mercy/Vineyard Publishing/Music
Services/Admin. by Copycare

I know a place, a wonderful place,
where accused and condemned
find mercy and grace.
Where the wrongs we have done
and the wrongs done to us
were nailed there with Him (You)
there on the cross.

MEN	*At the cross*
WOMEN	*At the cross*
ALL	*He (You) died for our sin.*
MEN	*At the cross*
WOMEN	*At the cross*
ALL	*He (You) gave us life again.*

269 Katherine Hankey (1834-1911)

1 I love to tell the story
    of unseen things above,
    of Jesus and His glory,
    of Jesus and His love.
    I love to tell the story
    because I know it's true.
    It satisfies my longings
    as nothing else can do.

I love to tell the story!
'Twill be my theme in glory
to tell the old, old story
of Jesus and His love.

2 I love to tell the story;
    more wonderful it seems
    than all the golden fancies
    of all our golden dreams.
    I love to tell the story,
    it did so much for me;
    and that is just the reason
    I tell it now to thee.

3 I love to tell the story;
    'tis pleasant to repeat
    what seems each time I tell it
    more wonderfully sweet.
    I love to tell the story,
    for some have never heard
    the message of salvation
    from God's own holy word.

4 I love to tell the story,
    for those who know it best
    seem hungering and thirsting
    to hear it like the rest.
    And when in scenes of glory
    I sing the new, new song,
    'twill be the old, old story
    that I have loved so long.

270 J B Pounds (1861-1921)

1 I must needs go home by the way of
        the cross;
    there's no other way but this,
    I shall ne'er get sight of the Gates of
        Light
    if the way of the cross I miss.

The way of the cross leads home,
the way of the cross leads home,
it is sweet to know, as I onward go,
the way of the cross leads home.

2 I must needs go on in the blood-
      sprinkled way,
   the path that the Saviour trod,
   if I ever climb to the heights sublime,
   where the soul is at home with God.

3 Then I bid farewell to the way of the
      world,
   to walk in it never more;
   for my Lord says "Come," and I seek
      my home,
   where He waits at the open door.

271 W A Ogden (1841-1897)

1 I've a message from the Lord,
      hallelujah!
   The message unto you I'll give,
   'tis recorded in His word, hallelujah!
   It is only that you "look and live."

   "Look and live," my brother, live,
   look to Jesus now and live,
   'tis recorded in His word;
      hallelujah!
   It is only that you "look and live."

2 I've a message full of love, hallelujah!
   A message, O my friend, for you.
   'Tis a message from above, hallelujah!
   Jesus said it, and I know 'tis true.

3 Life is offered unto you, hallelujah!
   Eternal life your soul shall have,
   if you'll only look to Him, hallelujah!
   Look to Jesus who alone can save.

272 Anna Olander tr., various
© Unidentified

1 If I gained the world but lost the
      Saviour,
      were my life worth living for a day?
   Could my yearning heart find rest and
      comfort
   in the things that soon must pass away?
   If I gained the world, but lost the
      Saviour,
      would my gain be worth the life-long
         strife?
   Are all earthly pleasures worth
      comparing
   for a moment with a Christ-filled life?

2 Had I wealth and love in fullest
      measure,
   and a name revered both far and near,
   yet no hope beyond, no harbour
      waiting
   where my storm-tossed vessel I could
      steer,
   if I gained the world, but lost the
      Saviour,
   who endured the cross and died for me,
   could then all the world afford a
      refuge,
   whither in my anguish I might flee?

3 O what emptiness without the Saviour
   mid the sins and sorrows here below!
   And eternity, how dark without Him,
   only night and tears and endless woe!
   What though I might live without the
      Saviour,
   when I come to die, how would it be?
   O to face the valley's gloom without
      Him!
   And without Him all eternity!

4 O the joy of having all in Jesus!
What a balm the broken heart to heal!
Ne'er a sin so great but He'll forgive it,
nor a sorrow that He does not feel!
If I have but Jesus, only Jesus,
nothing else in all the world beside,
O then everything is mine in Jesus,
for my needs and more He will provide.

273 Ruth Caye Jones
© Zondervan Corporation/Brentwood Benson
Music Publishing Inc./Admin. by Copycare

1 In times like these you need a Saviour,
in times like these you need an anchor;
be very sure, be very sure
your anchor holds and grips the Solid
Rock!

This Rock is Jesus, Yes, He's the One;
this Rock is Jesus, The only One!
Be very sure, be very sure
your anchor holds and grips the
Solid Rock!

2 In times like these you need the Bible,
in times like these O be not idle;
be very sure, be very sure
your anchor holds and grips the Solid
Rock!

3 In times like these I have a Saviour,
in times like these I have an anchor;
I'm very sure, I'm very sure
my anchor holds and grips the Solid
Rock!

This Rock is Jesus, Yes, He's the One;
this Rock is Jesus, The only One!
I'm very sure, I'm very sure
my anchor holds and grips the
Solid Rock!

274 F Bottome (1833-94)

1 Let us sing of His love once again,
of the love that can never decay,
of the blood of the Lamb who was slain,
till we praise Him again in that day.

I believe Jesus saves!
and His blood makes me whiter than
snow!
I believe Jesus saves!
and His blood makes me whiter than
snow!

2 There are cleansing and healing for all
who will wash in the life-giving flood;
there is perfect deliverance and joy
to be had in this world through the blood.
I believe Jesus saves ...

3 Even now, while we taste of His love,
we are filled with delight through His
name;
but what will it be when above,
we shall join in the song of the Lamb?
I believe Jesus saves ...

4 Then we'll march in His name till we
come,
at His bidding to cease from the fight,
and our Saviour shall welcome us home
To the regions of glory and light.
I believe Jesus saves ...

5 So with banner unfurled to the breeze,
our motto shall "Holiness" be,
till the crown from His hand we receive,
and the King in His glory we see!

I am sure we shall win,
for we fight in the strength of our King.
I am sure we shall win,
for we fight in the strength of our King.

275
James McGranahan (1840-1907)

1 O what a Saviour that He died for me!
From condemnation He hath made me
free;
"He that believeth on the Son," saith He,
"hath everlasting life."

"Verily, verily, I say unto you,
verily, verily," message ever new;
"He that believeth on the Son" 'tis true,
"hath everlasting life."

2 All my iniquities on Him were laid,
all my indebtedness by Him was paid;
all who believe on Him, the Lord hath
said,
"hath everlasting life."

3 Though poor and needy I can trust my
Lord,
though weak and sinful I believe His
word;
O glad message! every child of God,
"hath everlasting life."

4 Though all unworthy, yet I will not
doubt,
for him that cometh, He will not cast
out.
"He that believeth," O the good news
shout,
"hath everlasting life."

276
Gerrit Gustafson
© 1990 Integrity's Hosanna! Music/Admin. by
Kingsway's Thankyou Music

Only by grace can we enter,
only by grace can we stand;
not by our human endeavour,
but by the blood of the Lamb.

Into Your presence You call us,
You call us to come;
into Your presence You draw us,
and now by Your grace we come,
now by Your grace we come.

Lord, if You mark our transgressions,
who will stand?
Thanks to Your grace we are cleansed by
the blood of the Lamb.

(Repeat last stanza before returning
to parts one and two)

277
Frances Ridley Havergal (1836-79)

1 Precious, precious blood of Jesus
shed on Calvary;
shed for rebels, shed for sinners,
shed for thee!

Precious, precious blood of Jesus,
ever flowing free;
oh, believe it, oh, receive it,
'tis for thee.

2 Precious, precious blood of Jesus,
let it make thee whole;
let it flow in mighty cleansing
o'er thy soul.

3 Though thy sins are red like crimson,
deep in scarlet glow,
Jesus' precious blood shall wash thee
white as snow.

4 Precious blood that hath redeemed us!
All the price is paid!
Perfect pardon now is offered,
peace is made.

5 Now the holiest with boldness
   we may enter in;
   for the open fountain cleanseth
   from all sin.

6 Precious blood! by this we conquer
   in the fiercest fight,
   sin and Satan overcoming
   by its might.

7 Precious blood, whose full atonement
   makes us nigh to God!
   Precious blood, our way of glory,
   praise and laud!

278   Horatius Bonar (1808-89)

1 Rejoice and be glad! the Redeemer
   has come:
   go, look on His cradle, His cross, and
   His tomb.

   Sound His praises,
   tell the story of Him who was slain;
   sound His praises,
   tell with gladness He now lives
   again.

2 Rejoice and be glad! it is sunshine at last;
   the clouds have departed, the shadows
   are past.

3 Rejoice and be glad! for the blood has
   been shed;
   redemption is finished, the price has
   been paid.

4 Rejoice and be glad! now the pardon is
   free;
   the just for the unjust has died on the
   tree.

5 Rejoice and be glad! for the Lamb
   that was slain,
   o'er death is triumphant, and now lives
   again.

6 Rejoice and be glad! for our King is
   on high;
   He pleads now for us on His throne
   in the sky.

7 Rejoice and be glad! for He's coming
   again;
   He'll come in great glory, the Lamb
   that was slain.

279   Philip Paul Bliss (1838-76)

1 Sing them over again to me,
   wonderful words of life!
   Let me more of their beauty see,
   wonderful words of life!
   Words of life and beauty,
   teach me faith and duty.

   Beautiful words! Wonderful words!
   Wonderful words of life!
   Beautiful words! Wonderful words!
   Wonderful words of life

2 Christ, the Blessed One, gives to all
   Sinner, list to the loving call,
   All so freely given,
   wooing us to heaven!

3 Sweetly echo the gospel call,
   Offer pardon and peace to all,
   Jesus, only Saviour,
   sanctify for ever!

280 William Leslie
© Unidentified

1 Sound the gospel of grace abroad,
   there's life in the risen Lord!
   Spread the news of the gift of God,
   there's life in the risen Lord!
   God above desires it!
   Sinful man requires it!

   Tell it around, let it abound,
   there's life in the risen Lord.
   Tell it around, let it abound,
   there's life in the risen Lord.

2 All by nature are doomed to die,
   so saith the holy word;
   welcome therefore the joyful cry,
   there's life in the risen Lord!
   Welcome news of gladness -
   antidote for sadness.

3 Saints, apostles, and prophets all
   published with one accord,
   this deliverance from the fall,
   this life in the risen Lord.
   Glory be to Jesus,
   who from bondage frees us!

4 Pardon, power, and perfect peace
   the words of this life afford,
   never then let the tidings cease
   of life in the risen Lord.
   Open wide the portal
   unto every mortal.

281 Emily H Miller © Unidentified

1 I love to hear the story
   which angel voices tell,
   how once the King of Glory
   came down to earth to dwell;
   I am both weak and sinful,
   but this I surely know,
   the Lord came down to save me,
   because He loved me so.

2 I'm glad my blessed Saviour
   was once a child like me,
   to show how pure and holy
   His little ones might be;
   and if I try to follow
   His footsteps here below,
   He never will forget me,
   because He loved me so.

3 To sing His love and mercy,
   my sweetest songs I'll raise,
   and though I cannot see Him,
   I know He hears my praise!
   For He has kindly promised
   that I shall surely go
   to sing among His angels,
   because He loved me so.

282 Graham Kendrick
© 1989 Make Way Music

1 My Lord, what love is this
   that pays so dearly,
   that I, the guilty one,
   may go free!

   Amazing love,
   O what sacrifice,
   the Son of God given for me.
   My debt He pays,
   and my death He dies,
   that I might live, that I might live.

2 And so, they watched Him die
  despised, rejected:
  but oh, the blood He shed
  flowed for me!

3 And now this love of Christ
  shall flow like rivers;
  come wash your guilt away,
  live again!

283   Erdman Neumeister (1671-1756)

1 Sinners Jesus will receive;
  sound this word of grace to all
  who the heavenly pathway leave,
  all who linger, all who fall.

> *Sing it o'er and o'er again,*
> *Christ receiveth sinful men;*
> *make the message clear and plain,*
> *Christ receiveth sinful men.*

2 Come and He will give you rest;
  trust Him for His word is plain.
  He will take the sinfulest:
  Christ receiveth sinful men.

3 Now my heart condemns me not,
  pure before the law I stand;
  He who cleansed me from all spot
  satisfied its last demand.

4 Christ receiveth sinful men,
  even me with all my sin;
  purged from every spot and stain,
  Heaven with Him I enter in.

284   Kate Hankey (1834-1911)

1 Tell me the old, old story
  of unseen things above,
  of Jesus and His glory,
  of Jesus and His love.
  Tell me the story simply,
  as to a little child,
  for I am weak and weary,
  and helpless and defiled.

> *Tell me the old, old story,*
> *tell me the old, old story,*
> *tell me the old, old story*
> *of Jesus and His love.*

2 Tell me the story slowly,
  that I may take it in,
  that wonderful redemption,
  God's remedy for sin.
  Tell me the story often,
  for I forget so soon;
  "The early dew" of morning
  has passed away at noon.

3 Tell me the story softly,
  with earnest tones and grave;
  remember I'm the sinner
  whom Jesus came to save.
  Tell me that story always,
  if you would really be
  in any time of trouble
  a comforter to me.

4 Tell me the same old story,
  when you have cause to fear
  that this world's empty glory
  is costing me too dear.
  Yes, and when that world's glory
  is dawning on my soul,
  tell me the old, old story:
  "Christ Jesus makes you whole."

285 W H Parker (1845-1929) altd.
v. 6 Hugh Martin (1890-1964)
altered © 1986 Horrobin/Leavers

1 Tell me the stories of Jesus
   I love to hear;
   things I would ask Him to tell me
   if He were here;
   scenes by the wayside,
   tales of the sea,
   stories of Jesus,
   tell them to me.

2 First let me hear how the children
   stood round His knee;
   that I may know of His blessing
   resting on me;
   words full of kindness,
   deeds full of grace,
   signs of the love found
   in Jesus' face.

3 Tell me, in words full of wonder,
   how rolled the sea,
   tossing the boat in a tempest
   on Galilee.
   Jesus then doing
   His Father's will,
   ended the storm saying
   "Peace, peace, be still."

4 Into the city I'd follow
   the children's band,
   waving a branch of the palm-tree
   high in my hand;
   worshipping Jesus,
   yes, I would sing
   loudest hosannas,
   for He is King!

5 Show me that scene in the garden,
   of bitter pain;
   and of the cross where my Saviour
   for me was slain:

and, through the sadness,
help me to see
how Jesus suffered
for love of me.

6 Gladly I'd hear of His rising
   out of the grave,
   living and strong and triumphant,
   mighty to save:
   and how He sends us
   all men to bring
   stories of Jesus,
   Jesus, their King.

286 Francis Jane van Alstyne (1820-1915)
(Fanny J Crosby)

1 Tell me the story of Jesus,
   write on my heart every word!
   Tell me the story most precious,
   sweetest that ever was heard.
   Tell how the angels in chorus
   sang, as they welcomed His birth,
   "Glory to God in the highest,
   peace and good tidings to earth."

   Tell me the story of Jesus,
   write on my heart every word,
   tell me the story most precious,
   sweetest that ever was heard.

2 Fasting alone in the desert,
   tell of the days that He passed;
   how He was tried and was tempted,
   yet was triumphant at last.
   Tell of the years of His labours,
   tell of the sorrows He bore;
   He was despised and afflicted,
   homeless, rejected, and poor.

3 Tell of the cross where they nailed Him,
    dying in anguish and pain;
    tell of the grave where they laid Him;
    tell how He liveth again.
    Love, in that story so tender,
    clearer than ever I see;
    stay, let me weep while you whisper
    love paid the ransom for me.

287   Ira F Stanphill
© Singspiration Music/Brentwood Benson Music
Publishing Inc./Admin. by Copycare

1 The cross upon which Jesus died
    is a shelter in which we can hide;
    and its grace so free is sufficient for me,
    and deep is its fountain as wide as the
      sea.

    There's room at the cross for you,
    there's room at the cross for you;
    though millions have come,
    there's still room for one,
    yes, there's room at the cross for you.

2 Though millions have found Him a
      friend
    and have turned from the sins they have
      sinned,
    the Saviour still waits to open the
      gates
    and welcome a sinner before it's too
      late.

3 The hand of my Saviour is strong,
    and the love of my Saviour is long;
    through sunshine or rain, through loss
      or in gain,
    the blood flows from Calvary to cleanse
      every stain.

288   William Cowper (1731-1800)

1 There is a fountain filled with blood,
    drawn from Immanuel's veins,
    and sinners plunged beneath that flood
    lose all their guilty stains!
    Lose all their guilty stains,
    lose all their guilty stains
    and sinners plunged beneath that flood
    lose all their guilty stains!

2 The dying thief rejoiced to see
    that fountain in his day,
    and there may I, though vile as he,
    wash all my sins away.
    Wash all my sins away ...

3 I do believe, I will believe,
    that Jesus died for me!
    That on the cross He shed His blood,
      from sin to set me free.
    From sin to set me free ...

4 Dear dying Lamb! Thy precious blood
    shall never lose its power,
    till all the ransomed church of God
    be saved to sin no more.
    Be saved to sin no more ...

5 E'er since by faith I saw the stream
    Thy flowing wounds supply,
    redeeming love has been my theme,
    and shall be till I die.
    And shall be till I die ...

289   W A Williams
© Unidentified

1 There is a story sweet to hear,
    I love to tell it too;
    it fills my heart with hope and cheer,
    'tis old yet ever new.

'Tis old, yet ever new,
'tis old, yet ever new;
I know, I feel 'tis true,
'tis old, yet ever new.

2 It tells me God the Son came down
   from glory's throne to die,
   that I might live and wear a crown,
   and reign with Him on high.

3 It says He bore the Cross for me,
   and suffered in my place,
   that I from sin might ransomed be,
   and praise Him for His grace.

4 Oh wondrous love, so great, so vast,
   so boundless and so free!
   Lord, at Thy feet myself I cast;
   my all I give to Thee!

290   Elizabeth Clephane (1830-69)

1 There were ninety and nine that safely
      lay
   in the shelter of the fold;
   but one was out on the hills away,
   far off from the gates of gold,
   away on the mountains wild and bare,
   away from the tender Shepherd's care;
   away from the tender Shepherd's care.

2 "Lord, Thou hast here Thy ninety and
      nine;
   are they not enough for Thee?"
   But the Shepherd made answer, "This
      of Mine
   has wandered away from Me;
   and, although the road be rough and
      steep,
   I go to the desert to find My sheep,
   I go ...

3 But none of the ransomed ever knew
   how deep were the waters crossed,
   nor how dark was the night that the
      Lord passed through,
   ere He found His sheep that was lost;
   out in the desert He heard its cry,
   sick and helpless and ready to die,
   sick and ...

4 "Lord, whence are those blood-drops
      all the way,
   that mark out the mountain's track?"
   "They were shed for one who had gone
      astray,
   ere the Shepherd could bring him back."
   "Lord, whence are Thy hands so rent
      and torn?"
   "They are pierced tonight by many a
      thorn,
   they are ..."

5 But all through the mountains, thunder-
      riven,
   and up from the rocky steep,
   there arose a cry to the gate of heaven,
   "Rejoice, I have found My sheep!"
   And the angels echoed around the
      throne,
   "Rejoice, for the Lord brings back
      His own!
   Rejoice, for ..."

291   W E Littlewood (1831-86)

1 There is no love like the love of Jesus;
   never to fade or fall,
   till into the fold of the house of God
   He has gathered us all.

Jesus' love! precious love!
Boundless, and pure, and free;
oh, turn to that love, weary wandering
soul,
Jesus pleadeth for thee!

2 There is no heart like the heart of Jesus,
   filled with a tender love;
   no throb nor throe that our hearts can
   know,
   but He feels it above.

3 There is no eye like the eye of Jesus,
   piercing so far away;
   ne'er out of the sight of its tender light
   can the wanderer stray.

4 There is no voice like the voice of
   Jesus,
   tender and sweet its chime;
   like musical ring of a flowing spring
   in the bright summer time.

5 Oh, let us hark to the voice of Jesus!
   Then we shall never roam;
   and we shall rest on His loving breast,
   all the way to our heavenly home.

292 C B Gabriel (1856-1932)
Copyright Control

1 God is calling the prodigal
      come without delay
   hear, oh, hear Him calling, calling
      now for thee;
   though you've wandered so far from
      His presence, come today,
   hear His loving voice calling still.

Calling now for thee,
oh! weary prodigal come,
calling now for thee
oh! weary prodigal come.

2 Patient, loving tenderly still the
      Father pleads,
   hear, oh, hear Him calling, calling
      now for thee;
   oh return while the Spirit in mercy
      intercedes,
   hear His loving voice calling still.

3 Come, there's bread in the house of
      thy Father and to spare,
   hear, oh, hear Him calling, calling
      now for thee;
   lo! the table is spread and the feast
      is waiting there,
   hear His loving voice calling still.

293 Frederick William Faber (1814-63) altd.

1 There's a wideness in God's mercy
   like the wideness of the sea;
   there's a kindness in His justice
   which is more than liberty.

2 There is plentiful redemption
   in the blood that has been shed;
   there is joy for all the members
   in the sorrows of the Head.

3 There is grace enough for thousands
   of new worlds as great as this;
   there is room for fresh creations
   in that upper home of bliss.

4 For the love of God is broader
than the measures of man's mind;
and the heart of the Eternal
is most wonderfully kind.

5 But we make His love too narrow
by false limits of our own;
and we magnify His strictness
with a zeal He will not own.

6 If our love were but more simple
we should take Him at His word;
and our lives would be illumined
by the presence of our Lord.

294   Geoff Baker
© 1994 Sovereign Lifestyle Music UK

There's a wideness in God's mercy that
    is wider than the greatest sea;
and so I know it covers even me.
There's a depth to His compassion that is
    deeper than I'll understand;
and so my life is safe within His hands.
His love is deep enough for me,
to cause these blinded eyes to see,
to set this lowly captive free from sin.
His grace is flowing from above,
reflected in the Saviour's love
O precious Father, help me take it in.

295   D W Whittle (1840-1901)

1 When God of old the way of life
would teach to all His own,
He placed them safe beyond the reach
of death, by blood alone.

*It is His word, God's precious word,
it stands for ever true:
"When I the Lord shall see the blood,
I will pass over you."*

2 By Christ, the sinless Lamb of God,
the precious blood was shed
when He fulfilled God's holy word,
and suffered in our stead.

3 O soul, for thee salvation thus
by God is freely given;
the blood of Christ atones for sin,
and makes us meet for heaven.

4 The wrath of God that was our due,
upon the Lamb was laid;
and by the shedding of His blood
the debt for us was paid.

5 How calm the judgement hour shall pass
to all who do obey
the word of God, and trust the blood,
and make that word their stay!

296   D W Whittle (1840-1901)

1 When none was found to ransom me
He was found worthy;
to set a world of sinners free,
He was found worthy.

*Oh, the bleeding Lamb!
Oh, the bleeding Lamb!
Oh, the bleeding Lamb!
He was found worthy.*

2 To take the book and loose the seal,
to bruise the head that bruised His
heel.

3 To bridge the gulf 'twixt man and God,
   and save the rebels by His blood.

4 To open wide the gates of heaven;
   to Him all majesty is given.

5 To reign o'er all the ransomed race;
   I've tasted of His saving grace.

6 His blood has washed me white as snow,
   and all His fullness I shall know.

297 Philip Paul Bliss (1838-76)

1 "Whosoever heareth!" shout, shout
   the sound!
   Send the blessed tidings all the world
   around!
   Spread the joyful news wherever man
   is found;
   "Whosoever will may come."

   "Whosoever will!" "whosoever will!"
   Send the proclamation over vale and
   hill:
   'tis the loving Father calls the
   wanderer home:
   "Whosoever will may come."

2 Whosoever cometh need not delay;
   now the door is open, enter while you
   may:
   Jesus is the true and only Living Way,
   "Whosoever will may come."

3 "Whosoever will," the promise is secure;
   "Whosoever will," for ever shall endure;
   "Whosoever will" - 'tis life for
   evermore:
   "Whosoever will may come."

298 J G Badger
© Unidentified

1 Wondrous Love of Jesus! spread the
   news around,
   pardon freely offered, what a joyful
   sound!
   Jesus, loving Saviour, died to set me
   free;
   oh, that blessed "Whosoever," that
   means me.

   Pardon freely offered all who will
   believe;
   whosoever cometh Jesus will receive;
   Jesus, loving Saviour, died to set us
   free:
   hallelujah! "Whosoever" that means
   me.

2 Whosoever cometh may the promise
   claim,
   precious blood of Jesus cleanseth
   every stain.
   The Son of God has loved me,
   wonder can it be?
   "Whosoever," saith the Saviour, that
   means me.

3 Do not trust your feeling, trust His
   word alone.
   Prayers can never save you, tears
   cannot atone.
   "Finished!" cried the Saviour, nothing
   now to do.
   Come, believe this "Whosoever" -
   that means you.

299 R Lowry (1826-99)

1 What can wash away my stain?
Nothing but the blood of Jesus!
What can make me whole again?
Nothing but the blood of Jesus!

Oh, precious is the flow,
that makes me white as snow!
No other fount I know,
Nothing but the blood of Jesus!

2 For my cleansing this I see,
for my pardon this my plea.

3 Nothing can for sin atone,
nought of good that I have done.

4 This is all my hope and peace,
He is all my righteousness.

5 Now by this I overcome:
now by this I'll reach my home:

7.2   THE GOSPEL
Invitation

300 Philip Paul Bliss (1838-76)

1 "Almost persuaded" now to believe;
"Almost persuaded" Christ to receive.
seems now some soul to say?
"Go, Spirit, go Thy way:
some more convenient day
on Thee I'll call."

2 "Almost persuaded" come, come today!
"Almost persuaded" turn not away!
Jesus invites you here,
angels are ling'ring near,
prayers rise from hearts so dear,
O wanderer, come!

3 "Almost persuaded" harvest is past!
"Almost persuaded" doom comes at
    last!
"Almost" can not avail;
"Almost" is but to fail,
sad, sad, that bitter wail,
"Almost" - but lost!

301 Francis Jane van Alstyne (1820-1915)
(Fanny J Crosby)

1 Behold Me standing at the door,
and hear Me pleading evermore
with gentle voice - Oh, heart of sin,
may I come in? may I come in?

Behold Me standing at the door!
And hear Me pleading evermore:
say, weary heart, oppressed with sin,
may I come in? may I come in?

2 I bore the cruel thorns for thee,
I waited long and patiently:
say, weary heart, oppressed with sin,
may I come in? may I come in?

3 I would not plead with thee in vain;
remember all My grief and pain!
I died to ransom thee from sin:
may I come in? may I come in?

4 I bring thee joy from heaven above,
I bring thee pardon, peace, and love:
say, weary heart, oppressed with sin,
may I come in? may I come in?

302 Rev J H Stockton (1813-1877)

1 Come, every soul by sin oppressed,
there's mercy with the Lord;
and He will surely give you rest,
by trusting in His word.

Only trust Him, only trust Him,
only trust Him now!
He will save you, He will save you,
He will save you now!

2 For Jesus shed His precious blood
rich blessings to bestow:
plunge now into the crimson flood
that washes white as snow.

3 Yes, Jesus is the Truth, the Way
that leads you into rest;
believe in Him without delay,
and you are fully blest.

4 Come, then, and join this holy band,
and on to glory go,
to dwell in that celestial land
where joys immortal flow.

303 Robert Walmsley (1831-1905)

1 Come let us sing of a wonderful love,
tender and true;
out of the heart of the Father above,
streaming to me and to you:
wonderful love
dwells in the heart of the Father
above.

2 Jesus, the Saviour, this gospel to tell,
joyfully came;
came with the helpless and hopeless to
dwell,
sharing their sorrow and shame;
seeking the lost,
saving, redeeming at measureless cost.

3 Jesus is seeking the wanderers yet;
why do they roam?
Love only waits to forgive and forget;
home! weary wanderers, home!
Wonderful love
dwells in the heart of the Father above.

4 Come to my heart, O Thou wonderful
love,
come and abide,
lifting my life till it rises above
envy and falsehood and pride;
seeking to be
lowly and humble, a learner of Thee.

304 © Unidentified

1 Come, sinners, to Jesus! no longer
delay,
a full, free salvation He offers to-day;
arouse your dark spirits, awake from
your dream,
And Christ will support you in coming
to Him.

For the Lion of Judah shall break
every chain,
And give us the vict'ry again and
again.
For the Lion of Judah shall break
every chain,
And give us the vict'ry again and
again.

2 Our blessed Redeemer was nailed to
    the tree,
    to open a fountain for sinners like me,
    His blood is the fountain that pardon
      bestows,
    and cleanses the foulest wherever it
      flows.

3 And when I was willing with all things
    to part,
    He gave me my bounty, His love in my
      heart,
    so now I am joined with the conquering
      band,
    who are marching to glory at Jesus'
      command.

4 Though round me the storms of
    adversity roll,
    and the waves of destruction encompass
      my soul,
    in vain this frail vessel the tempest
      shall toss,
    my hopes rest secure on the blood of
      the cross.

5 And when with the ransomed of Jesus
    my Head,
    from fountain to fountain I then shall
      be led
    I'll fall at His feet and His mercy adore,
    and sing of the blood of the cross
      evermore.

305 G F Root (1820-95)

1 Come to the Saviour, make no delay;
    here in His word He has shown us the
      way;
    here in our midst He's standing today,
    tenderly saying, "Come."

Joyful, joyful will the meeting be,
when from sin our hearts are pure
and free,
and we shall gather, Saviour, with Thee,
in our eternal home.

2 "Suffer the children!" Oh, hear His
    voice,
    let every heart leap forth and rejoice;
    and let us freely make Him our choice.
    do not delay, but come.

3 Think once again, He's with us today;
    heed now His blest command, and obey;
    hear now His accents tenderly say,
    "Will you, My children, come?"

306 J Lawley (1859-1922)

1 Come with me, visit Calvary,
    where our Redeemer died;
    His blood, it fills the fountain,
    'tis full, 'tis deep, 'tis wide.
    He died from sin to sever
    our hearts and lives complete;
    He saves and keeps for ever
    those lying at His feet.

To the uttermost He saves,
to the uttermost He saves,
dare you now believe and His love
receive,
to the uttermost Jesus saves.

2 I will surrender fully,
    and do His blessed will;
    His blood doth make me holy,
    His presence me doth fill.
    He's saving, I'm believing,
    this blessing now I claim;
    His Spirit I'm receiving,
    my heart is in a flame.

3   I've wondrous peace through trusting,
a well of joy within;
this rest is everlasting,
each day I triumph win.
He gives me heavenly measure
pressed down and running o'er,
oh, what a priceless treasure,
glory for evermore!

307   John Morison (1750-98): as in Scottish Paraphrases, 1781

1   Come, let us to the Lord our God
with contrite hearts return:
our God is gracious, nor will leave
the desolate to mourn.

2   His voice commands the tempest forth,
and stills the stormy wave;
and though His arm be strong to smite,
'tis also strong to save.

3   Long hath the night of sorrow reigned;
the dawn shall bring us light;
God shall appear, and we shall rise
with gladness in His sight.

4   Our hearts, if God we seek to know,
shall know Him and rejoice;
His coming like the morn shall be,
like morning songs His voice.

5   As dew upon the tender herb,
diffusing fragrance round;
as showers that usher in the spring,
and cheer the thirsty ground.

6   So shall His presence bless our souls,
and shed a joyful light;
that hallowed morn shall chase away
the sorrows of the night.

308   William Cowper (1731-1800)

1   Hark, my soul! it is the Lord;
'tis thy Saviour, hear His word;
Jesus speaks, and speaks to thee,
"Say, poor sinner, lov'st thou Me?"

2   "I delivered thee, when bound,
and, when bleeding, healed thy wound;
sought thee wandering, set thee right,
turned thy darkness into light."

3   "Can a woman's tender care
cease toward the child she bare?
Yes! she may forgetful be,
yet will I remember thee."

4   "Mine is an unchanging love,
higher than the heights above,
deeper than the depths beneath,
free and faithful, strong as death."

5   "Thou shalt see My glory soon,
when the work of grace is done:
partner of My throne shalt be;
say, poor sinner, lov'st thou Me?"

309   Daniel W Whittle (1840-1901)

1   Have you any room for Jesus?
He who bore your load of sin;
as He knocks and asks admission,
sinner, will you let Him in?

Room for Jesus, King of glory!
Hasten now, His word obey,
swing your heart's door widely open,
bid Him enter while you may.

2 Room for pleasure, room for business,
but for Christ, the crucified,
not a place that He can enter,
in your heart for which He died?

3 Have you any time for Jesus,
as in grace He calls again?
Oh, today is time accepted,
tomorrow you may call in vain.

4 Room and time now give to Jesus,
soon will pass God's day of grace;
soon your heart be cold and silent,
and your Saviour's pleadings cease.

310 Annie L James
© Unidentified

1 Is there a heart that is waiting,
longing for pardon today?
Hear the glad message proclaiming,
Jesus is passing this way.

Jesus is passing this way,
this way, today,
Jesus is passing this way,
is passing this way today.

2 Is there a heart that has wandered?
Come with thy burden today;
mercy is tenderly pleading,
Jesus is passing this way.

3 Is there a heart that is broken?
Weary and sighing for rest?
Come to the arms of thy Saviour,
pillow thy head on His breast.

4 Come to thy only Redeemer,
come to His infinite love;
come to the gate that is leading
homeward to mansions above.

311 Anon.
© Unidentified

1 Jesus, my Saviour, to Bethlehem came,
born in a manger to sorrow and shame,
oh it was wonderful, blest be
His name,
seeking for me, for me!
Seeking for me, for me!
Seeking for me, for me!
Oh, it was wonderful, blest be
His name,
seeking for me, for me!

2 Jesus, my Saviour, on Calvary's tree,
paid the great debt, and my soul He set
free;
oh it was wonderful, how could it be?
dying for me, for me!
Dying for me...

3 Jesus, my Saviour, the same as of old,
while I was wand'ring afar from the fold
gently and long did He plead with my
soul,
calling for me, for me!
Calling for me...

4 Jesus, my Saviour, shall come from on
high,
sweet is the promise as weary years fly:
oh, I shall see Him descending the sky,
coming for me, for me!
Coming for me...

312 William Kirkpatrick (1838-1921)

1 Life at best is very brief,
   like the falling of a leaf,
   like the binding of a sheaf,
   be in time!
   Fleeting days are telling fast
   that the die will soon be cast,
   and the fatal line be passed,
   be in time!

   Be in time, be in time,
   while the voice of Jesus calls you,
   be in time!
   If in sin you longer wait,
   you may find no open gate,
   and your cry be just too late,
   be in time!

2 Fairest flowers soon decay,
   youth and beauty pass away,
   oh, you have not long to stay,
   be in time!
   While the Spirit bids you come,
   sinner, do not longer roam,
   lest you seal your hopeless doom,
   be in time!

3 Time is gliding swiftly by,
   death and judgement drawing nigh,
   to the arms of Jesus fly,
   be in time!
   Oh, I pray you, count the cost,
   ere the fatal line be crossed,
   and your soul in hell be lost!
   Be in time!

4 Sinner, heed the warning voice,
   make the Lord your final choice,
   then all heaven will rejoice,
   be in time!

Come from darkness into light,
come, let Jesus make you right,
come, and start for heaven tonight,
be in time!

313 Bill Harmon
© 1958 Renewed 1986 by Gospel Publishing House

Reach out and touch the Lord as He goes
   by;
you'll find He's not too busy to hear your
   heart's cry.
He's passing by this moment your needs
   to supply;
reach out and touch the Lord as He goes
   by.

314 Virginia W Moyer
© Unidentified

1 O sinner, the Saviour is calling for thee,
   long, long has He called thee in vain!
   He called thee when joy lent its crown
     to thy days,
   He called thee in sorrow and pain.

   O turn, while the Saviour in mercy
     is waiting,
   and steer for the harbour light!
   For how do you know but your soul
     may be drifting
   over the dead-line tonight?

2 O sinner, thine ears have been deaf
     to His voice,
   thine eyes to His glory been dim!
   The calls of thy Saviour have so
     wearied thee,
   oh what if they should weary Him?

3 O sinner, the Spirit is striving with thee!
   What if He should strive never more,
   but leave thee alone in thy darkness
     to dwell,
   in sight of the heavenly shore?

4 O sinner, God's patience may weary
     some day,
   and leave thy sad soul in the blast!
   By wilful resistance you've drifted away
   over the dead-line at last.

315 H E Govan (1866-1932)
          © The Faith Mission

1 O sinners, come to Jesus!
   All other trust is vain;
   your every hope must fail you
   unless you're born again.
   You need the cleansing fountain
   to purge your heart within,
   and purify your conscience
   from all the stains of sin.

2 You need to come to Jesus
   and find in Him your rest,
   confiding in His goodness,
   reclining on His breast.
   You need the voice of Jesus
   to whisper "Go in peace!"
   To calm the inward tempest
   and bid the conflict cease.

3 You need the power of Jesus
   to keep you day by day,
   to guard amid temptations
   and be your strength and stay.
   You need the love of Jesus:
   you need this faithful Friend,
   to cheer you and to bless you
   and guide you to the end.

4 Then will you come to Jesus,
   in spite of fear and doubt?
   He's waiting now to save you,
   and will not cast you out.
   He'll give you free forgiveness
   and full salvation now,
   if but, in true repentance,
   before His cross you bow.

316 D W Whittle (1840-1901)

1 Once again the Gospel message
   from the Saviour you have heard;
   Will you heed the invitation?
   Will you turn and seek the Lord?

   Come believing! come believing!
   Come to Jesus! look and live!
   Come believing! come believing!
   Come to Jesus! look and live!

2 Many summers you have wasted,
   ripened harvests you have seen;
   winter snows by spring have melted,
   yet you linger in your sin.

3 Jesus for your choice is waiting;
   tarry not; at once decide!
   While the Spirit now is striving,
   yield, and seek the Saviour's side.

4 Cease of fitness to be thinking;
   do not longer try to feel!
   It is trusting, and not feeling,
   that will give the Spirit's seal.

5 Let your will to God be given,
   trust in Christ's atoning blood;
   look to Jesus now in heaven,
   rest on His unchanging word.

317 G F Root (1820-95)

1 She only touched the hem of His
    garment
    as to His side she stole,
    amid the crowd that gathered around
    Him,
    and straightway she was whole.

Oh, touch the hem of His garment,
and thou, too, shalt be free;
His saving power this very hour
shall give new life to thee.

2 She came in fear and trembling before
    Him,
    she knew her Lord had come;
    she felt that from Him virtue had healed
    her,
    the mighty deed was done.

3 He turned with, "Daughter, be of good
    comfort,
    thy faith hath made thee whole";
    and peace that passeth all under-
    standing
    with gladness filled her soul.

318 W L Thompson (1847-1909)

1 Softly and tenderly Jesus is calling,
    calling for you and for me;
    see, on the portals He's waiting and
    watching,
    watching for you and for me.

Come home, come home;
you who are weary, come home!
Earnestly, tenderly, Jesus is calling,
calling, O sinner, come home!

2 Why should we tarry when Jesus is
    pleading,
    pleading for you and for me?
    Why should we linger and heed not
    His mercies,
    mercies for you and for me?

3 Time is now fleeting, the moments
    are passing,
    passing from you and from me;
    shadows are gathering, deathbeds
    are coming,
    coming for you and for me.

4 Oh, for the wonderful love He has
    promised,
    promised for you and for me;
    though we have sinned He has mercy
    and pardon,
    pardon for you and for me.

319 Francis Jane van Alstyne (1820-1915) (Fanny J Crosby)

1 Sinner, how thy heart is troubled!
    God is coming very near;
    do not hide thy deep emotion,
    do not check that falling tear.

Oh, be saved, His grace is free!
Oh, be saved, He died for thee!
Oh, be saved, He died for thee!

2 Art thou waiting till the morrow?
    Thou may'st never see its light;
    come at once! accept His mercy:
    He is waiting - come tonight!

3 With a lowly contrite spirit,
    kneeling at the Saviour's feet,
    thou canst feel, this very moment,
    pardon - precious, pure, and sweet.

4 Let the angels bear the tidings
   upward to the courts of heaven!
   Let them sing, with holy rapture,
   o'er another soul forgiven!

320 E H Swinstead
         © Unidentified

There's a way back to God from the
   dark paths of sin;
there's a door that is open and you may
   go in:
at Calvary's cross is where you begin,
when you come as a sinner to Jesus.

321 J C Bateman (1854-88)

1 There is a cleansing fountain,
   it flows from Calvary,
   'twas opened by the Saviour
   from sin each soul to free.
   And now His voice is calling
   with accents, oh so sweet!
   "Come to the cleansing river,
   down at the Mercy-seat."

   Oh! Calvary's stream is flowing,
   Calvary's stream is flowing,
   flowing so free for you and for me,
   Calvary's stream is flowing.

2 Though worn and heavy laden,
   and burdened with your sin,
   there's virtue in the river;
   oh, will you enter in?
   There's healing in its waters,
   there's cleansing in its stream;
   then look away to Calvary
   where mercy's light does beam.

3 This stream of life eternal
   for you is flowing free;
   oh, bow yourself for cleansing,
   and gain your liberty.
   Then Christ shall be your Saviour,
   and out of you shall flow
   a life of peace and heaven,
   God's Paradise below.

322 Amelia Matilda Hull (c1825-82)

1 There is life for a look at the Crucified
   One,
   there is life at this moment for thee;
   then look, sinner, look unto Him and
   be saved,
   unto Him who was nailed to the tree.

   Look, look, look and live,
   there is life for a look at the
   Crucified One,
   there is life at this moment for thee.

2 It is not thy tears of repentance nor
   prayers,
   but the blood that atones for the soul;
   on Him then believe, and a pardon
   receive,
   for His blood now can make thee quite
   whole.

3 We are healed by His stripes; wouldst
   thou add to the word?
   And He is our righteousness made;
   the best robe of heaven He bids thee
   to wear,
   oh, couldst thou be better arrayed?

4 Then doubt not thy welcome, since
   God has declared
there remaineth no more to be done;
that once in the end of the world He
   appeared,
and completed the work He begun.

5 But take, with rejoicing, from Jesus at
   once,
the life everlasting He gives:
and know with assurance thou never
   canst die,
since Jesus thy righteousness lives.

323   Lewis E Jones
         © Hope Publishing/Admin. by Copycare

1 Would you be free from your burden
   of sin?
   There's power in the blood, power in the
   blood;
   would you o'er evil a victory win?
   There's wonderful power in the blood.

   There is power, power, wonder-
     working power,
   in the blood of the Lamb;
   There is power, power, wonder-
     working power,
   in the precious blood of the Lamb.

2 Would you be free from your passion
   and pride?
   Come for a cleansing to Calvary's tide!

3 Would you be whiter, much whiter than
   snow?
   Sin-stains are lost in its life-giving flow.

4 Would you do service for Jesus your
   King?
   Would you live daily His praises to sing?

324   Lelia N Morris (1862-1929)
         © Unidentified

And the blood shall never lose its power,
no, never! no, never!
Jesus' blood avails for me forever,
and will never lose its power.

325   Elisha A Hoffman (1839-1929)
         © Unidentified

1 Where will you spend eternity?
   This question comes to you and me.
   Tell me, what shall your answer be?
   Where will you spend eternity?

   Eternity! eternity!
   Where will you spend eternity?

2 Many are choosing Christ today,
   turning from all their sins away:
   heaven shall their happy portion be;
   where will you spend eternity?

   Eternity! eternity!
   Where will you spend eternity?

3 Leaving the straight and narrow way,
   going the downward road today,
   sad will their final ending be -
   lost through a long eternity!

   Eternity! eternity!
   Lost through a long eternity!

4 Repent, believe, this very hour,
   trust in the Saviour's grace and power,
   then will your joyous answer be,
   saved through a long eternity!

   Eternity! eternity!
   Saved through a long eternity!

7.3 THE GOSPEL
Response

326 E R Latta (b. 1839)
Copyright Control

1 Blessed be the Fountain of blood,
to a world of sinners revealed:
blessed be the dear Son of God,
only by His stripes are we healed.
Though I've wandered far from His
    fold,
bringing to my heart pain and woe,
wash me in the blood of the Lamb,
and I shall be whiter than snow.

> *Whiter than the snow, whiter than the
> snow,*
> *wash me in the blood of the Lamb,*
> *and I shall be whiter than snow.*

2 Thorny was the crown that He wore,
and the cross His body o'ercame;
grievous were the sorrows He bore,
but He suffered thus not in vain.
May I to that fountain be led,
made to cleanse my sins here below;
wash me in the blood that He shed,
and I shall be whiter than snow.

3 Father, I have wandered from Thee,
often has my heart gone astray;
crimson do my sins seem to me,
water cannot wash them away.
Jesus, to that fountain of Thine,
leaning on Thy promise I go,
cleanse me by Thy washing divine,
and I shall be whiter than snow.

327 Charles Wesley (1707-88)

1 Depth of mercy! can there be
mercy still reserved for me?
Can my God His wrath forbear?
Me, the chief of sinners, spare?

2 I have long withstood His grace,
long provoked Him to His face;
would not hearken to His calls,
grieved Him by a thousand falls.

3 Whence to me this waste of love?
Ask my Advocate above!
See the cause in Jesus' face,
now before the throne of grace.

4 There for me the Saviour stands,
shows His wounds and spreads His
    hands.
God is love, I know, I feel,
Jesus lives, and loves me still.

5 If I rightly read Thy heart,
if Thou all compassion art,
bow Thine ear, in mercy bow,
pardon and accept me now!

328 Henry Williams Baker (1821-77)

1 God made me for Himself, to serve
    Him here,
with love's pure service and in filial
    fear;
to show His praise, for Him to labour
    now;
then see His glory where the angels
    bow.

2 All needful grace was mine through
   His dear Son,
   whose life and death my full
   salvation won;
   the grace that would have
   strengthened me, and taught;
   grace that would crown me when my
   work was wrought.

3 And I, poor sinner, cast it all away;
   lived for the toil or pleasure of each day;
   as if no Christ had shed His precious
   blood,
   as if I owed no homage to my God.

4 O Holy Spirit, with Thy fire divine,
   melt into tears this thankless heart of
   mine;
   teach me to love what once I seemed to
   hate,
   and live to God before it be too late.

329 Graham Kendrick & Steve Thompson
© 1991 Make Way Music

1 How can I be free from sin -
   lead me to the cross of Jesus,
   from the guilt, the power, the pain?
   Lead me to the cross of Jesus.
   There's no other way, no price that I
   could pay;
   simply to the cross I cling.
   This is all I need, this is all I plead,
   that His blood was shed for me.

2 How can I know peace within,
   lead me to the cross of Jesus,
   sing a song of joy again!
   Lead me to the cross of Jesus.
   Flowing from above, all forgiving love
   from the Father's heart to me!
   What a gift of grace His own
   righteousness
   clothing me in purity!

3 How can I live day by day -
   lead me to the cross of Jesus,
   following His narrow way?
   Lead me to the cross of Jesus.

330 Lewis Hartsough (1828-1919)

1 I hear Thy welcome voice,
   that calls me, Lord, to Thee,
   for cleansing in Thy precious blood,
   that flowed on Calvary.

   I am coming, Lord! coming now to
   Thee!
   Wash me, cleanse me in the blood
   that flowed on Calvary.

2 Though coming weak and vile,
   Thou dost my strength assure;
   Thou dost my vileness fully cleanse,
   till spotless all, and pure.

3 'Tis Jesus calls me on
   to perfect faith and love,
   to perfect hope, and peace, and trust,
   for earth and heaven above.

4 'Tis Jesus who confirms
   the blessed work within,
   by adding grace to welcomed grace,
   where reigned the power of sin.

5 All hail, atoning blood!
   All hail, redeeming grace!
   All hail, the gift of Christ our Lord,
   our Strength and Righteousness!

331 William J Kirkpatrick (1838-1921)

1 I've wandered far away from God,
   now I'm coming home;
   the paths of sin too long I've trod,
   Lord, I'm coming home.

   Coming home, coming home,
   never more to roam.
   To Thine open arms of love,
   Lord, I'm coming home!

2 I've wasted many precious years,
   now I'm coming home;
   I now repent with bitter tears,
   Lord, I'm coming home.

3 I'm tired of sin and straying, Lord,
   now I'm coming home;
   I'll trust Thy love, believe Thy word,
   Lord, I'm coming home.

4 My soul is sick, my heart is sore,
   now I'm coming home;
   My strength renew, my hope restore!
   Lord, I'm coming home.

332 Lucy Ann Bennett (1850-1927)

1 O teach me what it meaneth,
   that cross uplifted high,
   with One, the Man of Sorrows,
   condemned to bleed and die!
   O teach me what it cost Thee
   to make a sinner whole;
   and teach me, Saviour, teach me
   the value of a soul!

2 O teach me what it meaneth,
   that sacred crimson tide,
   the blood and water flowing
   from Thine own wounded side.
   Teach me that if none other
   had sinned, but I alone,
   yet still Thy blood, Lord Jesus,
   Thine only, must atone.

3 O teach me what it meaneth,
   Thy love beyond compare,
   the love that reacheth deeper
   than depths of self-despair!
   Yes, teach me, till there gloweth
   in this cold heart of mine,
   some feeble, pale reflection
   of that pure love of Thine.

4 O teach me what it meaneth,
   for I am full of sin;
   and grace alone can reach me,
   and love alone can win.
   O teach me, for I need Thee,
   I have no hope beside,
   the chief of all the sinners
   for whom the Saviour died!

5 O infinite Redeemer!
   I bring no other plea,
   because Thou dost invite me
   I cast myself on Thee.
   Because Thou dost accept me
   I love and I adore;
   because Thy love constraineth,
   I'll praise Thee evermore!

333 William True Sleeper (1819-1904)

1 Out of my bondage, sorrow, and night,
Jesus, I come! Jesus, I come!
Into Thy freedom, gladness, and light,
Jesus, I come to Thee!
Out of my sickness into Thy health,
out of my want and into Thy wealth,
out of my sin and into Thyself,
Jesus, I come to Thee!

2 Out of my shameful failure and loss,
Jesus, I come! Jesus, I come!
Into the glorious gain of Thy cross,
Jesus, I come to Thee!
Out of earth's sorrows into Thy balm,
out of life's storms and into Thy calm,
out of distress to jubilant psalm,
Jesus, I come to Thee!

3 Out of unrest and arrogant pride,
Jesus, I come! Jesus, I come!
Into Thy blessed will to abide,
Jesus, I come to Thee!
Out of myself to dwell in Thy love,
out of despair into raptures above,
upward for aye on wings like a dove,
Jesus, I come to Thee!

4 Out of the fear and dread of the tomb,
Jesus, I come! Jesus, I come!
Into the joy and light of Thy home,
Jesus, I come to Thee!
Out of the depths of ruin untold,
into the peace of Thy sheltering fold,
ever Thy glorious face to behold,
Jesus, I come to Thee!

334 Francis Jane van Alstyne (1820-1915)
(Fanny J Crosby)

1 Pass me not, O gentle Saviour,
hear my humble cry;
while on others Thou art calling,
do not pass me by.

Saviour, Saviour,
hear my humble cry;
while on others Thou art calling,
do not pass me by.

2 Let me, at Thy throne of mercy
find a sweet relief;
kneeling there in deep contrition,
help my unbelief.

3 Trusting only in Thy merit
would I seek Thy face;
heal my wounded, broken spirit,
save me by Thy grace.

4 Thou the spring of all my comfort,
more than life to me -
whom have I on earth beside Thee?
Whom in heaven but Thee?

335 Augustus Montague Toplady (1740-78)

1 Rock of Ages, cleft for me,
let me hide myself in Thee!
Let the water and the blood,
from Thy riven side which flowed,
be of sin the double cure,
cleanse me from its guilt and power.

2 Not the labours of my hands
can fulfil Thy law's demands;
could my zeal no respite know,
could my tears for ever flow,
all for sin could not atone;
Thou must save, and Thou alone.

3 Nothing in my hand I bring,
simply to Thy cross I cling;
naked, come to Thee for dress;
helpless, look to Thee for grace;
foul, I to the fountain fly;
wash me, Saviour! or I die.

4 While I draw this fleeting breath,
when my eyelids close in death,
when I soar through tracts unknown,
see Thee on Thy judgement throne,
Rock of Ages, cleft for me,
let me hide myself in Thee!

336 Merrill Dunlop
© Singspiration Music/Brentwood Benson
Music Publishing Inc./Admin. by Copycare

1 Show me the cross of Calvary,
open my eyes to see
Thy dying form in agony -
Lord, make it real to me.

Lord, make Calvary real to me!
Jesus, dying in agony,
Thy great sacrifice let me see:
Lord, make Calvary real to me!

2 Show me the cross of Calvary,
open my ears to Thy plea:
"Father, forgive them!" - can it be?
Lord, make it real to me.

3 Low at the cross of Calvary,
bowed is my heart as I see
grace that can save eternally -
Lord, make it real to me.

337 Leon Olguin
© 1990 Sound Truth Publishing/Maranatha!
Music/Admin. by Copycare

White as snow, white as snow,
though my sins were as scarlet Lord,
I know, Lord I know that I'm clean and
    forgiven,
through the power of Your blood,
through the wonder of Your love;
through faith in You I know that I can be
    white as snow.

338 Cornelius Elven (1797-1873)

1 With broken heart and contrite sigh,
a trembling sinner, Lord, I cry;
Thy pardoning grace is rich and free:
O God, O God be merciful to me!

2 I smite upon my troubled breast,
with deep and conscious guilt oppressed;
Christ and His Cross my only plea:
O God, O God be merciful to me!

3 Far off I stand with tearful eyes,
nor dare uplift them to the skies;
but Thou dost all my anguish see:
O God, O God be merciful to me!

4 Nor alms, nor deeds that I have done,
can for a single sin atone:
to Calvary alone I flee;
O God, O God merciful to me!

5 And when, redeemed from sin and hell,
with all the ransomed throng I dwell,
my raptured song shall ever be:
God has, God has been merciful to me!

339 Charlotte Elliot (1789-1871)

1 Just as I am, without one plea,
  but that Thy blood was shed for me,
  and that Thou bidst me come to Thee,
  O Lamb of God, I come! I come!

2 Just as I am, and waiting not
  to rid my soul of one dark blot.
  To Thee, whose blood can cleanse each
    spot,
  O Lamb of God, I come! I come!

3 Just as I am, though tossed about
  with many a conflict, many a doubt,
  fightings and fears within, without,
  O Lamb of God, I come! I come!

4 Just as I am, poor, wretched, blind;
  sight, riches, healing of the mind,
  yea, all I need in Thee to find,
  O Lamb of God, I come! I come!

5 Just as I am - Thou wilt receive,
  wilt welcome, pardon, cleanse, relieve;
  because Thy promise I believe,
  O Lamb of God, I come! I come!

6 Just as I am - Thy love unknown
  has broken every barrier down;
  now to be Thine, yea, Thine alone,
  O Lamb of God, I come! I come!

8.1   THE CHRISTIAN LIFE
Assurance

340 Anna Hudson (d. 1953)
© The Rodeheaver Co./Word Music/
Admin. by Copycare

1 Dear Saviour, Thou art mine,
  how sweet the thought to me!
  Let me repeat Thy name,
  and lift my heart to Thee.

   Mine! mine! mine!
   I know Thou art mine;
   Saviour, dear Saviour,
   I know Thou art mine.

2 Thou art the sinner's friend,
  so I Thy friendship claim,
  a sinner saved by grace,
  when Thy sweet message came.

3 My hardened heart was touched;
  Thy pardoning voice I heard;
  and joy and peace came in
  while listening to Thy word.

4 So, let me sing Thy praise,
  so, let me call Thee mine.
  I cannot doubt Thy word,
  I know that I am Thine.

341 Francis Jane van Alstyne (1820-1915)
(Fanny J Crosby)

1 A wonderful Saviour is Jesus, my Lord,
  a wonderful Saviour to me,
  He hideth my soul in the cleft of the
    rock,
  where rivers of pleasure I see.

*He hideth my soul in the cleft of the
    rock,
that shadows a dry thirsty land;
He hideth my life in the depths of
    His love,
and covers me there with His hand,
and covers me there with His hand.*

2 A wonderful Saviour is Jesus, my Lord,
    He taketh my burden away,
    He holdeth me up, and I shall not be
        moved,
    He giveth me strength as my day.

3 With numberless blessings each
        moment He crowns,
    and filled with His fullness divine,
    I sing in my rapture, oh, glory to God
    for such a Redeemer as mine!

4 When clothed in His brightness,
        transported I rise
    to meet Him in clouds of the sky,
    His perfect salvation, His wonderful
        love,
    I'll shout with the millions on high.

342 Francis Jane van Alstyne (1820-1915)
          (Fanny J Crosby)

1 Blessed assurance, Jesus is mine!
    Oh, what a foretaste of glory divine!
    Heir of salvation, purchase of God,
    born of His Spirit, washed in His blood.

    *This is my story, this is my song,
    praising my Saviour all the day long.
    This is my story, this is my song,
    praising my Saviour all the day long.*

2 Perfect submission, perfect delight,
    visions of rapture now burst on my
        sight;
    angels, descending, bring from above
    echoes of mercy, whispers of love.

3 Perfect submission, all is at rest;
    I in my Saviour am happy and blest,
    watching and waiting, looking above,
    filled with His goodness, lost in His love.

343 Daniel W Whittle (1840-1901)

1 Come sing, my soul, and praise the Lord,
    who hath redeemed thee by His blood;
    delivered thee from chains that bound,
    and brought thee to redemption ground.

    *Redemption ground, the ground of
        peace!
    Redemption ground, oh, wondrous
        grace!
    Here let our praise to God abound,
    who saves us on redemption ground.*

2 Once from my God I wandered far,
    and with His holy will made war:
    but now my songs to God abound;
    I'm standing on redemption ground.

3 Oh, joyous hour when God to me
    a vision gave of Calvary:
    my bonds were loosed, my soul unbound;
    I sang upon redemption ground.

4 No works of merit now I plead,
    but Jesus take for all my need;
    no righteousness in me is found,
    except upon redemption ground.

5   Come, weary soul, and here find rest;
    accept redemption, and be blest:
    the Christ, who died, by God is crowned
    to pardon on redemption ground.

5   Never a weakness that He doth not feel,
    never a sickness that He cannot heal;
    moment by moment, in woe or in weal,
    Jesus my Saviour abides with me still.

344   Daniel W Whittle (1840-1901)

1   Dying with Jesus, by death reckoned
      mine;
    living with Jesus a new life divine;
    looking to Jesus till glory doth shine;
    moment by moment, O Lord, I am
      Thine.

    Moment by moment I'm kept in His
      love,
    moment by moment I've life from
      above;
    looking to Jesus till glory doth shine;
    moment by moment, O Lord, I am
      Thine.

2   Never a battle with wrong for the right,
    never a contest that He doth not fight;
    lifting above us His banner so white
    moment by moment I'm kept in His
      sight.

3   Never a trial that He is not there,
    never a burden that He doth not bear,
    never a sorrow that He doth not share
    moment by moment I'm under His care.

4   Never a heart-ache, and never a groan,
    never a tear-drop, and never a moan;
    never a danger but there on the throne,
    moment by moment He thinks of His
      own.

345   D W Whittle (1840 - 1901)

1   I know not why God's wondrous grace
    to me has been made known;
    nor why - unworthy as I am -
    He claimed me for His own.

    But "I know whom I have believed;
    and am persuaded that He is able
    to keep that which I've committed
    unto Him against that day."

2   I know not how this saving faith
    to me He did impart;
    or how believing in His word
    wrought peace within my heart.

3   I know not how the Spirit moves,
    convincing men of sin;
    revealing Jesus through the word,
    creating faith in Him.

4   I know not what of good or ill
    may be reserved for me -
    of weary ways or golden days
    before His face I see.

346   Norman Clayton
    © Norman Clayton Publishing/Word Music/
    Admin. by Copycare

1   Jesus my Lord will love me for ever,
    from Him no power of evil can sever,
    He gave His life to ransom my soul,
    now I belong to Him:

Now I belong to Jesus,
Jesus belongs to me,
not for the years of time alone,
but for eternity.

2 Once I was lost in sin's degradation,
   Jesus came down to bring me salvation,
   lifted me up from sorrow and shame,
   now I belong to Him:

3 Joy floods my soul, for Jesus has saved
      me,
   freed me from sin that long had enslaved
      me,
   His precious blood He gave to redeem,
   now I belong to Him:

347 L H Edmonds (b. 19th c.)

1 My faith has found a resting place,
   not in device nor creed;
   I trust the ever-living One,
   His wounds for me shall plead.

   I need no other argument,
   I need no other plea,
   it is enough that Jesus died,
   and that He died for me.

2 Enough for me that Jesus saves,
   this ends my fear and doubt;
   a sinful soul I come to Him,
   He'll never cast me out.

3 My heart is leaning on the word,
   the written word of God,
   salvation by my Saviour's Name,
   salvation through His blood.

4 My great Physician heals the sick,
   the lost He came to save:
   for me His precious blood He shed,
   for me His life He gave.

348 Helen Lemmel © 1922 Singspiration Music/
Brentwood Benson Music Publishing Inc./
Admin. by Copycare

1 O soul, are you weary and troubled?
   No light in the darkness you see?
   There's light for a look at the Saviour,
   and life more abundant and free!

   Turn your eyes upon Jesus,
   look full in His wonderful face;
   and the things of earth will grow
      strangely dim
   in the light of His glory and grace.

2 Through death into life everlasting
   He passed and we follow Him there;
   over us sin no more hath dominion,
   for more than conquerors we are!

3 His word shall not fail you, He promised;
   believe Him, and all will be well:
   then go to a world that is dying,
   His perfect salvation to tell.

349 Francis Jane van Alstyne (1820-1915)
(Fanny J Crosby)

1 Redeemed, how I love to proclaim it,
   redeemed by the blood of the Lamb,
   redeemed through His infinite mercy;
   His child and for ever I am.

   Redeemed, Redeemed,
   redeemed by the blood of the Lamb;
   redeemed, redeemed,
   His child and for ever, I am.

2 Redeemed, and so happy in Jesus,
   no language my rapture can tell;
   I know that the light of His presence
   with me doth continually dwell.

3 I know I shall see in His beauty
the King in whose law I delight,
who lovingly guardeth my footsteps,
and giveth me songs in the night.

4 I know there's a crown that is waiting
in yonder bright mansion for me,
and soon with the spirits made perfect,
at home with the Lord I shall be.

350 Edward Henry Bickersteth (1825-1906)

1 Peace, perfect peace, in this dark world
of sin?
The blood of Jesus whispers peace
within.

2 Peace, perfect peace, by thronging
duties pressed?
To do the will of Jesus - this is rest.

3 Peace, perfect peace, with sorrows
surging round?
On Jesus' bosom nought but calm is
found.

4 Peace, perfect peace, with loved ones far
away?
In Jesus' keeping we are safe, and
they.

5 Peace, perfect peace, our future all
unknown?
Jesus we know; and He is on the
Throne.

6 Peace, perfect peace, death shadowing
us and ours?
Jesus has vanquished death and all
its powers.

7 It is enough; earth's struggles soon
shall cease,
and Jesus call us to heaven's perfect
peace.

351 Philip Paul Bliss (1838-76)

1 'Tis the promise of God full salvation
to give
unto him who on Jesus, His Son, will
believe.

Hallelujah! 'tis done, I believe on the
Son;
I am saved by the blood of the
crucified One.
Hallelujah! 'tis done, I believe on the
Son;
I am saved by the blood of the
crucified One.

2 Though the pathway be lonely and
dangerous too,
surely Jesus is able to carry me through.

3 Many loved ones have I in yon
heavenly throng,
they are safe now in glory, and this is
their song:

4 There are prophets and kings in that
throng I behold,
and they sing while they march
through the streets of pure gold:

5 There's a part in that chorus for you
and for me,
and the theme of our praises for ever
will be:

352 P P Bilhorn © Unidentified

1 There comes to my heart one sweet
     strain,
   a glad and a joyous refrain,
   I sing it again and again,
   sweet peace, the gift of God's love.

   Peace, peace, sweet peace,
   wonderful gift from above;
   oh, wonderful, wonderful peace,
   sweet peace, the gift of God's love.

2 By Christ on the cross peace was
     made,
   my debt by His death was all paid,
   no other foundation is laid
   for peace, the gift of God's love.

3 When Jesus as Lord I had crowned,
   my heart with this peace did abound,
   in Him the rich blessing I found,
   sweet peace, the gift of God's love.

4 In Jesus for peace I abide,
   and as I keep close to His side,
   there's nothing but peace doth betide,
   sweet peace, the gift of God's love.

353 Horatio Gates Spafford (1828-88)

1 When peace, like a river, attendeth
     my way,
   when sorrows like sea billows roll;
   whatever my lot, Thou hast taught
     me to know,
   it is well, it is well with my soul.

   It is well with my soul,
   it is well, it is well with my soul.

2 If Satan should buffet, if trials should
     come,
   let this blest assurance control,
   that Christ hath regarded my
     helpless estate,
   and hath shed His own blood for my
     soul.

3 My sin - oh, the bliss of this glorious
     thought -
   My sin - not in part, but the whole
   is nailed to His cross; and I bear it no
     more:
   praise the Lord, praise the Lord,
     O my soul!

4 For me be it Christ, be it Christ, hence
     to live!
   If Jordan above me shall roll,
   no pang shall be mine, for in death as
     in life,
   Thou wilt whisper Thy peace to my
     soul.

5 But Lord, 'tis for Thee, for Thy coming
     we wait,
   the sky, not the grave, is our goal;
   oh, trump of the angel! oh, voice of the
     Lord!
   Blessed hope! blessed rest of my soul!

8.2 THE CHRISTIAN LIFE
Witness and Testimony

354 Charles Wesley (1707-88)

1 And can it be that I should gain
an interest in the Saviour's blood?
Died He for me, who caused His pain?
For me, who Him to death pursued?
Amazing love! how can it be
that Thou, my God, shouldst die for me?

2 'Tis mystery all! The Immortal dies!
Who can explore His strange design!
In vain the first-born seraph tries
to sound the depths of love divine!
'Tis mercy all! let earth adore,
let angel minds inquire no more.

3 He left His Father's throne above,
so free, so infinite His grace;
emptied Himself of all but love,
and bled for Adam's helpless race:
'tis mercy all, immense and free;
for, O my God, it found out me.

4 Long my imprisoned spirit lay
fast bound in sin and nature's night;
Thine eye diffused a quickening ray,
I woke, the dungeon flamed with light;
my chains fell off, my heart was free;
I rose, went forth, and followed Thee.

5 No condemnation now I dread;
Jesus, and all in Him, is mine!
Alive in Him, my living Head,
and clothed in righteousness divine.
Bold I approach the eternal throne,
and claim the crown, through Christ
my own.

355 John Newton (1725-1807)

1 Amazing grace, how sweet the sound,
that saved a wretch like me!
I once was lost, but now am found,
was blind, but now I see.

2 'Twas grace that taught my heart to fear,
and grace my fears relieved;
how precious did that grace appear
the hour I first believed.

3 Through many dangers, toils and snares,
I have already come;
'tis grace hath brought me safe thus far,
and grace will lead me home.

4 When we've been there ten thousand
years
bright shining as the sun,
we've no less days to sing God's praise
than when we've first begun.

356 Major W T Maltby © Salvationist Publishing & Supplies/Admin. by Copycare

Christ is the answer to my every need;
Christ is the answer, He is my friend indeed.
Problems of life my spirit may assail,
with Christ my Saviour
I need never fail,
for Christ is the answer to my need.

357 Billy Funk © 1991 Integrity's Praise! Music/ Adm. by Kingsway's Thankyou Music

By Your blood You have saved us,
by Your blood You have freed us,
by Your blood we can enter into Your holy
place;
by Your blood You have raised us,
by Your blood, precious blood of the
Lamb.

Father God in heaven, precious Lamb of
    God,
we humbly bow before You and cry holy,
    holy.
All of heaven's singing the song of the
    redeemed,
giving glory to the Lamb.

By Your blood ...

358   Elisha A Hoffman (1839-1929)
                    Copyright Control

1   Christ has for sin atonement made,
    what a wonderful Saviour!
    We are redeemed! the price is paid!
    What a wonderful Saviour!

      What a wonderful Saviour is Jesus,
        my Jesus!
      What a wonderful Saviour is Jesus,
        my Lord!

2   I praise Him for the cleansing blood,
    that reconciled my soul to God.

3   He dwells within me day by day,
    and keeps me faithful all the way.

4   He gives me overcoming power,
    and triumph in each conflict hour.

5   To Him I've given all my heart;
    the world shall never share a part.

359   Isaac Watts (1674-1748)

1   Come, ye that love the Lord
    and let your joys be known;
    join in a song with sweet accord,
    join in a song with sweet accord
    and thus surround the throne,
    and thus surround the throne.

      We're marching to Zion!
      Beautiful, beautiful Zion!
      We're marching upward to Zion,
      the beautiful city of God!

2   Let those refuse to sing
    who never knew our God;
    but children of the heavenly King,
    but children of the heavenly King
    must speak their joys abroad,
    must speak their joys abroad.

3   The hill of Zion yields
    a thousand sacred sweets,
    before we reach the heavenly fields,
    before we reach the heavenly fields
    or walk the golden streets,
    or walk the golden streets.

4   Then let our songs abound
    and every tear be dry:
    we're marching through Immanuel's
    ground,
    we're marching through Immanuel's
    ground,
    to fairer worlds on high,
    to fairer worlds on high.

360 Elisha A Hoffman (1839-1929)

1 Down at the cross where my Saviour
    died,
  down where for cleansing from sin I
    cried,
  there to my heart was the blood applied;
  glory to His name!

  Glory to His name!
  Glory to His name!
  Now to my heart is the blood applied;
  Glory to His name!

2 I am so wondrously saved from sin,
  Jesus so sweetly abides within,
  here at the cross where He took me in;
  glory to His name!

3 Oh, precious fountain that saves from
    sin,
  I am so glad I have entered in;
  here Jesus saves me and keeps me clean;
  glory to His name!

4 Come to this fountain so rich and sweet,
  cast thy poor soul at the Saviour's feet,
  plunge in today and be made complete;
  glory to His name!

361 C Austin Miles © The Rodeheaver Co./Word
      Music/Admin. by Copycare

1 Far away the noise of strife upon my
    ear is falling,
  then I know the sins of earth beset on
    every hand;
  doubt and fear and things of earth in
    vain to me are calling,
  none of these shall move me from
    Beulah Land.

  I'm living on the mountain,
    underneath a cloudless sky,
  I'm drinking at the fountain that
    never shall run dry,
  oh, yes! I'm feasting on the manna
    from a bountiful supply,
  for I am dwelling in Beulah Land.

2 Far below the storm of doubt upon the
    world is beating,
  sons of men in battle long the enemy
    withstand;
  safe am I within the castle of God's
    Word retreating,
  nothing then can reach me, 'tis Beulah
    Land.

3 Let the stormy breezes blow, their cry
    cannot alarm me,
  I am safely sheltered here protected
    by God's hand;
  here the sun is always shining, here
    there's naught can harm me,
  I am safe for ever in Beulah Land.

4 Viewing here the works of God, I sink
    in contemplation,
  hearing now His blessed voice, I see
    the way is planned;
  dwelling in the Spirit, here I learn of
    full salvation,
  gladly will I tarry in Beulah Land.

362 Charles Gabriel (1856-1932)
      © Rodeheaver Co./Word Music/Admin. by
      Copycare

1 For all the Lord has done for me,
  I never will cease to praise Him;
  and for His grace so rich and free,
  I never will cease to praise Him.

I never will cease to praise Him,
my Saviour, my Saviour!
I never will cease to praise Him,
He's done so much for me.

2   He gives me strength for every day;
    He leads and guides me all the way.

3   Although the world His love neglect,
    I could not such a friend reject.

4   He saves me every day and hour;
    just now I feel His cleansing power.

5   While on my journey here below,
    And when to that bright world I go.

363   C.F.O.
          © Unidentified

1   Gone from my heart the world with all
      its charm;
    now through the blood I'm saved from
      sin's alarm;
    down at the cross my heart is bending
      low,
    the precious blood of Jesus washes
      white as snow.

    I love Him, I love Him, because He
      first loved me
    and purchased my salvation on
      Mount Calvary.

2   Once I was far away, deep down in sin,
    once was a slave to passions fierce
      within;
    once was afraid to meet an angry God,
    but now I'm cleansed from every stain
      through Jesus' blood.

3   Once I was bound, but now I am set free,
    once I was blind, but now the light I see;
    once I was dead, but now in God I live,
    and tell the world around the peace that
      He doth give.

364   Philip Doddridge (1702-51)
          and Augustus M Toplady (1740-78)

1   Grace! 'tis a charming sound,
    harmonious to the ear.
    Heaven with the echo shall resound,
    and all the earth shall hear.

    Saved by grace alone!
    This is all my plea:
    Jesus died for all mankind,
    and Jesus died for me.

2   'Twas grace that wrote my name
    in life's eternal book;
    'twas grace that gave me to the Lamb,
    who all my sorrows took.

3   Grace taught my wandering feet
    to tread the heavenly road,
    and new supplies each hour I meet,
    while pressing on to God.

4   Grace taught my soul to pray,
    and made mine eyes o'er flow;
    'tis grace has kept me to this day,
    and will not let me go.

5   Oh, let Thy grace inspire
    my soul with strength divine!
    May all my powers to Thee aspire,
    and all my days be Thine.

365 M. Warburton-Booth
© Africa Evangelical Fellowship

1 He is not a disappointment!
   Jesus is far more to me
   than in all my glowing daydreams
   I had fancied He could be;
   and the more I get to know Him,
   so the more I find Him true,
   and the more I long that others
   should be led to know Him too.

2 He is not a disappointment!
   He has saved my soul from sin;
   all the guilt and all the anguish
   which oppressed my heart within
   He has banished by His presence,
   and His blessed kiss of peace
   has assured my heart for ever
   that His love will never cease.

3 He is not a disappointment!
   He has sanctified my soul,
   cleansed me from my heart corruption,
   purified and made me whole;
   He removed the sinward proneness,
   stamped His image in its place,
   for He won me by the beauty
   and unveiling of His face.

4 He is not a disappointment!
   He is all in all to me,
   Saviour, Sanctifier, Healer;
   the unchanging Christ is He!
   He has won my heart's affections,
   and He meets my every need;
   He is not a disappointment,
   for He satisfies indeed.

(Repeat last 2 lines of each verse)

366 Julia Sterling © Unidentified

1 I am redeemed, oh, praise the Lord!
   My soul, from bondage free,
   has found at last a resting place
   in Him who died for me!

   I am redeemed! I am redeemed!
   I'll sing it o'er and o'er;
   I am redeemed! oh, praise the Lord!
   Redeemed for ever more!

2 I looked, and lo, from Calvary's cross
   a healing fountain streamed;
   it cleansed my heart, and now I sing,
   praise God, I am redeemed!

3 The debt is paid, my soul is free;
   and by His mighty power,
   the blood that washed my sins away
   still cleanseth every hour.

4 All glory be to Jesus' name!
   I know that He is mine!
   For on my heart the Spirit seals
   His pledge of love Divine.

5 And when I reach that world more bright
   than mortal ever dreamed,
   I'll cast my crown at Jesus' feet
   and cry, "Redeemed, redeemed!"

367 Marc Nelson
© 1985 Mercy/Vineyard Publishing/Music
Services/Admin. by Copycare

1 I believe in Jesus,
   I believe He is the Son of God.
   I believe He died and rose again,
   I believe He paid for us all.
   And I believe He's here now
   standing in our midst,
   here with the power to heal now
   and the grace to forgive.

2 I believe in You, Lord,
   I believe You are the Son of God;
   I believe You died and rose again:
   I believe You paid for us all:

MEN   And I believe You're here now,
WOMEN   I believe that You're here
ALL   standing in our midst.
MEN   Here with the power to heal now
WOMEN   with the power to heal
ALL   and the grace to forgive.

3 I believe in You, Lord,
   I believe You are the Son of God;
   I believe You died and rose again:
   I believe You paid for us all:

MEN   And I believe You're here now,
WOMEN   I believe that You're here
ALL   standing in our midst.
MEN   Here with the power to heal now
WOMEN   with the power to heal
ALL   and the grace to forgive.

   And I believe He's here now
   standing in our midst,
   here with the power to heal now
   and the grace to forgive.

368   Dora Greenwell (1821-82)

1 I am not skilled to understand
   what God hath willed, what God hath
      planned;
   I only know at His right hand
   stands One who is my Saviour.

2 I take Him at His word indeed;
   "Christ died for sinners," this I read;
   for in my heart I find a need
   of Him to be my Saviour.

3 That He should leave His place on high,
   and come for sinful man to die,
   you count it strange? so once did I
   before I knew my Saviour!

4 And oh, that He fulfilled may see
   the travail of His soul in me,
   and with His work contented be,
   as I with my dear Saviour!

5 Yea, living, dying, let me bring
   my strength, my solace, from this
      spring,
   that He who lives to be my King
   once died to be my Saviour.

369   Horatius Bonar (1808-89)

1 I heard the voice of Jesus say,
   "Come unto Me and rest;
   lay down, thou weary one, lay down,
   thy head upon My breast."
   I came to Jesus as I was,
   weary, and worn, and sad;
   I found in Him a resting place
   and He has made me glad.

2 I heard the voice of Jesus say,
   "Behold, I freely give
   the living water; thirsty one,
   stoop down and drink, and live."
   I came to Jesus, and I drank
   of that life-giving stream;
   my thirst was quenched, my soul
      revived,
   and now I live in Him.

3 I heard the voice of Jesus say,
  "I am this dark world's Light;
  look unto Me, thy morn shall rise,
  and all thy day be bright."
  I looked to Jesus, and I found
  in Him my Star, my Sun;
  and in that Light of life I'll walk
  till travelling days are done.

370 Robert Murray McCheyne (1813-43)

1 I once was a stranger
  to grace and to God,
  I knew not my danger
  and felt not my load;
  though friends spoke in rapture
  of Christ on the tree,
  Jehovah Tsidkenu
  was nothing to me.

2 Like tears from the daughters
  of Zion that roll,
  I wept when the waters
  went over His soul;
  yet thought not that my sins
  had nailed to the tree
  Jehovah Tsidkenu;
  'twas nothing to me.

3 When free grace awoke me
  by light from on high,
  then legal fears shook me,
  I trembled to die;
  no refuge, no safety
  in self could I see,
  Jehovah Tsidkenu
  my Saviour must be.

4 My terrors all vanished
  before the sweet name,
  my guilty fears banished,
  with boldness I came
  to drink at the fountain,
  life-giving and free,
  Jehovah Tsidkenu
  is all things to me.

5 E'en treading the valley,
  the shadow of death,
  this watchword shall rally
  my faltering breath;
  for when from life's fever
  my God sets me free,
  Jehovah Tsidkenu
  my deathsong shall be.

371 Walt Huntley
Copyright Control

1 I stood one day at Calvary
  where Jesus bled and died,
  I never knew He loved me so,
  for me was crucified;
  and as I stood there in my sin,
  His love reached down to me,
  and O the shame that filled my soul
  that day at Calvary!

2 I knelt one day at Calvary;
  my eyes were filled with tears
  to think such love I had refused
  through all these wasted years;
  and as I knelt I heard Him say,
  "I did it all for thee,"
  and O the love that filled my soul
  that day at Calvary!

3   I prayed one day at Calvary,
    "I'm Thine for evermore!
    Forgive me, Lord, for all my sin;
    my lost estate restore!"
    And as I prayed, to me He gave
    salvation full and free,
    and O the peace that filled my soul
    that day at Calvary!

372   Psalm 40 verses 1-5 (Scottish Psalter)

1   I waited for the Lord my God,
    and patiently did bear;
    at length to me He did incline
    my voice and cry to hear.

2   He took me from a fearful pit,
    and from the miry clay,
    and on a rock He set my feet,
    establishing my way.

3   He put a new song in my mouth,
    our God to magnify:
    many shall see it, and shall fear,
    and on the Lord rely.

4   O blessed is the man whose trust
    upon the Lord relies;
    respecting not the proud, nor such
    as turn aside to lies.

5   O Lord my God, full many are
    the wonders Thou hast done;
    Thy gracious thoughts to us-ward are
    above all thoughts are gone.

6   None can them reckon, unto Thee:
    if I would them declare.
    If I would speak of them, they more
    than can be numbered, are.

7   *To Father, Son and Holy Ghost*
    the God whom we adore
    be glory as it was, is now
    and shall be evermore.

373   tr. F Bevan (1827-1909)

1   I was journeying in the noontide,
    when His light shone o'er my road
    and I saw Him in that glory,
    saw Him, Jesus, Son of God.
    All around, in noonday splendour,
    earthly scenes lay fair and bright;
    but my eyes no longer see them
    for the glory of that light.

    I have seen the face of Jesus,
    tell me not of aught beside;
    I have heard the voice of Jesus,
    all my soul is satisfied.

2   Others, in the summer sunshine,
    wearily may journey on;
    I have seen a light from heaven,
    past the brightness of the sun;
    light that knows no cloud, no waning,
    light wherein I see His face,
    all His love's uncounted treasures,
    all the riches of His grace.

3   Marvel not that Christ in glory
    all my inmost heart hath won;
    not a star to cheer my darkness,
    but a light beyond the sun.
    All below lies dark and shadowed,
    nothing there to claim my heart,
    save the lonely track of sorrow
    where of old He walked apart.

4 Sinners, it was not to angels
all this wondrous love was given,
but to one who scorned, despised Him,
scorned and hated Christ in heaven.
From the lowest depths of evil,
to the throne in heaven above,
thus in me He told the measure
of His free unbounded love.

3 When the waves of sorrow roll,
when I am in distress,
Jesus takes my hand in His,
ever He loves to bless.
He will every fear dispel,
satisfy every need;
all who heed His loving call,
find rest indeed.

374 James Rowe (1865-1933)

1 I was sinking deep in sin,
sinking to rise no more,
overwhelmed by guilt within,
mercy I did implore.
Then the Master of the sea
heard my despairing cry,
Christ my Saviour lifted me,
now safe am I.

Love lifted me, love lifted me.
When no one but Christ could help,
love lifted me.
Love lifted me, Love lifted me.
When no one but Christ could help,
love lifted me!

2 Souls in danger, look above,
Jesus completely saves;
He will lift you by His love
out of the angry waves.
He's the Master of the sea,
billows His will obey;
He your Saviour wants to be,
be saved today!

375 Philip Paul Bliss (1838-76)

1 I will sing of my Redeemer
and His wondrous love to me:
on the cruel cross He suffered,
from the curse to set me free.

Sing, oh sing, of my Redeemer!
With His blood He purchased me!
On the cross He sealed my pardon,
paid the debt and made me free!

2 I will tell the wondrous story,
how, my lost estate to save,
in His boundless love and mercy
He the ransom freely gave.

3 I will praise my dear Redeemer,
His triumphant power I'll tell,
how the victory He giveth
over sin, and death, and hell.

4 I will sing of my Redeemer
and His heavenly love to me;
He from death to life hath brought me,
Son of God, with Him to be.

376 F H Rawley (1854-1952)
© Harper Collins Religious/Admin. by Copycare

1 I will sing the wondrous story
of the Christ who died for me,
how He left the realms of glory
for the cross on Calvary.
Yes, I'll sing the wondrous story
of the Christ who died for me,
sing it with His saints in glory,
gathered by the crystal sea.

2 I was lost: but Jesus found me,
found the sheep that went astray,
raised me up and gently led me
back into the narrow way.
Days of darkness still may meet me,
sorrow's path I oft may tread;
but His presence still is with me,
by His guiding hand I'm led.

3 He will keep me till the river
rolls its waters at my feet:
then He'll bear me safely over,
made by grace for glory meet.
Yes, I'll sing the wondrous story
of the Christ who died for me,
sing it with His saints in glory,
gathered by the crystal sea.

377 Rhea F Miller © The Rodeheaver Co./Word
Music/Admin. by Copycare

1 I'd rather have Jesus than silver or gold,
I'd rather be His than have riches
untold;
I'd rather have Jesus than houses or
lands,
I'd rather be led by His nail-pierced
hand.

Than to be the king of a vast domain
and be held in sin's dread sway;
I'd rather have Jesus than anything
this world affords today.

2 I'd rather have Jesus than men's
applause,
I'd rather be faithful to His dear cause;
I'd rather have Jesus than world-wide
fame,
I'd rather be true to His holy Name.

3 He's fairer than lilies of rarest bloom,
He's sweeter than honey from out the
comb;
He's all that my hungering spirit needs,
I'd rather have Jesus and let Him
lead.

378 C J Butler (d. 1877)

1 I was once far away from the Saviour
and as vile as a sinner could be;
and I wondered if Christ the Redeemer
could save a poor sinner like me.

2 I wandered on in the darkness,
not a ray of light could I see;
and the thought filled my heart with
sadness,
there's no hope for a sinner like me.

3 And then, in that dark lonely hour,
a voice sweetly whispered to me,
saying, "Christ the Redeemer has
power
to save a poor sinner like thee."

4   I listened: and lo! 'twas the Saviour
    that was speaking so kindly to me;
    I cried, "I'm the chief of sinners,
    Thou canst save a poor sinner like me!"

5   I then fully trusted in Jesus;
    and oh, what a joy came to me!
    My heart was filled with His praises
    for saving a sinner like me.

6   No longer in darkness I'm walking,
    for the light is now shining on me,
    and now unto others I'm telling
    how He saved a poor sinner like me.

7   And when life's journey is over,
    and I the dear Saviour shall see,
    I'll praise Him for ever and ever,
    for saving a sinner like me.

379   Isaac Watts (1674-1748)

1   I'm not ashamed to own my Lord,
    or to defend His cause;
    maintain the glory of His cross
    and honour all His laws.

2   Jesus, my Lord! I know His name,
    His name is all my boast;
    nor will He put my soul to shame,
    nor let my hope be lost.

3   I know that safe with Him remains,
    protected by His power,
    what I've committed to His hands
    till the decisive hour.

4   Then will He own His servant's name
    before His Father's face;
    and, in the new Jerusalem,
    appoint my soul a place.

(When sung to 379b add chorus)

At the cross, at the cross, where I
   first saw the light,
  and the burden of my heart rolled
   away,
  it was there by faith I received my
   sight,
  and now I am happy all the day.

380   L R Minor
             Copyright Control

1   I've something in my heart that Jesus
    gave to me,
    it makes me feel like singing glory all
    the day:
    He found my captive soul and gave
    me liberty,
    and now I feel like singing glory!

He makes the path grow brighter
   every passing day;
He makes the burden lighter, all
   along the way;
His Word is my delight, His will I now
   obey,
and all the time I'm singing glory!

2   My Saviour loosed my tongue that I
    might speak His praise;
    since then I have been singing glory
    all the day;
    I love to tell the lost of Jesus and His
    ways,
    and oh, it keeps me singing glory!

3 My Saviour took my feet from out the
      miry clay;
   since then I have been singing glory
      all the day:
   He placed them on the Rock that
      shall not pass away
   I cannot keep from singing glory!

4 O weary heart and sad, O heavy laden
      soul,
   if you would feel like singing glory all
      the day,
   just let the Saviour in and let Him take
      control:
   then you will feel like singing glory!

381 Charles H Gabriel (1856-1932)
         Copyright Control

1 In loving-kindness Jesus came,
   my soul in mercy to reclaim,
   and from the depths of sin and shame
   through grace He lifted me.

   From sinking sand He lifted me;
   with tender hand He lifted me;
   from shades of night to plains of light,
   O praise His name, He lifted me!

2 He called me long before I heard,
   before my sinful heart was stirred;
   but when I took Him at His word,
   forgiven He lifted me.

3 His brow was pierced with many a thorn,
   His hands by cruel nails were torn,
   when from my guilt and grief, forlorn,
   in love He lifted me.

4 Now on a higher plane I dwell,
   and with my soul I know 'tis well;
   yet how or why, I cannot tell,
   He should have lifted me.

382 W Spencer Walton (1850-1906)

1 In tenderness He sought me,
   weary and sick with sin,
   and on His shoulders brought me
   back to His fold again;
   while angels in His presence sang
   until the courts of heaven rang.

   Oh, the love that sought me!
   Oh, the blood that bought me!
   Oh, the grace that brought me to the
      fold,
   wondrous grace, that brought me to
      the fold!

2 He washed the bleeding sin-wounds,
   and poured in oil and wine;
   He whispered to assure me,
   "I've found thee, thou art Mine"
   I never heard a sweeter voice;
   it made my aching heart rejoice.

3 He pointed to the nail-prints,
   for me His blood was shed,
   a mocking crown so thorny
   was placed upon His head;
   I wondered what He saw in me,
   to suffer such deep agony.

4 I'm sitting in His presence,
   the sunshine of His face,
   while with adoring wonder
   His blessings I retrace.
   It seems as if eternal days
   are far too short to sound His praise.

5 So, while the hours are passing,
   all now is perfect rest;
   I'm waiting for the morning,
   the brightest and the best,
   when He will call us to His side,
   to be with Him, His spotless bride.

383

1 It was down at the feet of Jesus,
O the happy, happy day!
that my soul found peace in believing,
and my sins were washed away.

Let me tell the old, old story
of His grace so full and free,
for I feel like giving Him the glory
for His wondrous love to me.

2 It was down at the feet of Jesus,
where I found such perfect rest,
where the light first dawned on my
 spirit,
and my soul was truly blessed.

3 It was down at the feet of Jesus,
where I brought my guilt and sin,
that He cancelled all my transgressions,
and salvation entered in.

384

1 Love Divine, so great and wondrous,
deep and mighty, pure, sublime!
Coming from the heart of Jesus,
just the same through tests of time.

He the pearly gates will open,
so that I may enter in;
for He purchased my redemption
and forgave me all my sin.

2 Like a dove when hunted, frightened
as a wounded fawn was I;
broken-hearted, yet He healed me,
He will heed the sinner's cry.

3 Love Divine, so great and wondrous,
all my sins He then forgave.
I will sing His praise forever,
for His blood, His power to save.

4 In life's eventide, at twilight,
at His door I'll knock and wait;
by the precious love of Jesus
I shall enter heaven's gate.

385

1 My happy soul rejoices,
the sky is bright above;
I'll join the heavenly voices
and sing redeeming love.

For there's power in Jesus' blood,
power in Jesus' blood,
there's power in Jesus' blood
to wash me white as snow.

2 I heard the blessed story
of Him who died to save;
the love of Christ swept o'er me,
my all to Him I gave.

3 His gracious words of pardon
were music to my heart;
He took away my burden,
and bade my fears depart.

4 I plunge beneath this fountain,
that cleanseth white as snow;
it pours from Calvary's mountain,
with blessings in its flow.

5 Oh, crown Him King for ever,
my Saviour and my Friend.
By Zion's crystal river
His praise shall never end.

386 Sally Ellis
© 1986 Kingsway's Thankyou Music

It is no longer I that liveth but Christ that
    liveth in me;
it is no longer I that liveth but Christ that
    liveth in me.
He lives, He lives,
Jesus is alive in me;
it is no longer I that liveth but Christ that
    liveth in me.

387 E Mote (1797-1874)

1   My hope is built on nothing less
    than Jesus' blood and righteousness;
    I dare not trust the sweetest frame,
    but wholly lean on Jesus' name.

    On Christ, the solid rock, I stand;
    all other ground is sinking sand.
    All other ground is sinking sand.

2   When darkness seems to veil His face
    I rest on His unchanging grace;
    in every high and stormy gale,
    my anchor holds within the veil.

3   His oath, His covenant, and blood,
    support me in the 'whelming flood;
    when all around my soul gives way,
    He then is all my hope and stay.

    (Omit last line of chours when using
    the tune "St. Catherine")

388 James M Gray
© Hope Publishing/Harper Collins Religious/
Admin. by Copycare

1   Naught have I gotten but what I received;
    grace hath bestowed it since I have
        believed;
    boasting excluded, pride I abase;
    I'm only a sinner saved by grace!

    Only a sinner saved by grace!
    Only a sinner saved by grace!
    This is my story; to God be the glory,
    I'm only a sinner saved by grace!

2   Once, I was foolish and sin ruled my
        heart,
    causing my footsteps from God to
        depart;
    Jesus hath found me, happy my case,
    I now am a sinner saved by grace!

3   Tears unavailing, no merit had I;
    mercy had saved me, or else I must die;
    sin had alarmed me, fearing God's face;
    but now I'm a sinner saved by grace!

4   Suffer a sinner whose heart overflows,
    loving his Saviour, to tell what he
        knows;
    once more to tell it, would I embrace
    I'm only a sinner saved by grace!

389 Mark Altrogge © 1990 Integrity's Hosanna!
Music/People of Destiny Int./Adm. by
Kingsway's Thankyou Music

No eye has seen and no ear has heard,
and no mind has ever conceived
the glorious things that You have prepared
for everyone who has believed;
You brought us near and You called us
    Your own,
and made us joint heirs with Your Son.
    How high and how wide,
    how deep and how long,
    how sweet and how strong, is Your
    love;
    how lavish your grace,
    how faithful Your ways,
    how great is Your love, O Lord!

Objects of mercy who should have known
wrath,
we're filled with unspeakable joy,
riches of wisdom, unsearchable wealth,
and the wonder of knowing your voice;
You are our treasure and our great reward,
our hope and our glorious King.
How high and how wide ...

390 © Colin N Peckham

1 'Tis the mystery of the ages,
hid from prophets, priests and sages,
God my seeking heart engages,
He stoops down to dwell in me!

2 Christ in you the hope of glory,
tell the world the wondrous story,
see Him come, His is the victory!
God stoops down to dwell in me!

3 God is for us; yea, but in us,
naught but sin does He take from us,
then His life He giveth to us,
God stoops down to dwell in me!

4 We partake of His own nature,
thus to grow to His own stature,
while beholding Him in rapture,
God stoops down to dwell in me!

391 © Unidentified

1 O Christ, in Thee my soul hath found,
and found in Thee alone,
the peace, the joy, I sought so long,
the bliss till now unknown.

Now none but Christ can satisfy,
none other Name for me!
There's love, and life, and lasting joy,
Lord Jesus, found in Thee!

2 I sighed for rest and happiness,
I yearned for them, not Thee,
but while I passed my Saviour by,
His love laid hold on me.

3 I tried the broken cisterns, Lord,
but, ah! the waters failed!
E'en as I stooped to drink they fled
and mocked me as I wailed.

4 The pleasures lost I sadly mourned,
but never wept for Thee,
till grace the sightless eyes received
Thy loveliness to see.

392 Philip Doddridge (1702-51)

1 Oh, happy day that fixed my choice
on Thee, my Saviour and my God.
Well may this glowing heart rejoice;
and tell its raptures all abroad.

Happy day! happy day!
When Jesus washed my sins away.
He taught me how to watch and pray,
and live rejoicing every day.
Happy day! happy day!
When Jesus washed my sins away.

2 'Tis done, the great transaction's done!
I am my Lord's, and He is mine:
He drew me, and I followed on,
charmed to confess the voice divine.

3 Now rest, my long-divided heart,
fixed on this blissful centre, rest:
nor ever from thy Lord depart,
with Him of every good possessed.

4 High heaven, that heard the solemn vow,
that vow renewed shall daily hear,
till in life's latest hour I bow
and bless in death a bond so dear.

393 Mary D James (1810-83)

1 Oh, this uttermost salvation!
'Tis a fountain full and free,
pure, exhaustless, ever flowing,
wondrous grace, it reaches me.

It reaches me, it reaches me.
Wondrous grace, it reaches me.
Pure, exhaustless, ever flowing,
wondrous grace, it reaches me.

2 How amazing God's compassion,
that so vile a worm should prove
this stupendous bliss of heaven,
this unmeasured wealth of love.

3 Jesus, Saviour, I adore Thee,
Now Thy love I will proclaim;
I will tell the blessed story,
I will magnify Thy name.

394 L.M. Rouse © Unidentified

1 Precious Saviour, Thou hast saved me,
Thine and only Thine I am;
oh, the cleansing blood has reached me,
glory, glory to the Lamb.

Glory, glory, hallelujah!
Glory, glory to the Lamb!
Oh, the cleansing blood has reached
me!
Glory, glory to the Lamb!

2 Long my yearning heart was striving
to obtain this precious rest;
but when all my struggles ended,
simply trusting, I was blest.

3 Consecrated to Thy service,
I will live and die to Thee;
I will witness to Thy glory
of salvation, full and free.

4 Yes, I will stand up for Jesus,
He has sweetly saved my soul,
cleansed my heart from sin's corruption,
sanctified, and made me whole.

5 Glory to the Lord who bought me.
Glory for His saving power.
Glory to the Lord who keeps me.
Glory, glory, evermore.

395 Mike Kerry
© 1984 Kingsway's Thankyou Music

1 Reconciled, I'm reconciled,
I'm reconciled to God for ever;
know He took away my sin,
I know His love will leave me never.
Reconciled, I am His child,
I know it was on me He smiled;
I'm reconciled, I'm reconciled to God,
hallelujah!

2 I'm justified, I'm justified,
it's just as if I'd never sinned;
and once I knew such guilty fear,
but now I know His peace with me.
Justified, I'm justified,
it's all because my Jesus died;
I'm justified, I'm justified by God,
hallelujah!

3 I'll magnify, I'll magnify,
I'll magnify His name for ever;
wear the robe of righteousness
and bless the name of Jesus, Saviour;
magnify the One who died,
the One who reigns for me on high;
I'll magnify, I'll magnify my God.

396 William & Gloria Gaither
© 1971 Gaither Music Company/WJG Inc./
Admin. by Kingsway's Thankyou Music

1 Shackled by a heavy burden,
'neath a load of guilt and shame,
then the hand of Jesus touched me,
and now I am no longer the same.

*He touched me, O He touched me,
and O the joy that floods my soul;
something happened, and now I know,
He touched me and made me whole.*

2 Since I met this blessed Saviour,
since He cleansed and made me whole,
I will never cease to praise Him:
I'll shout it while eternity rolls.

397 Charles Butler
© Hope Publishing/Admin. by Copycare

1 Since Christ my soul from sin set free,
this world has been a heaven to me;
amid earth's sorrows and its woe,
'tis heaven my Jesus here to know.

*O hallelujah, yes, 'tis heaven!
'Tis heaven to know my sins forgiven;
on land or sea, what matters where,
where Jesus is, 'tis heaven there.*

2 Once heaven seemed a far-off place,
till Jesus showed His smiling face;
now it's begun within my soul,
'twill last while endless ages roll.

3 What matters where on earth we dwell -
on mountain top, or in the dell,
in cottage, or a mansion fair?
Where Jesus is, 'tis heaven there.

398 William J Gaither
© Gaither Music Company/WJG Inc./Admin.
by Kingsway's Thankyou Music

1 Since I started for the Kingdom,
since my life He controls,
since I gave my heart to Jesus,
the longer I serve Him, the sweeter He
grows.

*The longer I serve Him the sweeter He
grows,
the more that I love Him, more love
He bestows;
each day is like heaven, my heart
overflows,
the longer I serve Him the sweeter He
grows.*

2 Every need He is supplying,
plenteous grace He bestows;
every day my way gets brighter,
the longer I serve Him, the sweeter He
grows.

399 John W Peterson ©John W Peterson Company/
Admin. by Copycare

1 O what a wonderful, wonderful day,
day I will never forget;
after I'd wandered in darkness away,
Jesus my Saviour I met.
O what a tender, compassionate friend
He met the need of my heart;
shadows dispelling, with joy I am
telling,
He made all the darkness depart!

Heaven came down and glory filled
my soul,
when at the cross the Saviour made
me whole;
my sins were washed away
and my night was turned to day;
heaven came down and glory filled
my soul!

2   Born of the Spirit with life from above
into God's family divine,
justified fully through Calvary's love,
O what a standing is mine!
And the transaction so quickly was made
when as a sinner I came,
took of the offer of grace He did
proffer;
He saved me, O praise His dear name!

3   Now I've a hope that will surely endure
after the passing of time;
I have a future in Heaven for sure,
there in those mansions sublime.
And it's because of that wonderful day,
when at the cross I believed;
riches eternal and blessings supernal
from His precious hand I received.

400   Mark Pendergras
© Birdwing/BMG Songs Inc./Garden Valley/
Admin. by Copycare

1   The greatest thing in all my life is
knowing You;
the greatest thing in all my life is
knowing You;
I want to know You more;
I want to know You more.
The greatest thing in all my life is
knowing You.

2   The greatest thing in all my life is
loving You;
the greatest thing in all my life is
loving You;
I want to love You more;
I want to love You more.
The greatest thing in all my life is
loving You.

3   The greatest thing in all my life is
serving You;
the greatest thing in all my life is
serving You;
I want to serve You more;
I want to serve You more.
The greatest thing in all my life is
serving You.

401   v1 & 2 Seth Sykes; v3 Glyn L Taylor
© Singspiration Music/Brentwood Benson
Music Publishing Inc./Admin. by Copycare

1   The world was in darkness, in sin and
shame;
mankind was lost, and then Jesus came.
He carried our sins to Calvary's tree,
He hung there, and bled there, for you
and me.

Thank You, Lord, for saving my soul.
Thank You, Lord, for making me
whole.
Thank You, Lord, for giving to me
Thy great salvation so rich and free.

2   Lord Jesus came down from His throne
on high;
ready to live and willing to die.
For all of the pain and the suffering He
bore,
I'll love Him and thank Him for
evermore.

3   To You I surrender my all today,
    the debt I owe I ne'er could repay,
    I'll serve You with joy wherever You
        lead,
    with this great assurance, You'll meet
        my need.

402 John W Peterson ©1961 John W Peterson
         Company/Admin. by Copycare

1   There will never be a sweeter story,
    story of the Saviour's love divine;
    love that brought Him from the realms
        of glory,
    just to save a sinful soul like mine.

    *Isn't the love of Jesus something
        wonderful,
    wonderful, wonderful?
    oh, isn't the love of Jesus something
        wonderful?
    Wonderful it is to me.*

2   Boundless as the universe around me,
    reaching to the farthest soul away;
    saving, keeping love it was that found
        me,
    that is why my heart can truly say:

3   Love beyond our human comprehending,
    love of God in Christ how can it be!
    This will be my theme and never
        ending,
    great redeeming love of Calvary.

403 Francis Jane van Alstyne (1820-1915)
         (Fanny J Crosby)

1   We are never, never weary of the
        grand old song;
    glory to God, hallelujah!
    We can sing it loud as ever, with our
        faith more strong:
    glory to God, hallelujah!

    *Oh, the children of the Lord have a
        right to shout and sing,
    for the way is growing bright and
        our souls are on the wing;
    we are going by and by to the
        palace of a King!
    glory to God, hallelujah!*

2   We are going to a palace that is built
        of gold;
    where the King in all His splendour
    we shall soon behold.

3   There we'll shout redeeming mercy in
        a glad new song;
    there we'll sing the praise of Jesus
    with the blood-washed throng.

404 Graham Kendrick
         © 1988 Make Way Music

    *We shall stand with our feet on the
        Rock;
    whatever men may say,
    we'll lift Your name up high,
    and we shall walk through the darkest
        night;
    setting our faces like flint, we'll walk
        into the light!*

1 Lord, You have chosen me for
    fruitfulness
  to be transformed into Your likeness:
  I'm going to fight on through till I see
    You face to face.
  We shall stand ...

2 Lord, as Your witnesses You've
    appointed us,
  and with Your Holy Spirit anointed us:
  and so I'll fight on through till I see
    You face to face.
  We shall stand ...

4 There's a light in the valley of death
    now for me,
  since Jesus came into my heart!
  And the gates of the city beyond I can
    see,
  since Jesus came into my heart!

5 I shall go there to dwell in that city,
    I know,
  since Jesus came into my heart!
  and I'm happy, so happy, as onward
    I go,
  since Jesus came into my heart!

405 Rufus H McDaniel (1850-1940)
©Word Music (UK)/The Rodeheaver Co./
Admin. by Copycare

1 What a wonderful change in my life
    has been wrought,
  since Jesus came into my heart!
  I have light in my soul for which long I
    had sought,
  since Jesus came into my heart!

  Since Jesus came into my heart,
  since Jesus came into my heart,
  floods of joy o'er my soul
  like the sea billows roll,
  since Jesus came into my heart!

2 I have ceased from my wand'ring
    and going astray,
  since Jesus came into my heart!
  And my sins which were many are all
    washed away,
  since Jesus came into my heart!

3 I'm possessed of a hope that is
    steadfast and sure,
  since Jesus came into my heart!
  And no dark clouds of doubt now my
    pathway obscure,
  since Jesus came into my heart!

406 Bryn and Sally Haworth © 1983 Signalgrade/
Admin. by Kingsway's Thankyou Music

1 What kind of love is this,
    that gave itself for me?
  I am the guilty one,
    yet I go free.
  What kind of love is this?
  A love I've never known.
  I didn't even know His name,
  what kind of love is this?

2 What kind of man is this,
    that died in agony?
  He who had done no wrong
    was crucified for me.
  What kind of man is this,
    who laid aside His throne
  that I may know the love of God?
  What kind of man is this?

3 By grace I have been saved,
    it is the gift of God.
  He destined me to be His son,
    such is His love.
  No eye has ever seen,
  no ear has ever heard,
  nor has the heart of man conceived,
  what kind of love is this?

407 Mrs M J Harris © Unidentified

1 When I saw the cleansing fountain
 open wide for all my sin,
 I obeyed the Spirit's wooing
 when He said "Wilt thou be clean?"

  I will praise Him, I will praise Him,
  praise Him, praise the Lamb for
    sinners slain!
  Give Him glory all ye people,
  for His blood has washed away my
    stain.

2 Though the way seemed straight and
   narrow,
 all I claimed was swept away;
 my ambition, plans and wishes,
 at my feet in ashes lay.

3 Then God's fire upon the altar
 of my heart was set aflame;
 I shall never cease to praise Him:
 glory! glory! to His name.

4 Blessed be the name of Jesus,
 I'm so glad He took me in;
 He has pardoned my transgressions,
 He has cleansed my heart from sin.

408 Thoro Harris
  © Nazarene Publishing/Admin. by Copycare

1 Who can cheer the heart like Jesus,
 by His presence all divine?
 True and tender, pure and precious,
 O how blessed to call Him mine!

  All that thrills my soul is Jesus;
  He is more than life to me;
  and the fairest of ten thousand,
  in my blessed Lord I see.

2 Love of Christ so freely given,
 grace of God beyond degree,
 mercy higher than the heaven,
 deeper than the deepest sea.

3 What a wonderful redemption!
 Never can a mortal know
 how my sin, though red like crimson,
 can be whiter than the snow.

4 Every need His hand supplying,
 every good in Him I see;
 on His strength divine relying,
 He is all in all to me.

5 By the crystal flowing river,
 with the ransomed I will sing,
 and for ever and for ever,
 praise and glorify the King.

409 Constance B Ried © 1949 Singspiration Music/
  Brentwood Benson Music Publishing Inc./
  Admin. by Copycare

1 Wonderful love that rescued me,
 sunk deep in sin,
 guilty and vile as I could be,
 no hope within;
 when every ray of light had fled,
 O glorious day,
 raising my soul from out the dead,
 love found a way.

  Love found a way to redeem my soul,
  love found a way that could make
    me whole;
  love sent my Lord to the cross of
    shame,
  love found a way, O praise His holy
    name!

2 Love brought my Saviour here to die
on Calvary,
for such a sinful wretch as I,
how can it be?
Love bridged the gulf 'twixt me and
heaven,
taught me to pray;
I am redeemed, set free, forgiven,
love found a way.

3 Love opened wide the gates of light
to heaven's domain,
where in eternal power and might
Jesus shall reign;
love lifted me from depths of woe
to endless day,
there was no help in earth below,
love found a way.

410 William R Newell (1868-1956)
© Unidentified

1 Years I spent in vanity and pride,
caring not my Lord was crucified,
knowing not it was for me He died
on Calvary.

*Mercy there was great and grace
was free,
pardon there was multiplied to me,
there my burdened soul found liberty,
at Calvary.*

2 By God's Word at last my sin I learned,
then I trembled at the law I'd spurned,
till my guilty soul, imploring turned,
to Calvary.

3 Now I've given to Jesus everything,
now I gladly own Him as my King,
now my raptured soul can only sing
of Calvary.

4 Oh! the love that drew salvation's plan,
oh! the grace that brought it down to
man,
oh! the mighty gulf that God did span
at Calvary.

8.3   THE CHRISTIAN LIFE
Growth

411 Johann C Lavater (1741-1801)
tr. Elizabeth L Smith (1817-98)

1 O Jesus Christ, grow Thou in me
and all things else recede!
My heart be daily nearer Thee,
from sin be daily freed.

2 Each day let Thy supporting might
my weakness still embrace;
my darkness vanish in Thy light,
Thy life my death efface.

3 In Thy bright beams which on me fall
fade every evil thought;
that I am nothing, Thou art all,
I would be daily taught.

4 More of Thy glory let me see,
Thou Holy, Wise, and True!
I would Thy living image be,
in joy and sorrow too.

5 Fill me with gladness from above,
hold me by strength Divine;
Lord, let the glow of Thy great love
through my whole being shine.

6 Make this poor self grow less and less,
be Thou my life and aim;
oh, make me daily through Thy grace
more meet to bear Thy name!

412 Charles Price Jones (b. 20th c)
© Unidentified

1 Deeper, deeper in the love of Jesus
daily let me go;
higher, higher in the school of wisdom,
more of grace to know.

O deeper yet I pray,
and higher every day,
and wiser, blessed Lord,
in Thy precious, holy word.

2 Deeper, deeper! blessed Holy Spirit,
take me deeper still,
till my life is wholly lost in Jesus
and His perfect will.

3 Deeper, deeper! though it cost hard
trials,
deeper let me go!
Rooted in the holy love of Jesus,
let me fruitful grow.

4 Deeper, higher every day in Jesus,
till all conflict past,
finds me conqueror, and in His own
image
perfected at last.

413 Johnson Oatman Jnr & Ada R Habershon
©Maranatha! Music/Admin. by Copycare

1 I'm pressing on the upward way,
new heights I'm gaining every day;
still praying as I onward bound,
"Lord, plant my feet on higher
ground."

Lord, lift me up and let me stand,
by faith, on heaven's table-land;
where love, and joy, and light
abound,
Lord, plant my feet on higher
ground.

2 My heart has no desire to stay
where doubts arise, and fears dismay;
though some may dwell where these
abound,
my constant aim is higher ground.

3 Beyond the mist I fain would rise,
to rest beneath unclouded skies,
above earth's turmoil peace is found
by those who dwell on higher ground.

4 I long to scale the utmost height,
though rough the way and hard the
fight,
my song, while climbing, shall resound,
Lord, lead me on to higher ground.

5 Lord, lead me up the mountain side,
I dare not climb without my Guide;
And, heaven gained, I'll gaze around,
with grateful heart from higher
ground.

414 Eliza Edmunds Hewitt (1851-1920)

1 More about Jesus would I know,
more of His grace to others show;
more of His saving fullness see,
more of His love Who died for me.

More, more about Jesus!
More, more about Jesus!
More of His saving fullness see,
more of His love Who died for me.

2 More about Jesus let me learn,
   more of His holy will discern;
   Spirit of God, my teacher be,
   showing the things of Christ to me.

3 More about Jesus in His word,
   holding communion with my Lord;
   hearing His voice in every line,
   making each faithful saying mine.

4 More about Jesus on His throne,
   riches in glory all His own,
   more of His kingdom's sure increase;
   more of His coming, Prince of Peace.

415 Theodore Monod (1836-1921)

1 Oh! the bitter shame and sorrow,
   that a time could ever be,
   when I let the Saviour's pity
   plead in vain, and proudly answered,
   "All of self, and none of Thee."

2 Yet He found me: I beheld Him
   bleeding on the cursed tree,
   heard Him pray, "Forgive them, Father!"
   And my wistful heart said faintly:
   "Some of self, and some of Thee."

3 Day by day His tender mercy,
   healing, helping, full and free,
   sweet and strong, and ah! so patient,
   brought me lower, while I whispered,
   "Less of self, and more of Thee."

4 Higher than the highest heavens,
   deeper than the deepest sea,
   Lord, Thy love at last hath conquered!
   Grant me now my soul's petition:
   "None of self, and all of Thee."

(Tune 2 repeat last line of each verse.)

416 V1 © Wild Goose Resource Group. Reproduced
by Permission. V2 © Sovereign Music UK
V3 © Colin M Peckham

1 We are marching in the light of God,
   we are marching in the light of God,
   we are marching in the light of God,
   we are marching in the light of God.
     We are marching (marching;
         we are marching) - Oh,
     we are marching (marching;
     we are marching) - Oh,
     we are marching in the light of God!

2 We are living in the love of God,
   we are living in the love of God,
   we are living in the love of God,
   we are living in the love of God,
     We are living (living;
         we are living) - Oh,
     we are living in the love of God
     we are living (living;
     we are living) - Oh,
     we are living in the love of God!

3 We will follow in the will of God,
   we will follow in the will of God,
   we will follow in the will of God,
   we will follow in the will of God
     We will follow (follow;
         we will follow) - Oh,
     we will follow in the will of God
     we will follow (follow;
     we will follow) - Oh,
     we will follow in the will of God!

8.4 THE CHRISTIAN LIFE
Guidance and Security

417 Henry Francis Lyte (1793-1847)

1 Abide with me! fast falls the eventide;
   the darkness deepens; Lord with me
   abide!

When other helpers fail and comforts
  flee,
help of the helpless, oh, abide with me!

2 Swift to its close ebbs out life's little day,
earth's joys grow dim, its glories pass
   away:
change and decay in all around I see;
O Thou who changest not, abide with
  me.

3 I need Thy presence every passing hour,
what but Thy grace can foil the
   tempter's power?
Who like Thyself my guide and stay can
  be?
Through cloud and sunshine, oh, abide
  with me!

4 I fear no foe, with Thee at hand to bless,
ills have no weight and tears no
   bitterness:
where is death's sting? where, grave,
  thy victory?
I triumph still, if Thou abide with me.

5 Keep Thou Thy cross before my
   closing eyes,
shine through the gloom and point me
  to the skies:
Heaven's morning breaks and earth's
  vain shadows flee;
in life, in death, O Lord, abide with me.

418   Francis Jane van Alstyne (1820-1915)
       (Fanny J Crosby)

1 All the way my Saviour leads me:
what have I to ask beside?
Can I doubt His tender mercy,
who through life has been my Guide?
Heavenly peace, divinest comfort,
here, by faith, in Him to dwell!
For I know whate'er befall me,
Jesus doeth all things well.

2 All the way my Saviour leads me;
cheers each winding path I tread;
gives me grace for every trial,
feeds me with the living bread.
Though my weary steps may falter,
and my soul athirst may be,
gushing from the rock before me,
lo! a spring of joy I see.

3 All the way my Saviour leads me:
oh, the fullness of His love!
Perfect rest to me is promised
in my Father's house above.
When my spirit, clothed immortal,
wings its flight to realms of day,
this, my song through endless ages:
Jesus led me all the way.

419   A B Simpson (1834-1919)

1 Are you now in depths of sorrow,
where no arm can reach so low?
There is One whose arms almighty
reach beyond your deepest woe.
God Eternal is your refuge.
Let it still your wild alarms;
underneath your deepest sorrow
are the everlasting arms.

2 Other arms grow faint and weary,
these can never faint nor fail:
others reach our mounts of blessing,
these our lowest, loneliest vale.
Oh, that all might know His friendship!
Oh, that all might see His charms!
Oh, that all might have beneath them
Jesus' everlasting arms!

3   Underneath us, oh, how easy!
    We have not to mount on high,
    but to sink into His fullness,
    and in trustful weakness lie.
    And we find our humbling failures
    save us from the strength that harms,
    we may fail, but underneath us
    are the everlasting arms.

4   Arms of Jesus! fold me closer
    to Thy strong and loving breast,
    till my spirit on Thy bosom
    finds its everlasting rest;
    and when time's last sands are sinking,
    shield my heart from all alarms,
    softly whispering, "Underneath you
    are the everlasting arms."

420 William Williams (1717-91) altd.

1   Guide me, O Thou great Jehovah,
    pilgrim through this barren land;
    I am weak, but Thou art mighty;
    hold me with Thy powerful hand:
    Bread of heaven, Bread of heaven
    feed me till I want no more;
    feed me till I want no more.

2   Open now the crystal fountain,
    whence the healing stream shall flow:
    let the fire and cloudy pillar
    lead me all my journey through:
    strong Deliverer, strong Deliverer
    be Thou still my strength and shield;
    be Thou still my strength and shield.

3   When I tread the verge of Jordan,
    bid my anxious fears subside;
    death of death, and hell's destruction,
    land me safe on Canaan's side:
    songs of praises, songs of praises
    I will ever give to Thee;
    I will ever give to Thee!

421 Gloria and William Gaither
© Gaither Music Company/WJG Inc./Admin.
by Kingsway's Thankyou Music

Gentle Shepherd, come and lead us,
for we need You to help us find our way.
Gentle Shepherd, come and feed us,
for we need Your strength from day to
    day.
There's no other we can turn to
who can help us face another day.
Gentle Shepherd, come and lead us,
for we need You to help us find our way.

422 Jeremiah E Rankin (1828-1904)

1   God be with you till we meet again;
    by His counsels guide, uphold you;
    with His sheep securely fold you;
    God be with you till we meet again.

    *Till we meet, till we meet, till we meet
    at Jesus' feet,
    till we meet, till we meet, God be with
    you till we meet again!*

2   God be with you till we meet again;
    'neath His wings securely hide you;
    daily manna still provide you;
    God be with you till we meet again.

3   God be with you till we meet again;
    when life's perils thick confound you;
    put His loving arms around you;
    God be with you till we meet again.

4   God be with you till we meet again;
    keep love's banner floating o'er you;
    smite death's threatening wave before
    you;
    God be with you till we meet again.

423 J H Gilmore (1834-1918)

1 He leadeth me! O blessed thought,
   O words with heavenly comfort fraught;
   whate'er I do, where'er I be,
   still 'tis God's hand that leadeth me.

   He leadeth me! He leadeth me!
   By His own hand He leadeth me;
   His faithful follower I would be,
   for by His hand He leadeth me.

2 Sometimes 'mid scenes of deepest
      gloom,
   sometimes where Eden's bowers bloom,
   by waters still, o'er troubled sea,
   still 'tis His hand that leadeth me.

3 Lord, I would clasp Thy hand in mine,
   nor ever murmur or repine;
   content, whatever lot I see,
   since 'tis my God that leadeth me.

4 And when my task on earth is done,
   when, by Thy grace, the victory's won,
   e'en death's cold wave I will not flee,
   since Thou through Jordan leadest me.

3 Assuredly He shall thee save,
   and give deliverance
   both from the fowler's snare, and from
   the noisome pestilence.

4 His feathers shall thee hide; thy trust
   under His wings shall be:
   His faithfulness shall be a shield
   and buckler unto thee.

5 Thou shalt not need to be afraid
   for terrors of the night;
   nor for the arrow that doth fly
   by day, while it is light;

6 Nor for the pestilence, that walks
   in darkness secretly;
   nor for destruction that doth waste
   at noon-day openly.

7 Because on me He set His love,
   deliver him will I;
   because my great name he hath known,
   I will him set on high.

8 He'll call on me, I'll answer him;
   I will be with him still
   in trouble, to deliver him,
   and honour him I will.

424 Psalm 91 v 1-6; 14, 15 (Scottish Psalter)

1 He that doth in the secret place
   of the Most High reside,
   under the shade of Him that is
   the Almighty shall abide.

2 I of the Lord my God will say,
   He is my refuge still,
   He is my fortress and my God,
   and in Him trust I will.

425 Alfred B Smith & Eugene Clarke
© Singspiration Music/Brentwood Benson
Music Publishing Inc./Admin. by Copycare

1 I do not know what lies ahead,
   the way I cannot see;
   yet One stands near to be my guide,
   He'll show the way to me:

   I know who holds the future,
   and He'll guide me with His hand;
   with God things don't just happen,
   everything by Him is planned.

So as I face tomorrow,
with its problems large and small,
I'll trust the God of miracles,
give to Him my all.

2 I do not know how many days
of life are mine to spend;
but One who knows and cares for me
will keep me to the end:

3 I do not know the course ahead,
what joys and griefs are there;
but One is near who fully knows,
I'll trust His loving care:

426 Leonard Weaver © Unidentified

1 I have a Shepherd, One I love so well;
how He has blessed me tongue can never
tell;
on the Cross He suffered, shed His blood
and died,
that I might ever in His love confide.

Following Jesus, ever day by day,
nothing can harm me when He
leads the way;
darkness or sunshine, whate'er befall,
Jesus, the Shepherd, is my all in all.

2 Pastures abundant doth His hand
provide,
still waters flowing ever at my side,
goodness and mercy follow on my track,
with such a Shepherd nothing can I lack.

3 When I would wander from the path
astray,
then He will draw me back into the way;
in the darkest valley I need fear no ill,
for He, my Shepherd, will be with me
still.

4 When labour's ended and the journey
done,
then He will lead me safely to my home;
there I shall dwell in rapture sure and
sweet,
with all the loved ones gathered round
His feet.

427 © Christopher Idle/Jubilate Hymns

1 I love You, O Lord, You alone,
my refuge on whom I depend;
my Maker, my Saviour, my own,
my hope and my trust without end.
The Lord is my strength and my song,
defender and guide of my ways;
my Master to whom I belong,
my God who shall have all my praise.

2 The dangers of death gathered round,
the waves of destruction came near;
but in my despairing I found
the Lord who released me from fear.
I called for His help in my pain,
to God my salvation I cried;
He brought me His comfort again,
I live by the strength He supplied.

3 The earth and the elements shake
with thunder and lightning and hail;
the cliffs and the mountain-tops break
and mortals are feeble and pale.
His justice is full and complete,
His mercy to us has no end;
the clouds are a path for His feet,
He comes on the wings of the wind.

4 My hope is the promise He gives,
   my life is secure in His hand;
   I shall not be lost, for He lives!
   He comes to my side - I shall stand!
   Lord God, You are powerful to save,
   Your Spirit will spur me to pray;
   Your Son has defeated the grave:
   I trust and I praise You today!

428 Psalm 121 (Scottish Psalter)

1 I to the hills will lift mine eyes,
   from whence doth come mine aid?
   My safety cometh from the Lord,
   who heaven and earth hath made.

2 Thy foot He'll not let slide, nor will
   He slumber that thee keeps.
   Behold, He that keeps Israel,
   He slumbers not, nor sleeps.

3 The Lord thee keeps, the Lord thy shade
   on thy right hand doth stay:
   the moon by night thee shall not smite,
   nor yet the sun by day.

4 The Lord shall keep thy soul; He shall
   preserve thee from all ill.
   Henceforth thy going out and in
   God keep for ever will.

5 *To Father, Son, and Holy Ghost,*
   the God whom we adore,
   be glory, as it was, and is,
   and shall be evermore.

429 G A Young (19th c)

1 In shady, green pastures, so rich and so
      sweet,
   God leads His dear children along;
   where the water's cool flow bathes the
      weary one's feet,
   God leads His dear children along.

   Some through the waters,
   *   some through the flood,*
   some through the fire,
   *   but all through the blood;*
   some through great sorrow,
   *   but God gives a song,*
   in the night season and all the day
   *   long.*

2 Sometimes on the mount where the sun
      shines so bright,
   God leads His dear children along;
   sometimes in the valley, in darkest of
      night,
   God leads His dear children along.

3 Though sorrows befall us and evils
      oppose,
   God leads His dear children along;
   through grace we can conquer,
      defeat all our foes,
   God leads His dear children along.

430 David J Hadden & Bob Silvester
© 1983 Restoration Music Ltd., admin. by
Sovereign Music UK

1 Living under the shadow of His wing,
   we find security.
   Standing in His presence, we will bring
   our worship, worship, worship to the
      King.

2 Bowed in adoration at His feet,
  we dwell in harmony.
  Voices joined together that repeat,
  "worthy, worthy, worthy is the Lamb."

3 Heart to heart embracing in His love
  reveals His purity.
  Soaring in my spirit like a dove;
  holy, holy, holy is the Lord.

431   E Hopper (1818-88)

1 Jesus, Saviour, pilot me
  over life's tempestuous sea!
  Unknown waves before me roll,
  hiding rocks and treacherous shoal;
  chart and compass come from Thee;
  Jesus, Saviour, pilot me!

2 As a mother stills her child,
  Thou canst hush the ocean wild;
  boisterous waves obey Thy will
  when Thou say'st to them, "Be still!"
  Wondrous Sovereign of the sea,
  Jesus, Saviour, pilot me!

3 When at last I near the shore,
  and the fearful breakers roar
  'twixt me and the peaceful rest,
  then, while leaning on Thy breast,
  may I hear Thee say to me,
  "Fear not, I will pilot thee!"

432   W F Lloyd (1791-1853)

1 My times are in Thy hand;
  my God, I wish them there;
  my life, my friends, my soul I leave
  entirely to Thy care.

2 My times are in Thy hand,
  whatever they may be,
  pleasing or painful, dark or bright,
  as best may seem to Thee.

3 My times are in Thy hand;
  why should I doubt or fear?
  My Father's hand will never cause
  His child a needless tear.

4 My times are in Thy hand,
  Jesus, the crucified!
  Those hands my cruel sins had pierced
  are now my guard and guide.

5 My times are in Thy hand;
  I'll always trust in Thee;
  and, after death, at Thy right hand
  I shall for ever be.

433   William Orcutt Cushing (1823-1903)

1 Oh, safe to the Rock that is higher
  than I,
  my soul in its conflicts and sorrows
  would fly;
  so sinful, so weary, Thine, Thine would
  I be;
  Thou blessed Rock of Ages, I'm hiding
  in Thee.

  Hiding in Thee,
  hiding in Thee,
  Thou blest Rock of Ages,
  I'm hiding in Thee.

2 In the calm of the noontide, in sorrow's
  lone hour,
  in times when temptation casts o'er me
  its power;

in the tempests of life, on its wide
  heaving sea,
Thou blesst Rock of Ages, I'm hiding
  in Thee.

3 How oft in the conflict, when pressed
    by the foe,
  I have fled to my Refuge and breathed
    out my woe;
  how often when trials like sea billows
    roll,
  have I hidden in Thee, O Thou Rock
    of my soul.

434 Charles H Gabriel (1856-1932)
      © Unidentified

1 Sweet is the promise, "I will not forget
    thee,"
  nothing can molest or turn my soul
    away;
  e'en though the night be dark within the
    valley,
  just beyond is shining an eternal day.

    I will not forget thee or leave thee,
    in My hands I'll hold thee, in My
      arms I'll fold thee;
    I will not forget thee or leave thee
    I am thy Redeemer, I will care for thee.

2 How can I show my gratitude to Jesus,
  for His love unfailing and His tender
    care?
  I will proclaim to others His salvation,
  that they may accept Him and His
    promise share.

3 Trusting the promise, "I will not forget
    thee,"
  onward will I go with songs of joy and
    praise;
  though earth despise me, though my
    friends forsake me,
  Jesus will be near me, gladdening my
    days.

4 When at the golden portals I am
    standing,
  all my tribulations, all my sorrows past,
  how sweet to hear the blessed
    proclamation:
  "Enter faithful servant, welcome
    home at last."

435 Philip Doddridge (1702-51) alt.

1 O God of Bethel! by whose hand
  Thy people still are fed;
  who through this weary pilgrimage
  hast all our fathers led:

2 Our vows, our prayers, we now present
  before Thy throne of grace:
  God of our fathers! be the God
  of their succeeding race.

3 Through each perplexing path of life
  our wandering footsteps guide;
  give us each day our daily bread,
  and raiment fit provide.

4 O spread Thy covering wings around,
  till all our wanderings cease,
  and at our Father's loved abode
  our souls arrive in peace.

5 Such blessings from Thy gracious hand
  our humble prayers implore;
  and Thou shalt be our chosen God
  and portion evermore.

436
B Mansell Ramsey (1849-1923)

1 Teach me Thy way, O Lord,
   teach me Thy way!
   Thy gracious aid afford,
   teach me Thy way!
   Help me to walk aright,
   more by faith, less by sight;
   lead me with heavenly light:
   teach me Thy way!

2 When doubts and fears arise,
   teach me Thy way!
   When storms o'erspread the skies,
   teach me Thy way!
   Shine through the cloud and rain,
   through sorrow, toil, and pain;
   make Thou my pathway plain:
   teach me Thy way!

3 Long as my life shall last,
   teach me Thy way!
   Where'er my lot be cast,
   teach me Thy way!
   Until the race is run,
   until the journey's done,
   until the crown is won,
   teach me Thy way!

437
Henry Williams Baker (1821-77)

1 The King of love my Shepherd is,
   whose goodness faileth never!
   I nothing lack if I am His,
   and He is mine for ever.

2 Where streams of living water flow
   my ransomed soul He leadeth,
   and where the verdant pastures grow
   with food celestial feedeth.

3 Perverse and foolish oft I strayed,
   but yet in love He sought me,
   and on His shoulder gently laid,
   and home rejoicing brought me.

4 In death's dark vale I fear no ill
   with Thee, dear Lord, beside me,
   Thy rod and staff my comfort still,
   Thy Cross before to guide me.

5 And so, through all the length of days,
   Thy goodness faileth never.
   Good Shepherd, may I sing Thy praise
   within Thy house for ever!

438
Francis Rous (1579-1659) revised for
Scottish Psalter, 1650, from Psalm 23

1 The Lord's my Shepherd, I'll not want:
   He makes me down to lie
   in pastures green: He leadeth me
   the quiet waters by.

2 My soul He doth restore again;
   and me to walk doth make
   within the paths of righteousness,
   e'en for His own name's sake.

3 Yea, though I walk in death's dark vale,
   yet will I fear none ill;
   for Thou art with me; and Thy rod
   and staff me comfort still.

4 My table Thou hast furnished
   in presence of my foes;
   my head Thou dost with oil anoint,
   and my cup overflows.

5 Goodness and mercy all my life
   shall surely follow me;
   and in God's house for evermore
   my dwelling-place shall be.

*(When using the tune "Orlington"
repeat third line of each verse)*

439 Ann S Murphy (d.1942)
© Unidentified

1 There's a peace in my heart that the
     world never gave,
   a peace it can not take away;
   though the trials of life may surround
     like a cloud,
   I've a peace that has come there to stay.

   Constantly abiding, Jesus is
     mine;
   constantly abiding, rapture
     divine;
   He never leaves me lonely,
     whispers, O so kind:
   "I will never leave thee," Jesus is
     mine.

2 All the world seemed to sing of a
     Saviour and King,
   when peace sweetly came to my heart;
   troubles all fled away and my night
     turned to day,
   blessed Jesus, how glorious Thou art!

3 This treasure I have in a temple of clay,
   while here on His footstool I roam;
   but He's coming to take me some
     glorious day,
   over there to my heavenly home!

440 Johnson Oatman (1856-1922)

1 There's not a friend like the lowly
     Jesus,
   no, not one! no, not one!
   none else could heal all our soul's
     diseases,
   no, not one! no, not one!

   Jesus knows all about our struggles,
   He will guide till the day is done,
   there's not a friend like the lowly
     Jesus,
   no, not one! no, not one!

2 No friend like Him is so high and holy,
   and yet no friend is so meek and
   lowly.

3 There's not an hour that He is not near
     us,
   no night so dark but His love can cheer
   us.

4 Did ever saint find this friend forsake
     him?
   Or sinner find that He would not take
   him?

5 Was e'er a gift like the Saviour given?
   Will He refuse us a home in heaven?

441 Francis Jane van Alstyne (1820-1915)
(Fanny J Crosby)

1 Thou my everlasting portion,
   more than friend or life to me,
   all along my pilgrim journey,
   Saviour, let me walk with Thee.

Close to Thee, close to Thee,
close to Thee, close to Thee,
all along my pilgrim journey,
Saviour, let me walk with Thee.

2 Not for ease or worldly pleasure,
not for fame my prayer shall be;
gladly will I toil and suffer,
only let me walk with Thee.

3 Lead me through this vale of shadows,
bear me o'er life's fitful sea;
then the gate of life eternal
may I enter, Lord, with Thee.

442 Nahum Tate (1652-1715) &
Nicholas Brady (1659-1726)

1 Through all the changing scenes of life,
in trouble and in joy,
the praises of my God shall still
my heart and tongue employ.

2 Of His deliverance I will boast,
till all that are distressed
from my example comfort take,
and charm their griefs to rest.

3 O magnify the Lord with me,
with me exalt His Name;
when in distress to Him I called,
He to my rescue came.

4 The hosts of God encamp around
The dwellings of the just;
Deliverance He affords to all
Who on His succour trust.

5 O make but trial of His love,
experience will decide
how blessed are they, and only they,
who in His truth confide.

6 Fear Him, ye saints, and you will then
have nothing else to fear;
make you His service your delight,
your wants shall be His care.

443 Mary Peters (1813-56)

1 Through the love of God our Saviour,
all will be well.
Free and changeless is His favour;
all, all is well.
Precious is the blood that healed us,
perfect is the grace that sealed us,
strong the hand stretched forth to
   shield us;
all must be well.

2 Though we pass through tribulation,
all will be well.
Ours is such a full salvation,
all, all is well.
Happy, still in God confiding,
fruitful, if in Christ abiding,
holy, through the Spirit's guiding;
all must be well.

3 We expect a bright tomorrow,
all will be well.
Faith can sing through days of sorrow,
all, all is well.
On our Father's love relying,
Jesus every need supplying,
or in living or in dying,
all must be well.

444 W C Martin (d. 1935)
© Hope Publishing/Admin. by Copycare

1 Where He may lead me I will go,
for I have learned to trust Him so,
and I remember 'twas for me,
that He was slain on Calvary.

Jesus shall lead me night and day,
Jesus shall lead me all the way;
He is the truest Friend to me,
for I remember Calvary.

2 O I delight in His command,
love to be led by His dear hand,
His divine will is sweet to me,
hallowed by blood-stained Calvary.

3 Onward I go, nor doubt nor fear,
happy with Christ, my Saviour near,
trusting some day that I shall see,
Jesus, my Friend of Calvary.

445 Priscilla Jane Owens (1829-99)

1 Will your anchor hold in the storms of
life,
when the clouds unfold their wings of
strife?
When the strong tides lift, and the
cables strain,
will your anchor shift, or firm remain?

We have an anchor that keeps the soul
steadfast and sure while the billows
roll,
fastened to the Rock which cannot
move,
grounded firm and deep in the
Saviour's love.

2 It is safely moored, 'twill the storm
withstand,
for 'tis well secured by the Saviour's
hand;
and the cables passed from His heart
to mine
can defy the blast, through strength
divine.

3 It will firmly hold in the straits of fear,
when the breakers have told that the
reef is near;
though the tempest rave and the wild
winds blow,
not an angry wave shall our bark
o'erflow.

4 It will surely hold in the floods of death,
when the waters cold chill our latest
breath;
on the rising tide it can never fail,
while our hopes abide within the veil.

5 When our eyes behold through the
gathering night
the city of gold, our harbour bright,
we shall anchor fast by the heavenly
shore,
with the storms all past for evermore.

446 Joseph Addison (1672-1719)

1 When all Your mercies, Ө my God,
my rising soul surveys,
transported with the view, I'm lost
in wonder, love, and praise.

2 Unnumbered comforts on my soul
Your tender care bestowed,
before my infant heart conceived
from whom those comforts flowed.

3 Ten thousand thousand precious gifts
   my daily thanks employ,
   nor is the least a cheerful heart
   that tastes those gifts with joy.

4 Through every period of my life
   Your goodness I'll pursue
   and, after death, in distant worlds,
   the glorious theme renew.

5 Through all eternity to You
   a joyful song I'll raise;
   for, oh, eternity's too short
   to utter all Your praise!

2 He speaks, and by His word is given
   His peace, a rich foretaste of heaven!
   Not as the world He peace doth give;
   'tis through this hope my soul shall live.

3 I live; not I; 'tis He alone
   by whom the mighty work is done;
   dead to myself, alive to Him,
   I count all loss His rest to gain.

4 Now rest, my heart, the work is done,
   I'm saved through the Eternal Son!
   Let all my powers my soul employ,
   to tell the world my peace and joy.

8.5   THE CHRISTIAN LIFE:
Obedience and Trust

447   W O Cushing (1823-1902)

Follow, follow, I will follow Jesus,
anywhere, everywhere I will follow on;
follow, follow, I will follow Jesus,
everywhere He leads me I will follow on.

448   Charles B J Root
       © Unidentified

1 Abiding, oh, so wondrous sweet;
   I'm resting at the Saviour's feet!
   I trust in Him, I'm satisfied,
   I'm resting in the Crucified!

   Abiding, abiding, oh so
     wondrous sweet!
   I'm resting, resting at the
     Saviour's feet.

449   Katharina von Schlegel (b 1697)
       tr. Jane Laurie Borthwick (1813-97)

1 Be still, my soul: the Lord is on thy side;
   bear patiently the cross of grief or pain;
   leave to thy God to order and provide;
   in every change He faithful will remain.
   Be still, my soul: thy best, thy heavenly
     Friend
   through thorny ways leads to a joyful
     end.

2 Be still, my soul: thy God doth
     undertake
   to guide the future as He has the past.
   Thy hope, thy confidence, let nothing
     shake;
   all now mysterious shall be bright at last.
   Be still, my soul: the waves and winds
     still know
   His voice who ruled them while He
     dwelt below.

3 Be still, my soul: the hour is hastening
   on
  when we shall be for ever with the Lord,
  when disappointment, grief and fear are
   gone,
  sorrow forgot, love's purest joys restored.
  Be still, my soul: when change and tears
   are past,
  all safe and blessed we shall meet at last.

450 H E Govan (1866-1932)
       © The Faith Mission

1 Doubt Him not, although He leadeth
  other ways than hope had said;
  all the grace thy spirit needeth
  dwells in Him. Be not afraid!

    I will trust Thee - yes, will trust Thee!
    Nought I need of other aid;
    All sufficient Thou, my Saviour!
    Never will I be afraid.

2 Fret thee not about the morrow;
  faint thou not for hope delayed;
  He will lead, through joy, through
   sorrow
  to thy Home. Be not afraid!

3 Does some fierce temptation try thee?
  Look to Him who bruised its head;
  see the Conqueror standing by thee;
  trust in Him. Be not afraid!

4 Faileth all of earth's reliance?
  Do thy "vine and fig-tree" fade?
  Thou canst bid all foes defiance
  through thy Lord. Be not afraid!

5 Does there come a time of testing,
  when thine all of strength seems fled?
  His strength then on thee is resting
  if thou trust. Be not afraid!

6 Trusting thus and trusting ever,
  on the Lord Jehovah stayed.
  Thou at last shall ford the river
  safe, through Him. Be not afraid!

451 John Eddison © Scripture Union

1 Father, although I cannot see
  the future You have planned,
  and though the path is sometimes dark
  and hard to understand:
  yet give me faith, through joy and pain,
  to trace Your loving hand.

2 When I recall that in the past
  Your promises have stood
  through each perplexing circumstance
  and every changing mood,
  I rest content that all things work
  together for my good.

3 Whatever, then, the future brings
  of good or seeming ill,
  I ask for strength to follow You
  and grace to trust You still;
  and I would look for no reward,
  except to do Your will.

452 Jenny Hewer
       © 1975 Kingsway's Thankyou Music

1 Father, I place into Your hands
  the things that I can't do.
  Father, I place into Your hands
  the times that I've been through.
  Father, I place into Your hands
  the way that I should go,
  for I know I always can trust You.

2   Father, I place into Your hands
    my friends and family.
    Father, I place into Your hands
    the things that trouble me.
    Father, I place into Your hands
    the person I would be,
    for I know I always can trust You.

3   Father, we love to seek Your face,
    we love to hear Your voice.
    Father, we love to sing Your praise,
    and in Your name rejoice.
    Father, we love to walk with You
    and in Your presence rest,
    for we know we always can trust You.

4   Father, I want to be with You
    and do the things You do.
    Father, I want to speak the words
    that You are speaking too.
    Father, I want to love the ones
    that You will draw to You,
    for I know that I am one with You.

453   Mrs F W Suffield
© Unidentified

God is still on the throne,
and He will remember His own,
though trials oppress us, and burdens
    distress us,
He never will leave us alone.
God is still on the throne,
and He will remember His own,
His promise is true,
He will not forget you,
God is still on the throne.

454   © Unidentified

1   I am weak but Thou art strong,
    Jesus keep me from all wrong;
    I'll be satisfied as long
    as I walk, let me walk, close with Thee.

    Just a closer walk with Thee,
    grant it Jesus, this my plea;
    daily walking close with Thee,
    let it be, dear Lord, let it be.

2   Through this world of toils and snares,
    if I falter, Lord, who cares?
    Who with me my burden shares?
    None but Thee, dear Lord, none but
        Thee.

3   When my feeble life is o'er,
    time for me will be no more,
    guide me gently, safely home,
    to Thy kingdom's shore, to Thy shore.

455   Mrs I. Shorey
© Unidentified

1   I have a Friend so precious,
    so very dear to me,
    He loves me with such tender love,
    He loves so faithfully;
    I could not live apart from Him,
    I love to feel Him nigh,
    and so we dwell together,
    my Lord and I.

2   He knows how much I love Him,
    He knows I love Him well;
    but with what love He loveth me
    my tongue can never tell;
    it is an everlasting love,
    in ever rich supply,
    and so we love each other,
    my Lord and I.

3 He knows how I am longing
some weary soul to win,
and so He bids me go and speak
the loving word for Him;
He bids me tell His wondrous love,
and why He came to die,
and so we work together,
my Lord and I.

4 So up into the mountains
of heaven's cloudless light,
or away into the valleys
of darkness or of night.
Though round us tempests gather
and storms are raging high,
we'll travel on together,
my Lord and I.

5 And when the journey's ended,
in rest and peace at last,
when every thought of danger
and weariness is past,
in the Kingdom of the future,
in the glory by and by,
we'll live and reign together,
my Lord and I.

2 I lay my wants on Jesus,
all fullness dwells in Him:
He heals all my diseases,
He doth my soul redeem.
I lay my griefs on Jesus,
my burdens and my cares;
He from them all releases;
He all my sorrows shares.

3 I rest my soul on Jesus,
this weary soul of mine;
His right hand me embraces,
I on His breast recline.
I love the name of Jesus,
Immanuel, Christ, the Lord:
like fragrance on the breezes,
His name abroad is poured.

4 I long to be like Jesus,
meek, loving, lowly, mild;
I long to be like Jesus,
the Father's holy child.
I long to be with Jesus
amid the heavenly throng,
to sing with saints His praises,
to learn the angels' song.

456 Horatius Bonar (1808-89)

1 I lay my sins on Jesus,
the spotless Lamb of God;
He bears them all, and frees us
from the accursed load.
I bring my guilt to Jesus,
to wash my crimson stains
white in His blood most precious,
till not a spot remains.

457 Lizzie Edwards
© Unidentified

1 I must have the Saviour with me
for I dare not walk alone,
I must feel His presence near me,
and His arm around me thrown.

*Then my soul shall fear no ill,
let Him lead me where He will,
I will go without a murmur,
and His footsteps follow still.*

2   I must have the Saviour with me
    for my faith at best is weak;
    He can whisper words of comfort,
    that no other voice can speak.

3   I must have the Saviour with me
    in the onward march of life,
    through the tempest and the sunshine,
    through the battle and the strife.

4   I must have the Saviour with me,
    and His eye the way must guide,
    till I reach the vale of Jordan,
    till I cross the rolling tide.

458   Edward Turney
          Salvationist Publishing & Supplies/Admin. by
          Copycare

1   I will go in the strength of the Lord,
    in the path He hath marked for my feet,
    I will follow the light of His word,
    nor shrink from the dangers I meet.
    His presence my steps shall attend;
    His fullness my wants shall supply;
    on Him, till my journey shall end,
    my hope shall securely rely.

2   I will go in the strength of the Lord,
    to the work He appoints me to do;
    in the joy which His smile shall afford
    my soul shall her vigour renew.
    His power will protect me from harm,
    His grace my sufficiency prove;
    I will trust His omnipotent arm,
    I will rest in His covenant love.

3   I will go in the strength of the Lord
    to each conflict which faith may require;
    His grace as my shield and reward,
    my courage and zeal shall inspire.

If He issue the word of command
to meet and encounter the foe,
though with sling and with stone in
    my hand,
in the strength of the Lord I will go.

459   Frances Ridley Havergal (1836-79)

1   Like a river, glorious,
    is God's perfect peace,
    over all victorious
    in its bright increase;
    perfect, yet it floweth
    fuller every day,
    perfect, yet it groweth
    deeper all the way.

    Stayed upon Jehovah,
    hearts are fully blest;
    finding, as He promised,
    perfect peace and rest.

2   Hidden in the hollow
    of His blessed hand,
    never foe can follow,
    never traitor stand;
    not a surge of worry,
    not a shade of care,
    not a blast of hurry
    touch the spirit there.

3   Every joy or trial
    falleth from above,
    traced upon our dial
    by the Sun of Love,
    we may trust Him fully,
    all for us to do;
    they who trust Him wholly
    find Him wholly true.

460 © Child Evangelism Fellowship, Press

Let the Lord have His way
in your life every day,
there's no rest,
there's no peace until the Lord has His way;
place your life in His hands,
rest secure in His plan,
let the Lord,
let the Lord have His way.

461 Frances Ridley Havergal (1836-79)

1 Master, speak! Thy servant heareth,
waiting for Thy gracious word,
longing for Thy voice that cheereth;
Master, let it now be heard.
I am listening, Lord, for Thee;
what hast Thou to say to me?

2 Speak to me by name, O Master!
let me know it is to me;
speak, that I may follow faster,
with a step more firm and free,
where the Shepherd leads the flock
in the shadow of the rock.

3 Master, speak! though least and lowest,
let me not unheard depart;
Master, speak! for O Thou knowest
all the yearning of my heart;
knowest all its truest need;
speak, and make me blest indeed.

4 Master, speak! and make me ready,
when Thy voice is truly heard,
with obedience glad and steady
still to follow every word.
I am listening, Lord, for Thee;
Master, speak, O speak to me!

462 Richard Dukes
© Unidentified

1 My heart is fixed, eternal God,
fixed on Thee, fixed on Thee,
and my unchanging choice is made:
Christ for me!
He is my Prophet, Priest, and King,
who did for me salvation bring;
and while I've breath I mean to sing:
"Christ for me, Christ for me."

2 Let others boast of heaps of gold,
Christ for me, Christ for me.
His riches never can be told,
Christ for me.
Their gold will waste and wear away,
their honours perish in a day,
my portion never can decay;
Christ for me, Christ for me.

3 At home, abroad, by night, by day,
Christ for me, Christ for me,
Where'er may lead my pilgrim way,
Christ for me.
Him first and last, Him all day long,
my strength and shield, my fortress
    strong,
this evermore my hope and song,
Christ for me, Christ for me.

4 Now who can sing my song and say:
"Christ for me, Christ for me,
my life and truth, my light and way
Christ for me?"
Then here's my heart and here's my
    hand,
we'll form a daring, happy band,
and shout aloud throughout the land:
"Christ for me, Christ for me!"

463 George Matheson (1842-1906)

1 O Love that wilt not let me go,
I rest my weary soul in Thee;
I give Thee back the life I owe,
that in Thine ocean depths its flow
may richer, fuller be.

2 O Light, that followest all my way,
I yield my flickering torch to Thee;
my heart restores its borrowed ray,
that in Thy sunshine's blaze its day
may brighter, fairer be.

3 O Joy, that seekest me through pain,
I cannot close my heart to Thee;
I trace the rainbow through the rain,
and feel the promise is not vain
that morn shall tearless be.

4 O Cross, that liftest up my head,
I dare not ask to fly from Thee;
I lay in dust, life's glory dead,
and from the ground there blossoms red
life that shall endless be.

3 From fears and phantoms of the night,
from foes about my way,
    I trust in Him,
    I trust in Him,
by darkness as by day.

4 His holy angels keep my feet
secure from every stone;
    I trust in Him,
    I trust in Him,
and unafraid go on.

5 Strong in the everlasting name,
and in my Father's care,
    I trust in Him,
    I trust in Him,
who hears and answers prayer.

6 Safe in the shadow of the Lord,
possessed by love divine,
    I trust in Him,
    I trust in Him,
and meet His love with mine.

464 © Timothy Dudley-Smith (based on Psalm 91)

1 Safe in the shadow of the Lord
beneath His hand and power,
    I trust in Him,
    I trust in Him,
my fortress and my tower.

2 My hope is set on God alone
though Satan spreads his snare,
    I trust in Him,
    I trust in Him,
to keep me in His care.

465 E Page (1836-1921)

1 Simply trusting every day,
trusting through a stormy way;
even when my faith is small,
trusting Jesus, that is all.

    Trusting as the moments fly;
    trusting as the days go by;
    trusting Him whate'er befall;
    trusting Jesus, that is all.

2 Brightly doth His Spirit shine
   into this poor heart of mine.
   While He leads I cannot fall;
   trusting Jesus, that is all.

3 Singing if my way is clear;
   praying if the path be drear;
   if in danger, for Him call;
   trusting Jesus, that is all.

4 Trusting Him while life shall last,
   trusting Him till earth be past,
   till within the jasper wall:
   trusting Jesus, that is all.

466 B B McKinney © Unidentified

1 "Take up thy cross and follow Me,"
   I heard my Master say;
   "I gave My life to ransom thee
   surrender your all today."

   Wherever He leads I'll go,
   wherever He leads I'll go;
   I'll follow my Christ who loves me so,
   wherever He leads I'll go.

2 He drew me closer to His side,
   I sought His will to know;
   and in that will I now abide
   wherever He leads I'll go.

3 It may be through the shadows dim
   or o'er the stormy sea;
   I take my cross and follow Him
   wherever He leadeth me.

4 My heart, my life, my all I bring
   to Christ who loves me so;
   He is my Master, Lord, and King
   wherever He leads I'll go.

467 Stuart Hamblen © 1950 Duchess Music Corporation, USA. MCA Music Ltd. Used by permission of Music Sales Ltd. All rights reserved. International Copyright Secured

1 The chimes of time ring out the news;
   another day is through.
   Someone slipped and fell.
   Was that someone you?
   You may have longed for added strength,
   your courage to renew.
   Do not be disheartened,
   for I have news for you.

   It is no secret what God can do.
   What He's done for others,
   He'll do for you.
   With arms wide open,
   He'll pardon you;
   it is no secret what God can do.

2 There is no night, for in His light
   you'll never walk alone.
   Always feel at home wherever you may
      roam.
   There is no power can conquer you,
   while God is on your side.
   Just take Him at His promise;
   don't run away and hide.

468 Edith Gilling Cherry (1872-97)

1 We rest on Thee, our shield and our
      defender!
   we go not forth alone against the foe;
   strong in Thy strength, safe in Thy
      keeping tender,
   we rest on Thee, and in Thy name we go.
   Strong in Thy strength, safe in Thy
      keeping tender,
   we rest on Thee, and in Thy name we go.

2 Yes, in Thy name, O Captain of
    salvation!
  in Thy dear name, all other names above;
  Jesus our righteousness, our sure
    foundation,
  our Prince of glory and our King of
    love.
  Jesus our righteousness, our sure
    foundation,
  our Prince of glory and our King of
    love.

3 We go in faith, our own great weakness
    feeling,
  and needing more each day Thy grace
    to know:
  yet from our hearts a song of triumph
    pealing,
  "We rest on Thee, and in Thy name we
    go."
  Yet from our hearts a song of triumph
    pealing,
  "We rest on Thee, and in Thy name
    we go."

4 We rest on Thee, our shield and our
    defender!
  Thine is the battle, Thine shall be the
    praise;
  when passing through the gates of
    pearly splendour,
  victors, we rest with Thee, through
    endless days.
  When passing through the gates of
    pearly splendour,
  victors, we rest with Thee, through
    endless days.

469   John Henry Sammis (1846-1919)

1 When we walk with the Lord
  in the light of His word,
  what a glory He sheds on our way;
  while we do His good will
  He abides with us still,
  and with all who will trust and obey.

    *Trust and obey, for there's no other
      way
    to be happy in Jesus but to trust
      and obey.*

2 Not a shadow can rise,
  not a cloud in the skies,
  but His smile quickly drives it away;
  not a doubt nor a fear,
  not a sigh nor a tear,
  can abide while we trust and obey.

3 Not a burden we bear,
  not a sorrow we share,
  but our toil He doth richly repay;
  not a grief nor a loss,
  not a frown nor a cross
  but is blest if we trust and obey.

4 But we never can prove
  the delights of His love
  until all on the altar we lay,
  for the favour He shows
  and the joy He bestows
  are for them who will trust and obey.

5 Then in fellowship sweet
  we will sit at His feet
  or we'll walk by His side in the way,
  what He says we will do,
  where He sends we will go,
  never fear, only trust and obey.

470 Mildred Duff © Unidentified

1 When you feel weakest, dangers
   surround,
  subtle temptations, troubles abound,
  nothing seems hopeful, nothing seems
   glad,
  all is despairing, even-time sad.

    Keep on believing, Jesus is near,
    keep on believing, there's nothing to
     fear;
    keep on believing, this is the way,
    faith in the night, as well as the day.

2 If all were easy, if all were bright,
  where would the cross be? Where
   would the fight?
  But in the hardness, God gives to you
  chances of proving that you are true.

3 God is your Wisdom, God is your Might,
  God's ever near you, guiding you right;
  He understands you, knows all you need;
  trusting in Him you'll surely succeed.

4 Let us press on, then, never despair,
  live above feeling, victory's there;
  Jesus can keep us so near to Him
  that nevermore our faith shall grow dim.

8.6   THE CHRISTIAN LIFE
Conflict and Triumph

471 Freda Hanbury Allen (b. 1926)
© Unidentified

1 A life of overcoming,
  a life of ceaseless praise,
  be this thy blessed portion,
  throughout the coming days.
  The victory was purchased
  on Calv'ry's cross for thee,
  sin shall not have dominion,
  the Son hath made thee free.

2 And would'st thou know the secret
  of constant victory?
  Let in the Overcomer,
  and He will conquer thee!
  Thy broken spirit, taken
  in sweet captivity,
  shall glory in His triumph
  and share His victory.

3 Then from thy life ascending
  one triumph note of praise,
  (for they who always conquer
  a victor's song must raise,)
  shall echo on unceasing
  till Satan's host doth flee
  before our glorious watchword,
  "Lord, victory for me."

4 Though all the path before thee
  the host of darkness fill,
   look to thy Father's promise,
  and claim the victory still.
  Faith sees the heavenly legions,
  where doubt sees nought but foes,
  and through the very conflict
   her life the stronger grows.

5 More stern will grow the conflict
  as nears our King's return,
and they alone can face it
who this great lesson learn:
that from them God asks nothing
but to unlatch the door
admitting Him, who through them
will conquer evermore.

one moment will not linger,
but, spite of hell, shall have its course;
'tis written by His finger.
And though they take our life,
goods, honour, children, wife,
yet is their profit small;
these things shall vanish all,
the city of God remaineth.

472 Martin Luther (1483-1546)
vs 2-4 tr. Thomas Carlyle (1796-1881)

1 A mighty fortress is our God,
  a bulwark never failing;
our helper He amid the flood
of mortal ills prevailing.
For still our ancient foe
doth seek to work us woe;
His craft and power are great,
and, armed with cruel hate,
on earth is not His equal.

2 With force of arms we nothing can,
  full soon were we down ridden;
but for us fights the proper Man
whom God Himself has bidden.
Ask ye: Who is this same?
Christ Jesus is His name,
the Lord Sabaoth's Son;
He, and no other one,
shall conquer in the battle.

3 And were this world all devils o'er,
  and watching to devour us,
we lay it not to heart so sore;
not they can overpower us.
And let the prince of ill
look grim as e'er he will,
he harms us not a whit;
for why? His doom is writ;
a word shall quickly slay him.

4 God's word, for all their craft and force,

473 Isaac Watts (1483-1546)

1 Am I a soldier of the cross
  a follower of the Lamb?
And shall I fear to own His cause
or blush to speak His name?

In the name, the precious name
of Him who died for me,
through grace I'll win the promised
   crown,
whate'er my cross may be.

2 Must I be carried to the skies
  on flowery beds of ease,
while others fought to win the prize,
and sailed through bloody seas?

3 Are there no foes for me to face?
  Must I not stem the flood?
Is this vile world a friend to grace,
to help me on to God?

4 Since I must fight if I would reign,
  increase my courage, Lord!
I'll bear the toil, endure the pain
supported by Thy word.

474 Herbert H Booth (1862-1926)

1 Blessed Lord, in Thee is refuge,
  safety for my trembling soul,
  power to lift my head when drooping,
  'midst the angry billows' roll.
  I will trust Thee, I will trust Thee,
    I will trust Thee,
  all my life Thou shalt control.

2 In the past too unbelieving
  'midst the tempest I have been,
  and my heart has slowly trusted
  what my eyes have never seen.
  Blessed Jesus, blessed Jesus,
    blessed Jesus,
  teach me on Thine arm to lean.

3 Oh, for trust that brings the triumph,
  when defeat seems strangely near!
  Oh, for faith that changes fighting
  into victory's ringing cheer!
  Faith triumphant! faith triumphant!
    faith triumphant!
  knowing not defeat or fear.

4 Faith triumphant - blessed victory!
  Every barrier swept away!
  Heaven descending, joy and fullness,
  dawn of everlasting day!
  Jesus only, Jesus only,
    Jesus only,
  Him to love and Him obey.

475 © Unidentified

1 Forward, soldiers, bold and fearless,
  hear the call of God;
  prove your courage in the conflict,
  tread where brave men trod.

Lift aloft the cross of Jesus!
Hold it high and strong;
sound the praise of Him who saves us,
swell the battle song!

2 Faith our shield, and hope our helmet,
  Satan's host we face;
  marshalled in the might of Jesus,
  win we by His grace.

3 Catch the order of our Captain,
  wield the Spirit's sword;
  onward, fearless, press to conquer,
  slaying with His word.

4 Sharers in the glad hosanna,
  all who will believe.
  They who joyful bear His banner,
  crowns of life receive.

476 © Unidentified

In the name of Jesus, in the name of Jesus,
  we have the victory.
In the name of Jesus, in the name of Jesus,
  demons will have to flee.
Who can tell what God can do?
Who can tell of His love for you?
In the name of Jesus, Jesus, we have the
  victory.

477 Annie Johnson Flint
© Lillenas Publishing Co./Admin. by Copycare

1 He giveth more grace when the burdens
    grow greater,
  He sendeth more strength when the
    labours increase;
  to added affliction He addeth His mercy,
  to multiplied trials, His multiplied peace.

His love has no limit, His grace has
no measure,
His power has no boundary known
unto men;
for out of His infinite riches in Jesus
He giveth, and giveth, and giveth
again!

2 When we have exhausted our store
of endurance,
when our strength has failed ere the
day is half done,
when we reach the end of our hoarded
resources,
our Father's full giving is only begun.

478 Anon.
© Unidentified

1 Jesus hath died and hath risen again,
pardon and peace to bestow;
fully I trust Him; from sin's guilty stain
Jesus saves me now.

Jesus saves me now!
Jesus saves me now!
Yes, Jesus saves me all the time,
Jesus saves me now!

2 Sin's condemnation is over and gone,
Jesus alone knoweth how;
life and salvation my soul hath put on;
Jesus saves me now.

3 Jesus is stronger than Satan and sin,
Satan to Jesus must bow,
therefore I triumph without and within;
Jesus saves me now.

4 Sorrow and pain may beset me about,
nothing can darken my brow;
battling in faith I can joyfully shout:
Jesus saves me now.

479 R Johnson
Copyright Control

1 Marching on in the light of God,
marching on, I'm marching on;
up the path that the Master trod,
marching, marching on.

A robe of white, a crown of gold,
a harp, a home, a mansion fair,
a victor's palm, a joy untold,
are mine when I get there.
For Jesus is my Saviour, He's washed
my sins away,
paid my debt on Calvary's mountain;
happy in His dying love, singing all
the day,
I'm living, yes, I'm living in the
fountain.

2 Marching on through the hosts of sin,
victory's mine while I've Christ within.

3 Marching on while the worldlings sneer,
perfect love casteth out all fear.

4 Marching on in the Spirit's might,
more than conqueror in every fight.

5 Marching on to the realms above,
there to sing of redeeming love.

480 Julia Ward Howe (1819-1910)

1 Mine eyes have seen the glory of the
coming of the Lord;
He is trampling out the vintage where
the grapes of wrath are stored;
He hath loosed the fateful lightning
of His terrible, swift sword:
our God is marching on.

Glory, glory! Hallelujah!
Glory, glory! Hallelujah!
Glory, glory! Hallelujah!
Our God is marching on.

2 He has sounded forth the trumpet that
    shall never call retreat;
    He is sifting out the hearts of men
    before His judgement seat:
    oh, be swift, my soul, to answer Him!
    be jubilant, my feet!
    our God is marching on.

3 In the beauty of the lilies, Christ was
    born across the sea,
    with a glory in His bosom that
    transfigures you and me:
    as He died to make men holy, let us
    live to make men free,
    Our God is marching on.

481 S Baring-Gould (1834-1924)

1 Onward Christian soldiers, marching
    as to war,
    with the cross of Jesus going on before.
    Christ the royal Master leads against the
    foe;
    forward into battle, see, His banners go!

    Onward, Christian soldiers, marching
        as to war,
    with the cross of Jesus going on
        before.

2 At the name of Jesus Satan's legions
    flee;
    on then, Christian soldiers, on to victory.
    Hell's foundations quiver at the shout of
    praise;
    brothers, lift your voices, loud your
    anthems raise.

3 Like a mighty army moves the church
    of God;
    brothers, we are treading where the
    saints have trod;
    we are not divided, all one body we,
    one in hope and calling, one in charity.

4 Crowns and thrones may perish,
        kingdoms rise and wane,
    but the Church of Jesus constant will
    remain;
    gates of hell can never 'gainst that
    Church prevail;
    we have Christ's own promise, and
    that cannot fail.

5 Onward, then, ye people, join our happy
    throng,
    blend with ours your voices in the
    triumph song;
    glory, praise and honour unto Christ
    the King;
    this through countless ages men and
    angels sing.

482 Charles Wesley (1707-88)

1 Soldiers of Christ, arise
    and put your armour on!
    Strong in the strength which God
        supplies
    through His eternal Son.
    Strong in the Lord of hosts,
    and in His mighty power;
    who in the strength of Jesus trusts
    is more than conqueror.

2 Stand, then, in His great might,
   with all His strength endued;
   and take, to arm you for the fight,
   the panoply of God.
   To keep your armour bright,
   attend with constant care,
   still walking in your Captain's sight
   and watching unto prayer.

3 From strength to strength go on;
   wrestle, and fight, and pray;
   tread all the powers of darkness down
   and win the well-fought day;
   That, having all things done,
   and all your conflicts past,
   ye may o'ercome through Christ alone
   and stand complete at last.

3 Stand up, stand up for Jesus!
   Stand in His strength alone;
   the arm of flesh will fail you,
   ye dare not trust your own:
   put on the gospel armour,
   and, watching unto prayer,
   where duty calls or danger,
   be never wanting there.

4 Stand up, stand up for Jesus!
   The strife will not be long;
   this day the noise of battle,
   the next, the victor's song;
   to him that overcometh,
   a crown of life shall be;
   He with the King of glory
   shall reign eternally!

483 George Duffield (1818-88)

1 Stand up, stand up for Jesus!
   ye soldiers of the cross;
   lift high His royal banner,
   it must not suffer loss;
   from victory unto victory
   His army shall He lead,
   till every foe is vanquished,
   and Christ is Lord indeed.

   Stand up for Jesus!
   ye soldiers of the cross;
   lift high His royal banner,
   it must not, it must not suffer loss.

2 Stand up, stand up for Jesus!
   The trumpet call obey;
   forth to the mighty conflict
   in this His glorious day;
   ye that are men now serve Him
   against unnumbered foes;
   let courage rise with danger,
   and strength to strength oppose.

484 W A Garratt (b. 1846)
© Unidentified

1 We never need be vanquished,
   we never need give in,
   though waging war with Satan,
   and compassed round by sin.
   Temptations will beset us,
   allurements oft assail,
   but in the name of Jesus
   we shall, we must prevail.

2 God wills not that His people
   by sin enthralled should be,
   but that their lives, as ransomed,
   be lives of victory;
   and so at our disposal
   He places all His power,
   that we from its resources
   may draw in danger's hour.

3 Herein is hid the secret
of an all-glorious life
whereby we conquer Satan,
and rise above sin's strife.
Abiding in the Saviour,
self prostrate in the dust,
we live to do His bidding
in glad perpetual trust.

4 We in ourselves are nothing,
a small and feeble host,
nor have we aught of prowess
wherein to make our boast.
Our stronghold is Christ Jesus,
His grace alone we plead,
His name our shield and banner,
Himself, just all we need.

485 Frances Ridley Havergal (1836-79)

1 Who is on the Lord's side?
Who will serve the King?
Who will be His helpers,
other lives to bring?
Who will leave the world's side?
Who will face the foe?
Who is on the Lord's side?
Who for Him will go?
By Thy call of mercy,
by Thy grace divine,
we are on the Lord's side,
Saviour, we are Thine!

2 Not for weight of glory,
not for crown and palm,
enter we the army,
raise the warrior psalm;
but for love that claimeth
lives for whom He died:
He whom Jesus nameth
must be on His side!

By Thy love constraining,
by Thy grace divine,
we are on the Lord's side,
Saviour, we are Thine.

3 Jesus, Thou has bought us,
not with gold or gem,
but with Thine own life-blood
for Thy diadem;
with Thy blessing filling
all who come to Thee,
Thou hast made us willing,
Thou hast made us free.
By Thy grand redemption,
by Thy grace divine,
we are on the Lord's side,
Saviour, we are Thine!

4 Fierce may be the conflict,
strong may be the foe;
but the King's own army
none can overthrow:
round His standard ranging,
victory is secure,
for His truth unchanging
makes the triumph sure.
Joyfully enlisting,
by Thy grace divine,
we are on the Lord's side,
Saviour, we are Thine!

5 Chosen to be soldiers
in an alien land,
chosen, called, and faithful,
for our captain's band;
in the service royal
let us not grow cold;
let us be right loyal,
noble, true and bold.
Master, Thou wilt keep us,
by Thy grace divine,
always on the Lord's side,
Saviour, always Thine.

486 John Bunyan (1628-88) and H. E. Govan
(1866-1932) (verse 3) © The Faith Mission

1 Who would true valour see,
   let him come hither;
   one here will constant be,
   come wind, come weather;
   there's no discouragement
   shall make him once relent
   his first avowed intent
   to be a pilgrim.

2 Who so beset him round
   with dismal stories,
   do but themselves confound;
   His strength the more is.
   No lion can him fright,
   he'll with a giant fight,
   but he will have a right
   to be a pilgrim.

3 Fair gleams his home at length
   to pilgrim weary,
   who in Jehovah's strength
   has battled bravely.
   Nor surging torrents roar
   can fray him from that shore;
   full soon he passes o'er
   oh, happy pilgrim.

487 H R Palmer (1834-1907)

1 Yield not to temptation, for yielding is
     sin,
   each victory will help you some other
     to win;
   fight manfully onward, dark passions
     subdue,
   look ever to Jesus, He'll carry you
     through.

   Ask the Saviour to help you,
   comfort, strengthen, and keep you;
   He is willing to aid you,
   He will carry you through.

2 Shun evil companions, bad language
     disdain,
   God's name hold in reverence, nor take
     it in vain;
   be thoughtful and earnest, kind-hearted
     and true,
   look ever to Jesus, He'll carry you
     through.

3 To him that o'ercometh God giveth a
     crown,
   through faith we shall conquer, though
     often cast down;
   He who is our Saviour our strength will
     renew,
   look ever to Jesus, He'll carry you
     through.

488 Rev H J Zelley (1859-1942)
© Unidentified

1 When Israel out of bondage came,
   a sea before them lay;
   the Lord reached down His mighty
     hand
   and rolled the sea away.

   Then forward still, 'tis Jehovah's will,
   though the billows dash and spray;
   with a conquering tread we will push
   ahead,
   He'll roll the sea away.

2 Before me was a sea of sin,
   so great I feared to pray;
   my heart's desire the Saviour read
   and rolled the sea away.

3 When sorrows dark, like stormy waves
  were dashing o'er my way,
  again the Lord in mercy came
  and rolled the sea away.

4 And when I reach the sea of death,
  for needed grace I'll pray;
  I know the Lord will quickly come
  and roll the sea away.

8.7 THE CHRISTIAN LIFE:
Fellowship

489 © Unidentified

1 Be still and know that I am God.
  Be still and know that I am God.
  Be still and know that I am God.

2 I am the Lord that healeth thee.
  I am the Lord that healeth thee.
  I am the Lord that healeth thee.

3 In Thee, O Lord, I put my trust.
  In Thee, O Lord, I put my trust.
  In Thee, O Lord, I put my trust.

490 From John 13
Copyright Control

A new commandment I give unto you,
that you love one another as I have loved
  you,
that you love one another as I have loved
  you.
By this shall all men know that you are
  My disciples,
if you have love one for another.
By this shall all men know that you are
  My disciples,
if you have love one for another.

491 Jessie Pounds (1861-1921)

1 Anywhere with Jesus I can safely go,
  anywhere He leads me in this world
    below,
  anywhere without Him, dearest joys
    would fade,
  anywhere with Jesus I am not afraid.

    *Anywhere! anywhere! fear I cannot
      know,
    anywhere with Jesus I can safely go.*

2 Anywhere with Jesus I am not alone,
  other friends may fail me, He is still
    my own.
  Though His hand may lead me over
    drearest ways,
  anywhere with Jesus is a house of praise.

3 Anywhere with Jesus I can go to sleep,
  when the darkling shadows round
    about me creep.
  Knowing I shall waken never more to
    roam.
  anywhere with Jesus will be home,
    sweet home.

492 Dave Bilbrough
© 1983 Kingsway's Thankyou Music

I am a new creation,
no more in condemnation,
here in the grace of God I stand.
My heart is over-flowing,
my love just keeps on growing,
here in the grace of God I stand.

And I will praise You, Lord,
yes, I will praise You, Lord,
and I will sing of all that You have done.
A joy that knows no limit,
a lightness in my spirit,
here in the grace of God I stand.

493 Psalm 73:23-28 (Scottish Psalter)

1 Nevertheless continually,
   O Lord, I am with Thee:
   Thou dost me hold by my right hand,
   and still upholdest me.

2 Thou, with Thy counsel, while I live,
   wilt me conduct and guide;
   and to Thy glory afterwards
   receive me to abide.

3 Whom have I in the heavens high
   but Thee, O Lord, alone?
   and in the earth whom I desire
   besides Thee is none.

4 My flesh and heart doth faint and fail,
   but God doth fail me ne'er:
   for of my heart God is the strength
   and portion forever.

5 For, lo, they that are far from Thee
   for ever perish shall;
   Them that a whoring from Thee go
   thou hast destroyed all.

6 But surely it is good for me
   that I draw near to God:
   in God I trust, that all my works
   I may declare abroad.

494 Elton M Roth
© 1924 Hope Publishing/Admin. by Copycare

1 I have a song that Jesus gave me,
   it was sent from heaven above;
   there never was a sweeter melody,
   'tis a melody of love.

   In my heart there rings a melody,
   there rings a melody with heaven's
   *   harmony;*
   in my heart there rings a melody;
   there rings a melody of love.

2 I love the Christ that died on Calvary,
   for He washed my sins away;
   He put within my heart a melody,
   and I know it's there to stay.

3 'Twill be my endless theme in glory,
   with the angels I will sing;
   'twill be a song with glorious harmony,
   when the courts of heaven ring.

495 Frances Ridley Havergal (1836-79)

1 I know I love Thee better, Lord,
   than any earthly joy,
   for Thou hast given me the peace
   which nothing can destroy.

   The half has never yet been told
   of love so full and free.
   the half has never yet been told:
   the blood, it cleanseth me.

2 I know that Thou art nearer still
   than any earthly throng,
   and sweeter is the thought of Thee
   than any lovely song.

3 Thou hast put gladness in my heart;
then well may I be glad!
Without the secret of Thy love
I could not but be sad.

4 O Saviour, precious Saviour, mine!
What will Thy presence be,
if such a life of joy can crown
our walk on earth with Thee?

496 Charles Fry
© Salvationist Publishing & Supplies/Admin.
by Copycare

1 I've found a friend in Jesus, He's
everything to me;
He's the fairest of ten thousand to my
soul!
the Lily of the Valley, in Him alone I
see
all I need to cleanse and make me fully
whole:
in sorrow He's my comfort, in trouble
He's my stay;
He tells me every care on Him to roll.
He's the Lily of the Valley, the Bright
and Morning Star;
He's the fairest of ten thousand to my
soul.

2 He all my grief has taken and all my
sorrows borne;
in temptation He's my strong and
mighty tower;
I've all for Him forsaken, I've all my
idols torn
from my heart, and now He keeps
me by His power.
Though all the world forsake me and
Satan tempt me sore,
through Jesus I shall safely reach the
goal.

He's the Lily of the Valley, the Bright
and Morning Star;
He's the fairest of ten thousand to my
soul.

3 He'll never, never leave me, nor yet
forsake me here,
while I live by faith and do His blessed
will;
a wall of fire about me, I've nothing
now to fear;
with His manna He my hungry soul
shall fill.
Then sweeping up to glory, I'll see His
blessed face,
where rivers of delight shall ever roll.
He's the Lily of the Valley, the Bright
and Morning Star;
He's the fairest of ten thousand to my
soul.

497 James Small (1817-88)

1 I've found a Friend, oh, such a Friend!
He loved me ere I knew Him;
He drew me with the cords of love,
and thus He bound me to Him.
And round my heart still closely twine
those ties which nought can sever,
for I am His, and He is mine,
for ever and for ever!

2 I've found a Friend, oh, such a Friend!
He bled, He died to save me;
and not alone the gift of life,
but His own self He gave me,
nought that I have my own I call,
I hold it for the Giver:
my heart, my strength, my life, my all
are His, and His for ever!

3 I've found a Friend, oh, such a Friend!
  All power to Him is given
  to guard me on my onward course,
  and bring me safe to heaven.
  The eternal glories gleam afar
  to nerve my faint endeavour!
  So now to watch! to work! to war!
  And then to rest for ever!

4 I've found a Friend, oh, such a Friend!
  So kind, and true, and tender;
  so wise a Counsellor and Guide,
  so mighty a Defender!
  From Him who loves me now so well,
  what power my soul can sever?
  Shall life or death? or earth or hell?
  No! I am His for ever!

498   Anna L Waring (1823-1910)

1 In heavenly love abiding,
  no change my heart shall fear;
  and safe is such confiding,
  for nothing changes here.
  The storm may roar without me,
  my heart may low be laid,
  but God is round about me
  and can I be dismayed?

2 Wherever He may guide me,
  no want shall turn me back;
  my Shepherd is beside me,
  and nothing can I lack.
  His wisdom ever waketh,
  His sight is never dim,
  He knows the way He taketh,
  and I will walk with Him.

3 Green pastures are before me,
  which yet I have not seen;
  bright skies will soon be o'er me,
  where the dark clouds have been.
  My hope I cannot measure,
  my path to life is free,
  my Saviour has my treasure,
  and He will walk with me.

499   William Walsham How (1823-97)

1 It is a thing most wonderful,
  almost too wonderful to be,
  that God's own Son should come
      from heaven
  and die to save a child like me.

2 And yet I know that it is true;
  He chose a poor and humble lot,
  and wept, and toiled, and mourned,
      and died,
  for love of those who loved Him not.

3 I sometimes think about the cross,
  and shut my eyes and try to see
  the cruel nails and crown of thorns,
  and Jesus crucified for me.

4 But even could I see Him die,
  I could but see a little part
  of that great love, which, like a fire,
  is always burning in His heart.

5 I cannot tell how He could love
  a child so weak and full of sin;
  His love must be most wonderful,
  if He could die my love to win.

6 It is most wonderful to know
  His love for me so free and sure;
  but 'tis more wonderful to see
  my love for Him so faint and poor.

7 And yet I want to love Thee, Lord;
  O light the flame within my heart,
  and I will love Thee more and more,
  until I see Thee as Thou art.

500 Avis Christiansen
© Brentwood Benson Music Publishing Inc./
Admin. by Copycare

1 It is glory just to walk with Him whose
    blood has ransomed me;
  it is rapture for my soul each day.
  It is joy divine to feel Him near
    where'er my path may be.
  Bless the Lord, it's glory all the way!

  It is glory just to walk with Him.
  It is glory just to walk with Him.
  He will guide my steps aright,
  through the vale and o'er the height.
  It is glory just to walk with Him.

2 It is glory when the shadows fall, to
    know that He is near.
  Oh, what joy to simply trust and pray!
  It is glory to abide in Him when skies
    above are clear.
  Yes, with Him, it's glory all the way!

3 'Twill be glory when I walk with Him
    on heaven's golden shore,
  never from His side again to stray.
  'Twill be glory, wondrous glory with the
    Saviour ever more,
  everlasting glory all the way!

501 Jean Sophia Pigott (1845-82)

1 Jesus! I am resting, resting,
  in the joy of what Thou art;
  I am finding out the greatness
  of Thy loving heart.
  Thou hast bid me gaze upon Thee,
  and Thy beauty fills my soul,
  for, by Thy transforming power,
  Thou hast made me whole.

  Jesus! I am resting, resting,
  in the joy of what Thou art,
  I am finding out the greatness
  of Thy loving heart.

2 Oh, how great Thy loving kindness,
  vaster, broader than the sea!
  Oh, how marvellous Thy goodness,
  lavished all on me!
  Yes, I rest in Thee, Beloved,
  know what wealth of grace is Thine,
  know Thy certainty of promise,
  and have made it mine.

3 Simply trusting Thee, Lord Jesus,
  I behold Thee as Thou art,
  and Thy love so pure, so changeless,
  satisfies my heart;
  satisfies its deepest longings,
  meets, supplies its every need,
  compasseth me round with blessings:
  Thine is love indeed!

4 Ever lift Thy face upon me,
  as I work and wait for Thee;
  resting 'neath Thy smile, Lord Jesus,
  earth's dark shadows flee.
  Brightness of my Father's glory,
  sunshine of my Father's face,
  keep me ever trusting, resting,
  fill me with Thy grace.

502 J M Harris (d. 1931)
© Unidentified

1 Jesus my King, my wonderful Saviour,
all of my life is given to Thee;
I am rejoicing in Thy salvation,
Thy precious blood now maketh me free.

Wonderful Saviour, wonderful
Saviour,
Thou art so near, so precious to me;
wonderful Saviour, wonderful
Saviour,
my heart is filled with praises to Thee.

2 Freedom from sin, oh, wonderful story!
All of its stains washed whiter than
snow,
Jesus has come to live in His temple,
and with His love my heart is aglow.

3 Jesus my Lord, I'll ever adore Thee,
lay at Thy feet my treasures of love;
lead me in ways to show forth Thy glory,
ways that will end in heaven above.

4 When in that bright and beautiful city
I shall behold Thy glories untold,
I shall be like Thee, wonderful Saviour,
and I will sing while ages unfold.

503 Bernard of Clairvaux (1091-1153)
tr. Edward Caswell (1814-78)

1 Jesus, the very thought of Thee
with sweetness fills my breast;
but sweeter far Thy face to see,
and in Thy presence rest.

2 Nor voice can sing, nor heart can frame,
nor can the memory find
a sweeter sound than Thy blest name,
O Saviour of mankind!

3 O hope of every contrite heart,
O joy of all the meek,
to those who fall how kind Thou art,
how good to those who seek!

4 But what to those who find? Ah, this
nor tongue nor pen can show;
the love of Jesus, what it is,
none but His loved ones know.

5 Jesus, our only joy be Thou,
as Thou our prize wilt be;
Jesus, be Thou our glory now,
and through eternity.

504 Francis Jane van Alstyne (1820-1915)
(Fanny J Crosby)

1 Jesus, keep me near the Cross!
There a precious fountain,
free to all, a healing stream
flows from Calvary's mountain.

In the Cross, in the Cross
be my glory ever,
till my raptured soul shall find
rest beyond the river!

2 Near the Cross, a trembling soul,
love and mercy found me;
there the bright and morning star
shed its beams around me.

3 Near the Cross! O Lamb of God,
   bring its scenes before me!
   Help me walk from day to day
   with its shadow o'er me.

4 Near the Cross I'll watch and wait,
   hoping, trusting ever,
   till I reach the golden strand,
   just beyond the river.

*(When using Werner repeat last line of
each verse and use part of chorus:
In the cross, in the cross,
be my glory ever.)*

505 M P Ferguson (b. 1850)
© Unidentified

1 Joys are flowing like a river
   since the Comforter has come:
   He abides with us for ever,
   makes the trusting heart His home.

   *Blessed quietness! holy quietness!
   What assurance in my soul!
   On the stormy sea, speaking peace
     to me,
   how the billows cease to roll!*

2 Bringing life and health and gladness
   all around, this glorious Guest
   banished unbelief and sadness,
   changed our weariness to rest.

3 Like the rain that falls from heaven,
   like the sunlight from the sky,
   so the Holy Ghost is given,
   coming on us from on high.

4 See, a fruitful field is growing,
   blessed fruits of righteousness!
   And the streams of life are flowing
   in the lonely wilderness.

5 What a wonderful salvation,
   where we always see His face!
   What a peaceful habitation,
   what a quiet resting place!

506 George Wade Robinson (1838-77)

1 Loved with everlasting love,
   led by grace that love to know;
   Spirit, breathing from above,
   Thou hast taught me it is so!
   Oh, this full and perfect peace!
   Oh, this presence so divine!
   In a love which cannot cease
   I am His, and He is mine.

2 Heaven above is softer blue,
   earth around is sweeter green,
   something lives in every hue
   Christless eyes have never seen;
   birds with gladder songs o'erflow,
   flowers with deeper beauties shine,
   since I know, as now I know,
   I am His, and He is mine.

3 Things that once were wild alarms
   cannot now disturb my rest;
   closed in everlasting arms,
   pillowed on the loving breast.
   Oh to lie for ever here,
   doubt and care and self resign,
   while He whispers in my ear,
   I am His, and He is mine!

4 His for ever, only His;
   who the Lord and me shall part?
   Ah, with what a rest of bliss
   Christ can fill the loving heart!
   Heaven and earth may fade and flee,
   first-born light in gloom decline;
   but, while God and I shall be,
   I am His, and He is mine.

(Repeat last two lines of each verse)

507
William R Featherstone (1846-73)

1 My Jesus, I love Thee, I know Thou art
   mine;
   for Thee all the pleasures of sin I resign;
   my gracious Redeemer, my Saviour art
   Thou,
   if ever I loved Thee, my Jesus, 'tis
   now.

2 I love thee because Thou hast first loved
   me,
   and purchased my pardon on Calvary's
   tree;
   I love Thee for wearing the thorns on
   Thy brow;
   if ever I loved Thee, my Jesus, 'tis
   now.

3 I'll love Thee in life, I will love Thee in
   death,
   and praise Thee as long as Thou lendest
   me breath,
   and say when the death dew lies cold on
   my brow,
   if ever I loved Thee, my Jesus, 'tis
   now.

4 In mansions of glory and endless delight,
   I'll ever adore Thee in heaven so bright;
   I'll sing with the glittering crown on my
   brow,
   if ever I loved Thee, my Jesus, 'tis
   now.

508
© Unidentified

1 Not a sound invades the stillness,
   not a form invades the scene,
   save the voice of my Beloved
   and the person of my King.

   Precious, gentle, holy Jesus!
   Blessed Bridegroom of my heart,
   in Thy secret inner chamber,
   Thou wilt whisper what Thou art.

2 And within those heavenly places,
   calmly hushed in sweet repose,
   there I drink, with joy absorbing
   all the love Thou wouldst disclose.

3 Wrapped in deep adoring silence,
   Jesus, Lord, I dare not move,
   lest I lose the smallest saying
   meant to catch the ear of love.

4 Rest then, O my soul, contented:
   Thou hast reached thy happy place,
   in the bosom of thy Saviour,
   gazing up in His dear face.

(When using the tune "Kirstenbosch" chorus is
only sung after verses 2 & 4)

509
Francis Jane van Alstyne (1820-1915)
(Fanny J Crosby)

1 Rich are the moments of blessing
   Jesus my Saviour bestows;
   pure is the well of salvation
   fresh from His mercy that flows.

   Ever He walketh beside me,
   brightly His sunshine appears,
   spreading a beautiful rainbow
   over the valley of tears.

2 Rich are the moments of blessing,
   lovely, and hallowed, and sweet,
   when from my labour at noon-tide
   calmly I rest at His feet.

3 Why should I ever grow weary?
   Why should I faint by the way?
   Has He not promised to give me
   strength for the toils of the day?

4 Though by the mist and the shadow
   sometimes my sky may be dim,
   rich are the moments of blessing
   spent in communion with Him.

510 Bernard of Clairvaux (1091-1153)

1 Jesus, Thou joy of loving hearts,
   Thou fount of life, Thou light of men!
   From the best bliss that earth imparts
   we turn unfilled to Thee again.

2 Thy truth unchanged hath ever stood;
   Thou savest those that on Thee call;
   to them that seek Thee, Thou art good,
   to them that find Thee, All in all!

3 We taste Thee, O Thou living bread,
   and long to feast upon Thee still;
   we drink of Thee, the fountain head,
   and thirst our souls from Thee to fill.

4 Our restless spirits yearn for Thee;
   where'er our changeful lot is cast,
   glad when Thy gracious smile we see,
   blest when our faith can hold Thee fast.

5 O Jesus, ever with us stay!
   Make all our moments calm and bright;
   chase the dark night of sin away:
   shed o'er the world Thy holy light.

511 Cleland McAfee (1866-1944)
© Unidentified

1 There is a place of quiet rest,
   near to the heart of God;
   a place where sin cannot molest,
   near to the heart of God.

   O Jesus, blest Redeemer,
   sent from the heart of God;
   hold us, who wait before Thee,
   near to the heart of God.

2 There is a place of comfort sweet,
   near to the heart of God;
   a place where we our Saviour meet,
   near to the heart of God.

3 There is a place of full release,
   near to the heart of God;
   a place where all is joy and peace,
   near to the heart of God.

512 Francis Jane van Alstyne (1820-1915)
(Fanny J Crosby)

1 Take the world, but give me Jesus!
   All its joys are but a name,
   but His love abideth ever,
   through eternal years the same.

   Oh, the height and depth of mercy!
   Oh, the length and breadth of love!
   Oh, the fullness of redemption,
   pledge of endless life above!

2 Take the world, but give me Jesus,
   sweetest comfort of my soul;
   with my Saviour watching o'er me
   I can sing, though billows roll.

3 Take the world, but give me Jesus!
   Let me view His constant smile;
   then throughout my pilgrim journey
   light will cheer me all the while.

4 Take the world, but give me Jesus!
   In His cross my trust shall be,
   till, with clearer, brighter vision,
   face to face my Lord I see.

513 Leonard Bartlotti and Jan Harrington
© 1975 Celebration/Admin. by Kingsway's
Thankyou Music

Tell My people I love them,
tell My people I care;
when they feel far away from Me,
tell My people I am there.

1 Tell My people I came and died
   to give them liberty;
   and to abide in Me
   is to be really free.

2 Tell My people where'er they go
   My comfort they can know;
   My peace and joy and love
   I freely will bestow.

Then welcome, O Lord, to the throne
*   of my heart!*
I'd hail Thee my Saviour and
*   King!*
Be Thine all my service, for worthy
*   Thou art,*
and forever Thy praise I will sing,
and forever Thy praise I will sing.

2 There's truth in the heart when the
   Lord reigns within,
   in the heart and the life, day by day,
   with a conscience that seeks to be
   blameless from sin
   and His bidding alone to obey.

3 There's strength in the heart when
   the Lord is its king;
   not a task, but His grace will empower;
   not a foe, but His hand will deprive of
   its sting;
   blessed Shield and Protector and
   Tower!

4 There's joy in the heart that has
   Christ on the throne,
   such as none but Himself can impart;
   'tis a joy that remaineth when earth's
   joys are flown,
   'tis a fullness of joy in the heart.

514 H E Govan (1866-1932)
© The Faith Mission

1 There's peace in the heart that has
   Christ for its king;
   for His reign and His peace have no end:
   in His shelter secure and at rest we can
   sing,
   for His foes to His sceptre must bend.

515 Eliza Edmunds Hewitt (1851-1920)

1 There is sunshine in my soul today,
   more glorious and bright
   than glows in any earthly sky,
   for Jesus is my light.

Oh, there's sunshine, blessed sunshine
while the peaceful, happy moments
*   roll;*
when Jesus shows His smiling face,
there is sunshine in my soul.

2   There is music in my soul today,
    a carol to my King,
    and Jesus, listening, can hear
    the song I cannot sing.

3   There is spring-time in my soul today,
    for when the Lord is near,
    the dove of peace sings in my heart,
    the flowers of grace appear.

4   There is gladness in my soul today,
    and hope, and praise, and love,
    for blessings which He gives me now,
    for joys laid up above.

516   Elisha A Hoffman (1839-1929)
          Copyright Control

1   What a fellowship, what a joy divine,
    leaning on the everlasting arms;
    what a blessedness, what a peace is
        mine,
    leaning on the everlasting arms.

    Leaning, leaning,
    safe and secure from all alarms;
    leaning, leaning,
    leaning on the everlasting arms.

2   Oh, how sweet to walk in this pilgrim
        way!
    Oh, how bright the path grows from day
        to day!

3   What have I to dread, what have I to
        fear?
    I have blessed peace with my Lord so
        near.

517   Rev Johnson Oatman Jr. (1856-1922)

1   When upon life's billows you are
        tempest tossed,
    when you are discouraged, thinking
        all is lost,
    count your many blessings, name
        them one by one,
    and it will surprise you what the Lord
        hath done.

    Count your blessings, name them
    *   one by one,*
    count your blessings, see what God
    *   hath done;*
    count your blessings, name them
    *   one by one,*
    and it will surprise you what the Lord
    *   hath done.*

2   Are you ever burdened with a load of
        care?
    Does the cross seem heavy you are
        called to bear?
    Count your many blessings, every
        doubt will fly,
    and you will be singing as the days go
        by.

3   When you look at others with their
        lands and gold,
    think that Christ has promised you His
        wealth untold!
    Count your many blessings! Money
        cannot buy
    your reward in heaven nor your home
        on high.

4   So, amid the conflict, whether great
      or small,
    do not be discouraged, God is over all.
    Count your many blessings! Angels
      will attend,
    help and comfort give you to your
      journey's end.

8.8   THE CHRISTIAN LIFE
Prayer and Devotion

518   H Stowell (1799-1865)

1   From every stormy wind that blows,
    from every swelling tide of woes,
    there is a calm, a sure retreat;
    'tis found beneath the Mercy seat.

2   There is a place where Jesus sheds
    the oil of gladness on our heads;
    a place than all beside more sweet
    it is the blood-stained Mercy seat.

3   There is a scene where spirits blend,
    where friend holds fellowship with
      friend;
    though scattered far, by faith we meet
    around one common Mercy seat.

4   There, there, on eagle's wings we soar,
    till sense and sin molest no more,
    and heaven comes down our souls to
      greet,
    and glory crowns the Mercy seat!

519   Anon
         © Unidentified

1   Hast thou heard Him, seen Him,
      known Him?
    Is not thine a captured heart?
    Chief among ten thousand own Him,
    joyful choose the better part.

2   Idols once they won thee, charmed thee,
    lovely things of time and sense;
    gilded thus does sin disarm thee,
    honeyed lest thou turn thee thence.

3   What has stripped the seeming beauty
    from the idols of the earth?
    Not a sense of right or duty,
    but the sight of peerless worth.

4   Not the crushing of those idols,
    with its bitter void and smart;
    but the beaming of His beauty
    the unveiling of His heart.

5   Who extinguishes their taper
    till they hail the rising sun?
    Who discards the garb of winter
    till the summer has begun?

6   'Tis that look that melted Peter,
    'tis that face that Stephen saw,
    'tis that heart that wept with Mary,
    can alone from idols draw:

7   Draw and win and fill completely,
    till the cup o'erflow the brim;
    what have we to do with idols
    who have companied with Him?

520 Annie Sherwood Hawkes (1835-1918)

1 I need Thee every hour, most gracious
    Lord;
    no tender voice like Thine can peace
    afford.

    I need Thee, oh, I need Thee, every
      hour I need Thee;
    oh, bless me now, my Saviour!
      I come to Thee!

2 I need Thee every hour, stay Thou near
    by;
    temptations lose their power when
      Thou art nigh.

3 I need Thee every hour, in joy or pain;
    come quickly and abide, or life is vain.

4 I need Thee every hour, teach me Thy
    will;
    and Thy rich promises in me fulfil.

5 I need Thee every hour, most Holy One:
    oh, keep me Thine indeed, Thou blessed
    Son!

521 William Pennefather (1816-73)

1 Jesus, stand among us
    in Thy risen power,
    let this time of worship
    be a hallowed hour.

2 Breathe Thy Holy Spirit
    into every heart,
    bid the fears and sorrows
    from each soul depart.

3 Thus with quickened footsteps
    we'll pursue our way,
    watching for the dawning
    of eternal day.

522 Charles Wesley (1707-88)

1 Jesus, lover of my soul,
    let me to Thy bosom fly,
    while the nearer waters roll,
    while the tempest still is high;
    hide me, O my Saviour, hide,
    till the storm of life is past;
    safe into the haven guide;
    oh, receive my soul at last.

2 Other refuge have I none;
    hangs my helpless soul on Thee;
    leave, ah! leave me not alone,
    still support and comfort me.
    All my trust on Thee is stayed;
    all my help from Thee I bring;
    cover my defenceless head
    with the shadow of Thy wing.

3 Thou, O Christ! art all I want:
    more than all in Thee I find;
    raise the fallen, cheer the faint,
    heal the sick and lead the blind.
    Just and holy is Thy name.
    I am all unrighteousness;
    false and full of sin I am,
    Thou art full of truth and grace.

4 Plenteous grace with Thee is found,
    grace to cover all my sin;
    let the healing streams abound,
    make and keep me pure within.
    Thou of life the fountain art,
    freely let me take of Thee;
    spring Thou up within my heart,
    rise to all eternity.

523 Alexander Stewart (1843-1923)

1 Lord Jesus Christ, we seek Thy face;
   within the veil we bow the knee;
   oh, let Thy glory fill the place,
   and bless us while we wait on Thee.

2 We thank Thee for the precious blood
   that purged our sins and brought us nigh;
   all cleansed and sanctified to God,
   Thy holy Name to magnify.

3 Shut in with Thee, far, far above
   the restless world that wars below:
   we seek to learn and prove Thy love,
   Thy wisdom and Thy grace to know.

4 The brow that once with thorns was
      bound,
   Thy hands, Thy side, we fain would see;
   draw near, Lord Jesus, glory crowned,
   and bless us while we wait on Thee.

524 © Timothy Dudley-Smith

1 Lord, for the years Your love has kept
      and guided,
   urged and inspired us, cheered us on
      our way,
   sought us and saved us, pardoned
      and provided,
   Lord of the years, we bring our thanks
   today.

2 Lord, for that Word, the Word of life
      which fires us,
   speaks to our hearts and sets our souls
      ablaze;
   teaches and trains, rebukes us and
      inspires us;
   Lord of the Word, receive Your people's
   praise.

3 Lord, for our land in this our
      generation,
   spirits oppressed by pleasure, wealth
      and care;
   for young and old, for commonwealth
      and nation,
   Lord of our land, be pleased to hear
      our prayer.

4 Lord, for our world; where we disown
      and doubt Him,
   loveless in strength, and comfortless in
      pain;
   hungry and helpless, lost indeed
      without Him:
   Lord of the world, we pray that Christ
      may reign.

5 Lord for ourselves; in living power
      remake us -
   self on the cross and Christ upon the
      throne,
   past put behind us, for the future take
   us,
   Lord of our lives, to live for Christ
   alone.

525 © Michael Saward/Jubilate Hymns

1 Lord of the cross of shame,
   set my cold heart aflame
   with love for You, my Saviour and my
      Master;
   who on that lonely day
   bore all my sins away,
   and saved me from the judgement
      and disaster.

2   Lord of the empty tomb,
    born of a virgin's womb,
    triumphant over death, its power
        defeated;
    how gladly now I sing
    Your praise, my risen King,
    and worship You, in heaven's
        splendour seated.

3   Lord of my life today,
    teach me to live and pray
    as one who knows the joy of sins
        forgiven;
    so may I ever be,
    now and eternally,
    one with my fellow citizens in heaven.

526   Clara Scott (1841-97)

1   Open my eyes that I may see
    glimpses of truth Thou hast for me;
    place in my hands the wonderful key
    that shall unclasp and set me free.

    Silently now I wait for Thee,
    ready, my God, Thy will to see;
    open my eyes, illumine me,
    Spirit divine!

2   Open my ears that I may hear
    voices of truth Thou sendest clear;
    and while the wave-notes fall on my ear,
    everything false will disappear.

3   Open my mouth and let me bear
    tidings of mercy everywhere;
    open my heart and let me prepare
    love with Thy children thus to share.

4   Open my mind, that I may read
    more of Thy love in word and deed:
    what shall I fear while yet Thou dost
        lead?
    Only for light from Thee I plead.

527   James Montgomery (1771-1854)

1   Prayer is the soul's sincere desire,
    uttered or unexpressed!
    The motion of a hidden fire,
    that trembles in the breast.

2   Prayer is the burden of a sigh,
    the falling of a tear,
    the upward glancing of an eye,
    when none but God is near.

3   Prayer is the simplest form of speech
    that infant lips can try;
    prayer, the sublimest strains that reach
    the Majesty on high.

4   Prayer is the Christian's vital breath,
    the Christian's native air,
    his watchword at the gates of death;
    he enters heaven with prayer.

5   The saints in prayer appear as one,
    in word, and deed, and mind;
    while with the Father and the Son,
    sweet fellowship they find.

6   O Thou by Whom we come to God,
    the Life, the Truth, the Way!
    The path of prayer Thyself hast trod,
    Lord, teach us how to pray!

528 Graham Kendrick
© 1988 Make Way Music

Soften my heart, Lord, soften my heart;
from all indifference set me apart;
to feel Your compassion,
to weep with Your tears -
come soften my heart, O Lord,
soften my heart.

529 W W Walford (1772-1850)

1 Sweet hour of prayer, sweet hour of
    prayer,
  that calls me from a world of care
  and bids me at my Father's throne
  make all my wants and wishes known!
  In seasons of distress and grief
  my soul has often found relief,
  and oft escaped the tempter's snare
  by thy return, sweet hour of prayer.

2 Sweet hour of prayer, sweet hour of
    prayer,
  the joy I feel, the bliss I share,
  of those whose anxious spirits burn
  with strong desires for thy return!
  With such I hasten to the place
  where God, my Saviour, shows His face,
  and gladly take my station there,
  and wait for thee, sweet hour of prayer.

3 Sweet hour of prayer, sweet hour of
    prayer,
  thy wings shall my petition bear
  to Him whose truth and faithfulness
  engage the waiting soul to bless;
  and since He bids me seek His face,
  believe His word, and trust His grace,
  I'll cast on Him my every care,
  and wait for thee, sweet hour of prayer.

530 Stuart Hamblen © 1984 Hamblen Music
U.S.A. All Rights Reserved. Reproduced by
kind permission of Carlin Music Corporation.

1 Teach me, Lord, to wait down on my
    knees
  till in Your own good time, You answer
    my pleas,
  teach me not to rely on what others do,
  but to wait in pray'r for an answer from
    You.

  They that wait upon the Lord shall
  renew their strength;
  they shall mount up with wings as
  *   eagles;*
  they shall run, and not be weary;
  they shall walk and not faint.
  Teach me, Lord, teach me, Lord, to
  *   wait.*

2 Teach me, Lord, to wait while hearts are
    aflame,
  let me humble my pride, and call on
    Your name,
  keep my faith renewed, my eyes on
    Thee,
  let me be on this earth what you want
    me to be.

531 Graham Kendrick
© 1988 Make Way Music

1 Who can sound the depths of sorrow
  in the Father heart of God,
  for the children we've rejected,
  for the lives so deeply scarred?
  And each light that we've extinguished
  has bought darkness to our land:
  upon the nation, upon the nation
  have mercy Lord!

2 We have scorned the truth You gave us,
we have bowed to other lords,
we have sacrificed the children
on the altars of our gods.
O let truth again shine on us,
let Your holy fear descend:
upon the nation, upon the nation
have mercy Lord!

MEN

3 Who can stand before Your anger;
who can face Your piercing eyes?
For You love the weak and helpless,
and You hear the victim's cries.

ALL

Yes, You are a God of justice,
and Your judgement surely comes:
upon the nation, upon the nation
have mercy Lord!

WOMEN

4 Who will stand against the violence?
Who will comfort those who mourn?
In an age of cruel rejection,
who will build for love a home?

ALL

Come and shake us into action,
come and melt our hearts of stone:
upon Your people, upon Your people,
have mercy Lord!

5 Who can sound the depths of mercy
in the Father heart of God?
For there is a Man of sorrows
who for sinners shed His blood.
He can heal the wounds of nations,
He can wash the guilty clean:
because of Jesus, because of Jesus,
have mercy Lord!

532 Joseph Medicott Scriven (1819-86)

1 What a Friend we have in Jesus,
all our sins and griefs to bear!
What a privilege to carry
everything to God in prayer!
Oh, what peace we often forfeit,
oh, what needless pain we bear,
all because we do not carry
everything to God in prayer!

2 Have we trials and temptations?
Is there trouble anywhere?
We should never be discouraged;
take it to the Lord in prayer.
Can we find a friend so faithful,
who will all our sorrows share?
Jesus knows our every weakness;
take it to the Lord in prayer.

3 Are we weak and heavy-laden,
cumbered with a load of care?
Precious Saviour, still our refuge,
take it to the Lord in prayer.
Do thy friends despise, forsake thee?
Take it to the Lord in prayer;
in His arms He'll take and shield thee,
thou wilt find a solace there.

8.9   THE CHRISTIAN LIFE
Future Life

533 Isaac Watts (1674-1748)

1 Sweet is the work, my God, my King,
to praise Thy name, give thanks and
sing,
to show Thy love by morning light,
and talk of all Thy truth at night.

2 Sweet is the day of sacred rest,
no mortal cares disturb my breast;
O may my heart in tune be found,
like David's harp of solemn sound.

3 My heart shall triumph in the Lord,
and bless His works, and bless His word;
Thy works of grace, how bright they
  shine,
how deep Thy counsels, how divine!

4 And I shall share a glorious part,
when grace has well refined my heart,
and fresh supplies of joy are shed,
like holy oil, to cheer my head.

5 Then shall I see and hear and know
all I desired or wished below;
and every power find sweet employ
in that eternal world of joy.

534 Carrie E Breck (1855-1934)
© Unidentified

1 Face to face with Christ my Saviour,
face to face: what will it be
when with rapture I behold Him,
Jesus Christ who died for me?

  Face to face shall I behold Him,
  far beyond the starry sky;
  face to face in all His glory,
  I shall see Him by and by!

2 Only faintly now I see Him,
with the darkling veil between,
but a blessed day is coming,
when His glory shall be seen.

3 What rejoicing in His presence,
when are banished grief and pain;
when the crooked ways are straightened
and the dark things shall be plain.

4 Face to face! O blissful moment!
Face to face, to see and know!
Face to face with my Redeemer,
Jesus Christ who loves me so.

535 J Montgomery (1771-1854)

1 For ever with the Lord!
Amen, so let it be;
life from the dead is in that word,
'tis immortality.
Here in the body pent,
absent from Him I roam,
yet nightly pitch my moving tent,
a day's march nearer home.

2 My Father's house on high,
home of my soul; how near
at times to faith's foreseeing eye
Thy golden gates appear:
my thirsty spirit faints
to reach the land I love;
the bright inheritance of saints,
Jerusalem above.

3 For ever with the Lord!
  Father, if 'tis Thy will,
  the promise of that faithful word
  e'en here to me fulfil!
  Be Thou at my right hand,
  then can I never fail;
  uphold Thou me so I shall stand,
  fight, and I must prevail.

4 So, when my latest breath
  shall rend the veil in twain,
  by death I shall escape from death
  and life eternal gain.
  Knowing as I am known,
  how shall I love that word!
  And oft repeat before the throne:
  For ever with the Lord!

536   Eliza Edmunds Hewitt (1851-1920)

1 Sing the wondrous love of Jesus,
  sing His mercy and His grace;
  in the mansions, bright and blessed,
  He'll prepare for us a place.

  When we all get to heaven,
  what a day of rejoicing that will be!
  When all see Jesus,
  we'll sing and shout the victory.

2 While we walk the pilgrim pathway,
  clouds will over-spread the sky;
  but when travelling days are over,
  not a shadow, not a sigh.

3 Let us, then, be true and faithful,
  trusting, serving every day;
  just one glimpse of Him in glory,
  will the toils of life repay.

4 Onward to the prize before us!
  Soon His beauty we'll behold;
  soon the pearly gates will open,
  we shall tread the streets of gold.

537   Mrs A R Cousin (1824-1909)

1 The sands of time are sinking,
  the dawn of heaven breaks;
  the summer morn I've sighed for,
  the fair sweet morn awakes;
  dark, dark hath been the midnight,
  but dayspring is at hand,
  and glory, glory dwelleth
  in Immanuel's land.

2 Oh, Christ, He is the fountain -
  the deep sweet well of love!
  The streams on earth I've tasted,
  more deep I'll drink above;
  there to an ocean fullness
  His mercy doth expand,
  and glory, glory dwelleth
  in Immanuel's land.

3 With mercy and with judgement
  my web of time He wove,
  and aye the dews of sorrow
  were lustred by His love;
  I'll bless the hand that guided,
  I'll bless the heart that planned,
  when throned where glory dwelleth
  in Immanuel's land.

4 The bride eyes not her garment,
  but her dear bridegroom's face;
  I will not gaze at glory
  but on my King of grace,
  not at the crown He giveth,
  but on His pierced hand;
  the Lamb is all the glory
  of Immanuel's land.

5   I've wrestled on towards heaven,
    'gainst storm and wind and tide;
    now like a weary traveller
    that leaneth on his guide,
    amid the shades of evening,
    while sinks life's lingering sand.
    I hail the glory, dawning
    in Immanuel's land.

538   Jim Hill
    © Ben Speer Music/Integrated Copyright
    Group/Admin. by Copycare

1   There is coming a day when no
    heartaches shall come,
    no more clouds in the sky, no more
    tears to dim the eye;
    all is peace forever more on that happy
    golden shore,
    what a day, glorious day that will be!

    What a day that will be when my
    Jesus I shall see,
    and I look upon His face, the One who
    saved me by His grace;
    when He takes me be the hand and
    leads me through the promised Land,
    what a day, glorious day that will be!

2   There'll be no sorrow there, no more
    burdens to bear,
    no more sickness, no pain, no more
    parting over there;
    and for ever I will be with the One who
    died for me
    what a day, glorious day that will be!

539   Ruth Lake © 1972 Scripture in Song, a division
    of Integrity Music/Adm. by Kingsway's
    Thankyou Music

Therefore the redeemed of the Lord shall
    return,
and come with singing unto Zion,
and everlasting joy shall be upon their
    head.
Therefore the redeemed of the Lord shall
    return,
and come with singing unto Zion,
and everlasting joy shall be upon their
    head.

They shall obtain gladness and joy,
and sorrow and mourning shall flee away.
Therefore the redeemed of the Lord shall
    return,
and come with singing unto Zion,
and everlasting joy shall be upon their
    head.

540   Francis Jane van Alstyne (1820-1915)
    (Fanny J Crosby)

1   When my life-work is ended, and I
    cross the swelling tide,
    when the bright and glorious morning
    I shall see;
    I shall know my Redeemer when I
    reach the other side,
    and His smile will be the first to
    welcome me.

    I shall know Him, I shall know Him
    as redeemed by His side I shall stand,
    I shall know Him, I shall know Him
    by the print of the nails in His hand.

2 Oh, the soul-thrilling rapture when I
    view His blessed face,
  and the lustre of His kindly beaming eye;
  how my full heart will praise Him for
    the mercy, love, and grace
  that prepares me for a mansion in the
    sky.

3 Oh, the dear ones in glory, how they
    beckon me to come,
  and our parting at the river I recall;
  to the sweet vales of Eden they will sing
    my welcome home,
  but I long to meet my Saviour first of
    all.

4 Through the gates to the city in a robe
    of spotless white,
  He will lead me where no tears shall ever
    fall;
  in the glad song of ages I shall mingle
    with delight;
  but I long to meet my Saviour first of
    all.

541 Arthur T Pearson (1837-1911)

1 With harps and with viols there stands
    a great throng
  in the presence of Jesus, and sings this
    new song:

  *Unto Him Who hath loved us and
    washed us from sin,
  unto Him be the glory for ever! Amen.*

2 All these once were sinners, defiled in
    His sight;
  now arrayed in pure garments, in praise
    they unite.

3 He maketh the rebel a priest and a king,
  He hath bought us and taught us this
    new song to sing.

4 How helpless and hopeless we sinners
    had been,
  if He never had loved us till cleansed
    from our sin.

5 Aloud in His praises our voices shall
    ring,
  so that others, believing, this new song
    shall sing.

542 Charles Gabriel (1856-1932)
  © Word Music/Admin. by Copycare

1 When all my labours and trials are o'er,
  and I am safe on that beautiful shore,
  just to be near the dear Lord I adore,
  will through the ages be glory for me.

  *Oh, that will be glory for me,
    glory for me, glory for me,
  when by His grace I shall look on
    His face,
  that will be glory, be glory for me.*

2 When, by the gift of His infinite grace,
  I am accorded in heaven a place,
  just to be there, and to look on His face,
  will through the ages be glory for me.

3 Friends will be there I have loved long
    ago;
  joy like a river around me will flow,
  yet, just a smile from my Saviour, I
    know,
  will through the ages be glory for me.

8.10 THE CHRISTIAN LIFE
Aspiration

543 John Newton (1725-1807)

1 Approach, my soul, the mercy-seat,
where Jesus answers prayer;
there humbly fall before His feet,
for none can perish there.

2 Thy promise is my only plea;
with this I venture nigh;
Thou callest burdened souls to Thee,
and such, O Lord, am I.

3 Bowed down beneath a load of sin,
by Satan sorely pressed,
by wars without, and fears within,
I come to Thee for rest.

4 Be Thou my shield and hiding-place,
that, sheltered near Thy side,
I may my fierce accuser face,
and tell Him Thou hast died.

5 Oh, wondrous love! to bleed and die,
to bear the Cross and shame,
that guilty sinners, such as I,
might plead Thy gracious Name.

544 Martin Nystrom
© 1983 Restoration Music Ltd., admin. by
Sovereign Music UK

1 As the deer pants for the water,
so my soul longs after You.
You alone are my heart's desire
and I long to worship You.

*You alone are my strength, my
shield,
to You alone may my spirit yield.
You alone are my heart's desire
and I long to worship You.*

2 I want You more than gold or silver,
only You can satisfy.
You alone are the real joy-giver
and the apple of my eye.

3 You're my Friend and You're my
Brother,
even though You are a king.
I love You more than any other,
so much more than anything.

545 John Daniels
© 1979 Word's Spirit of Praise Music/Admin.
by Copycare

As we are gathered, Jesus is here,
one with each other, Jesus is here;
joined by the Spirit,
washed in His Blood,
part of the Body,
the Church of God.
As we are gathered, Jesus is here,
one with each other, Jesus is here.

546 'A Prayer (Be Thou My Vision)' from THE
POEM BOOK OF THE GAEL. Selected and
Edited by Eleanor Hull.
Published by Chatto & Windus

1 Be Thou my vision, O Lord of my heart;
naught be all else to me, save that Thou
art;
Thou my best thought, by day or by
night,
waking or sleeping, Thy presence my
light.

2   Be Thou my wisdom, Thou my true
      Word;
    I ever with Thee, Thou with me, Lord;
    Thou my great Father, I Thy true son;
    Thou in me dwelling, and I with Thee
      one.

3   Be Thou my battle-shield, sword for
      the fight,
    be Thou my dignity, Thou my delight.
    Thou my soul's shelter, Thou my high
      tower:
    raise Thou me heavenward, O Power
      of my power.

4   Riches I heed not, nor man's empty
      praise,
    Thou mine inheritance, now and
      always:
    Thou and Thou only, first in my heart,
    High King of heaven, my treasure
      Thou art.

5   High King of heaven, after victory won,
    may I reach heaven's joys, O bright
      heaven's Sun!
    Heart of my own heart, whatever befall,
    still be my vision, O ruler of all.

547   T Binney (1798-1874)

1   Eternal Light! Eternal Light!
    How pure the soul must be,
    when, placed within Thy searching sight,
    it shrinks not, but, with calm delight,
    can live, and look on Thee!

2   The spirits that surround Thy throne
    may bear the burning bliss;
    but that is surely theirs alone,
    since they have never, never known
    a fallen world like this.

3   Oh, how shall I, whose native sphere
    is dark, whose mind is dim,
    before the Ineffable appear,
    and on my naked spirit bear
    the uncreated beam?

4   There is a way for man to rise
    to that sublime abode:
    an offering and a sacrifice,
    a Holy Spirit's energies,
    an advocate with God;

5   These, these prepare us for the sight
    of holiness above:
    the sons of ignorance and night
    may dwell in the eternal light,
    through the eternal love!

548   Robert Cameron
          © 1986 Word's Spirit of Praise Music/
          Admin. by Copycare

I want to worship the Lord with all of my
      heart,
give Him my all and not just a part,
lift up my hands to the King of kings,
praise Him in everything.

549   Richard Blanchard
          © Sacred Songs/Word Music/Admin. by
          Copycare

1   Like the woman at the well I was
      seeking
    for things that could not satisfy;
    and then I heard my Saviour speaking:
    "Draw from My well that never shall
      run dry."

Fill my cup, Lord, I lift it up, Lord!
Come and quench this thirsting of
my soul;
Bread of heaven, feed me till I want
no more;
fill my cup, fill it up and make me
whole!

2 There are millions in this world who are
craving
the pleasure earthly things afford;
but none can match the wondrous
treasure
that I find in Jesus Christ my Lord.

3 So, my brother, if the things this world
gave you
leave hungers that won't pass away,
my blessed Lord will come and save
you,
if you kneel to Him and humbly pray:

550 Psalm 63:1-8 (Scottish Psalter)

1 Lord, Thee my God, I'll early seek:
my soul doth thirst for Thee;
my flesh longs in a dry parched land,
wherein no waters be:

2 That I Thy power may behold,
and brightness of Thy face,
as I have seen Thee heretofore
within Thy holy place.

3 Since better is Thy love than life,
my lips Thee praise shall give.
I in Thy name will lift my hands,
and bless Thee while I live.

4 E'en as with marrow and with fat
my soul shall filled be;
then shall my mouth with joyful lips
sing praises unto Thee:

5 When I do Thee upon my bed
remember with delight,
and when on Thee I meditate
in watches of the night.

6 In shadow of Thy wings I'll joy,
for Thou mine help hast been.
My soul Thee follows hard; and me
Thy right hand doth sustain.

551 Kate B Wilkinson (1859-1928)
Copyright Control

1 May the mind of Christ my Saviour
live in me from day to day,
by His love and power controlling
all I do and say.

2 May the word of God dwell richly
in my heart from hour to hour,
so that all may see I triumph
only through His power.

3 May the peace of God my Father
rule my life in everything,
that I may be calm to comfort
sick and sorrowing.

4 May the love of Jesus fill me,
as the waters fill the sea;
Him exalting, self abasing,
this is victory.

5 May I run the race before me,
strong and brave to face the foe,
looking only unto Jesus,
as I onward go.

552 Ray Palmer (1808-1887)

1 My faith looks up to Thee,
   Thou Lamb of Calvary,
   Saviour Divine!
   Now hear me while I pray;
   take all my guilt away;
   oh, let me from this day
   be wholly Thine!

2 May Thy rich grace impart
   strength to my fainting heart,
   my zeal inspire;
   as Thou hast died for me,
   oh, may my love to Thee
   pure, warm, and changeless be,
   a living fire!

3 While life's dark maze I tread,
   and griefs around me spread,
   be Thou my Guide;
   bid darkness turn to day,
   wipe sorrow's tears away,
   nor let me ever stray
   from Thee aside.

4 When ends life's transient dream,
   when death's cold, sullen stream
   shall o'er me roll,
   blest Saviour, then, in love,
   fear and distrust remove,
   oh, bear me safe above,
   a ransomed soul!

553 Sarah Fuller Adams (1805-48)
v6 Arthur Tozer Russell (1806-74)

1 Nearer, my God, to Thee,
   nearer to Thee:
   e'en though it be a cross
   that raiseth me,
   still all my song shall be
   nearer, my God, to Thee,
   nearer, my God, to Thee,
   nearer to Thee.

2 Though, like a wanderer,
   the sun gone down,
   darkness be over me,
   my rest a stone,
   yet in my dreams I'd be
   nearer, my God, to Thee,
   nearer, my God, to Thee,
   nearer to Thee.

3 There let the way appear,
   steps unto heaven;
   all that Thou sendest me,
   in mercy given;
   angels to beckon me
   nearer, my God, to Thee,
   nearer, my God, to Thee,
   nearer to Thee.

4 Then, with my waking thoughts
   bright with Thy praise,
   out of my stony griefs
   Bethel I'll raise;
   so by my woes to be
   nearer, my God, to Thee,
   nearer, my God, to Thee,
   nearer to Thee.

5 Or, if on joyful wing
   cleaving the sky,
   sun, moon, and stars forgot,
   upward I fly,
   still all my song shall be,
   nearer, my God, to Thee,
   nearer, my God, to Thee,
   nearer to Thee.

554 Lelia N Morris
© 1994 C M Alexander's Copyright Trust
Harper Collins Religious/Admin. by Copycare

1 Nearer, still nearer, close to Thy heart,
   draw me, my Saviour, so precious Thou
   art;
   fold me, oh fold me close to Thy breast,
   shelter me safe in that haven of Rest.

2 Nearer, still nearer! Nothing I bring,
   naught as an offering to Jesus, my King,
   only my sinful, now contrite heart;
   grant me the cleansing Thy blood doth
   impart.

3 Nearer, still nearer! Lord to be Thine,
   sin with its follies I gladly resign;
   all of its pleasures, pomp, and its pride;
   give me but Jesus, my Lord crucified.

4 Nearer, still nearer, while life shall last,
   till all its struggles and trials are past;
   then through eternity, ever I'll be
   nearer, my Saviour, still nearer to Thee.

(Repeat the last line of each verse)

555 F Brook
© Unidentified

1 My goal is God Himself, not joy nor
   peace,
   nor even blessing, but Himself, my God:
   'tis His to lead me there, not mine, but
   His
   At any cost, dear Lord, by any road!

2 So faith bounds forward to its goal in
   God,
   and love can trust her Lord to lead her
   there;
   upheld by Him my soul is following
   hard,
   till God has full fulfilled my deepest
   prayer.

3 No matter if the way be sometimes
   dark,
   no matter though the cost be oft-times
   great,
   He knows how I best shall reach the
   mark,
   the way that leads to Him must needs
   be strait.

4 One thing I know, I cannot say Him nay;
   one thing I do, I press toward my Lord:
   my God, my glory here, from day to day,
   and in the glory there my Great Reward.

556 William Cowper (1731-1800)

1 O for a closer walk with God,
   a calm and heavenly frame,
   a light to shine upon the road
   that leads me to the Lamb.

2 Where is the blessedness I knew
   when first I saw the Lord?
   Where is that soul-refreshing view
   of Jesus and His word?

3 What peaceful hours I once enjoyed!
   How sweet their memory still!
   But they have left an aching void
   the world can never fill.

4 Return, O holy Dove! return,
   sweet messenger of rest!
   I hate the sins that made Thee mourn,
   and drove Thee from my breast.

5 The dearest idol I have known,
   whate'er that idol be,
   help me to tear it from Thy throne,
   and worship only Thee.

6 So shall my walk be close with God,
   calm and serene my frame;
   so purer light shall mark the road
   that leads me to the Lamb.

557 Joseph Templeton
        © Unidentified

Oh, for a new anointing,
oh, for a heavenly flame -
oh, for a new anointing,
to glorify Thy Name.
Oh, for sin and self to cease,
oh, for a sense of inward peace,
oh, for Thy glory to increase,
Saviour, anoint me now.

558 Robert Cull
        © 1976 Maranatha! Music/Admin. by Copycare

Open our eyes, Lord,
we want to see Jesus,
to reach out and touch Him
and say that we love Him.
Open our ears, Lord,
and help us to listen:
O open our eyes, Lord,
we want to see Jesus!

559 Chris Bowater
        © 1985 Sovereign Lifestyle Music

Reign in me, sovereign Lord, reign in me,
reign in me, sovereign Lord, reign in me.
Captivate my heart,
let Your kingdom come,
establish there Your throne,
let Your will be done!
Reign in me, sovereign Lord, reign in me,
Reign in me, sovereign Lord, reign in me.

560 E May Grimes (1868-1927)

1 Speak, Lord, in the stillness, while I
   wait on Thee;
   hush my heart to listen in expectancy.

2 Speak, O blessed Master, in this quiet
   hour;
   let me see Thy face, Lord, feel Thy touch
   of power.

3 For the words Thou speakest, they
   are life indeed;
   living bread from heaven, now my
   spirit feed!

4 Satiate my being, with Thy fullness
   fill;
   as the dew descending, let Thy speech
   distil.

5 All to Thee is yielded, I am not mine
   own;
   blissful, glad surrender, I am Thine
   alone.

6 Speak, Thy servant heareth; be not
   silent, Lord!
   Waits my soul upon Thee for the
   quickening word.

7 Fill me with the knowledge of Thy
   glorious will;
   all Thine own good pleasure in Thy
   child fulfil.

8 Like a watered garden full of
   fragrance rare,
   lingering in Thy presence let my life
   appear.

561

Karen Lafferty
© 1972 Maranatha! Music/Admin. by Copycare

1 Seek ye first the kingdom of God
   and His righteousness,
   and all these things shall be added unto
      you.
   Allelu, alleluia.
   Seek ye first . . .

2 Man shall not live by bread alone,
   but by every word
   that proceeds from the mouth of
      God.
   Allelu, alleluia.
   Man shall not live . . .

3 Ask and it shall be given unto you,
   seek and ye shall find;
   knock and the door shall be opened
   unto you.
   Allelu, alleluia.
   Ask and it shall . . .

3 Within the veil, His fragrance
      poured upon thee,
   without the veil, that fragrance
      shed abroad;
   Within the veil, His hand shall
      tune the music
   which sounds on earth the praises
      of thy Lord.

4 Within the veil, thy spirit deeply
   anchored,
   Thou walkest calm above a world of
      strife;
   Within the veil, thy soul with Him
   united,
   shall live on earth His resurrection life.

**9.1   CONSECRATION AND
        HOLINESS**
The Call to Holiness

562

Freda Hanbury Allen (b. 1926)
© Unidentified

1 Within the veil: Be this, beloved
      thy portion
   within the secret of thy Lord to dwell;
   beholding Him, until thy face His glory,
   thy life His love, thy lips His praise
      shall tell.

2 Within the veil, for only as thou
      gazest
   upon the matchless beauty of His face,
   canst thou become a living revelation
   of His great heart of love, His untold
      grace.

563

Charles Wesley (1707-88)

1 All things are possible to him
   that can in Jesus' name believe;
   Lord, I no more Thy name blaspheme,
   Thy truth I lovingly receive.
   I can, I do believe in Thee;
   all things are possible to me.

2 'Twas most impossible of all
   that here sin's reign in me should cease,
   yet shall it be, I know it shall;
   Jesus, I trust Thy faithfulness!
   If nothing is too hard for Thee,
   all things are possible to me.

3 Though earth and hell the Word
gainsay,
the Word of God shall never fail;
the Lord can break sin's iron sway;
'tis certain, though impossible.
The thing impossible shall be.
All things are possible to me.

4 All things are possible to God;
to Christ, the power of God in man;
to me, when I am all renewed,
in Christ am fully formed again,
and from the reign of sin set free,
all things are possible to me.

5 All things are possible to God;
to Christ, the power of God in me;
now shed Thy mighty Self abroad,
let me no longer live, but Thee;
give me this hour in Thee to prove
the sweet omnipotence of love.

564 Lelia N Norris (1862-1929) © Unidentified

1 Called unto holiness, Church of our
God,
purchase of Jesus, redeemed by His
blood;
called from the world and its idols to
flee,
called from the bondage of sin to be free.

"Holiness unto the Lord," is our
watchword and song,
"Holiness unto the Lord," as we're
marching along:
sing it, shout it, loud and long,
"Holiness unto the Lord," now and
for ever.

2 Called unto holiness, children of light,
walking with Jesus in garments of white;
raiment unsullied, nor tarnished with sin,
God's Holy Spirit abiding within.

3 Called unto holiness, praise His dear
name,
this blessed secret to faith now made
plain.
Not our own righteousness, but Christ
within,
living and reigning, and saving from sin.

4 Called unto holiness, glorious thought!
Up from the wilderness wanderings
brought
out from the shadows and darkness of
night
into the Canaan of perfect delight.

5 Called unto holiness, Bride of the
Lamb,
waiting the Bridegroom's returning
again;
lift up your heads, for the day draweth
near
when in His beauty the King shall
appear.

565 Lucy J Rider (1849-1922)

1 Ho, every one that is thirsty in spirit,
ho, every one that is weary and sad;
come to the fountain, there's fullness
in Jesus,
all that you're longing for, come and
be glad.

"*I will pour water on him that is
thirsty,
I will pour floods upon the dry
ground;
open your heart for the gift I am
bringing;
while ye are seeking Me, I will be
found.*"

2   Child of the world, are you tired of
your bondage?
Weary of earth-joys, so false, so
untrue?
Thirsting for God and His fullness of
blessing?
List to the promise, a message for you!

3   Child of the Kingdom, be filled with
the Spirit!
Nothing but fullness thy longing can
meet:
'tis the enduement for life and for
service;
thine is the promise, so certain, so
sweet.

566   E F Miller (1731-1807)

1   O mourner in Zion, how blessed art thou,
for Jesus is waiting to comfort thee now;
fear not to rely on the word of thy God;
*step out on the promise,
step out on the promise,
step out on the promise,
get under the blood.*

2   O ye that are hungry and thirsty, rejoice!
For ye shall be filled; do you hear that
sweet voice,
inviting you now to the banquet of God?
step out ...

3   Who sighs for a heart from iniquity free?
O, poor troubled soul! There's a
promise for thee;
there's rest, weary one, in the bosom
of God;
step out ...

4   The promise can't save, though the
promise is true;
'tis the blood we get under that
cleanses us through;
it cleanses me now, hallelujah to God!
*I rest on the promise,
I rest on the promise,
I rest on the promise,
I'm under the blood.*

567   William Dunn Longstaff (1822-94)

1   Take time to be holy! Speak oft with
thy Lord;
abide in Him always, and feed on His
Word.
Make friends of God's children; help
those who are weak;
forgetting in nothing His blessing to
seek.

2   Take time to be holy; the world rushes
on;
spend much time in secret with Jesus
alone;
by looking to Jesus, like Him thou shalt
be;
thy friends in thy conduct His
likeness shall see.

3 Take time to be holy! Be calm in thy soul;
each thought and each temper beneath
His control,
thus led by His Spirit to fountains of love,
thou soon shalt be fitted for service
above.

568 John George Govan (1861-1927)

1 There's a Saviour from all sin;
if you only let Him in
to your heart, He there will reign,
while you trust Him.
He will put the evil out,
save from every fear and doubt,
and you'll soon begin to shout,
"Hallelujah!"

Hallelujah! Hallelujah!
Jesus is my Saviour King,
He does full salvation bring,
Hallelujah! Hallelujah!
Now with heart and voice I sing
Hallelujah!

2 Jesus is a wondrous name,
now and evermore the same.
He can cleanse from every stain,
only trust Him.
He will fill your soul with joy,
and your talents will employ,
Satan's kingdom to destroy.
Hallelujah!

3 If from every sin you part,
and let Christ have all your heart,
you need fear no fiery dart,
while you trust Him.
For while Jesus reigns within,
you are proof against all sin,
and His perfect peace you win,
Hallelujah!

9.2 CONSECRATION AND HOLINESS
Longings for Holiness

569 Psalm 51 verses 1-7 (Scottish Psalter)

1 After Thy loving-kindness, Lord,
have mercy upon me:
for Thy compassions great, blot out
all mine iniquity.

2 Me cleanse from sin, and throughly wash
from mine iniquity:
for my transgressions I confess;
my sin I ever see.

3 'Gainst Thee, Thee only, have I sinned,
in Thy sight done this ill;
that when Thou speak'st Thou may'st be
just,
and clear in judging still.

4 Behold, I in iniquity
was formed the womb within;
My mother also me conceived
in guiltiness and sin.

5 Behold, Thou in the inward parts
with truth delighted art;
and wisdom Thou shalt make me know
within the hidden part.

6 Do Thou with hyssop sprinkle me,
I shall be cleansed so;
yea, wash Thou me, and then I shall
be whiter than the snow.

570
Edwin Hatch (1835-89)

1 Breathe on me, Breath of God,
fill me with life anew,
that I may love what Thou dost love,
and do what Thou wouldst do.

2 Breathe on me, Breath of God,
until my heart is pure;
until my will is one with Thine
to do and to endure.

3 Breathe on me, Breath of God,
till I am wholly Thine;
until this earthly part of me
glows with Thy fire divine.

4 Breathe on me, Breath of God,
so shall I never die,
but live with Thee the perfect life
of Thine eternity.

571
© Colin N Peckham

1 Before Your holiness I bow,
oh Jesus come and cleanse me now,
oh come and take away my sin,
and purify me deep within.
I grieve, I grieve, this dreadful state
the evil hid within, I hate,
the good I would, but cannot do,
I'm left the evil to pursue.

2 Defiled my very thoughts and mind,
within repulsive sin I find.
How sinful sickness dissipates,
and filthiness makes desolate!
Oh where is there escape for me?
Where can I find His purity?
Oh come Lord Jesus, set me free,
And by Your blood deliver me!

3 Your Word is surely ever true,
and what You promise You will do,
so when You claim to purify
this must be true; God cannot lie.
I come then, Jesus, and I stake
my all upon the Word I take.
It is enough! God's Word to me
will hold throughout eternity.

4 I claim in faith; the prayer prevails,
and as I trust the blood avails.
Sin's power is broken, and I know
my heart is cleansed as white as snow.
The Spirit speaks the Word to me
which gives me glorious liberty.
And all my heart is Yours to fill,
to live for ever in Your will.

572
R Kelso Carter (1849-1928)
© Unidentified

1 Breathe upon us, Lord, from heaven,
fill us with the Holy Ghost;
promise of the Father given,
send us now a Pentecost.

Breathe upon us, breathe upon us,
with Thy love our hearts inspire;
breathe upon us, breathe upon us,
Lord, baptise us now with fire.

2 While the Spirit hovers o'er us,
open all our hearts, we pray;
to Thine image, Lord, restore us,
witness in our souls today.

3 From all sin grant us exemption,
wash us in the cleansing flood;
let us know the full redemption
purchased for us by the blood.

4 Lift us, Lord, oh, lift us higher,
    from the carnal mind set free;
    fill us with refining fire,
    give us perfect liberty.

573   Frances Ridley Havergal (1836-79)

1 Church of God, beloved and chosen,
    church of God for whom Christ died,
    claim thy gifts and praise the Giver!
    Ye are washed and sanctified!
    Sanctified by God the Father,
    and by Jesus Christ His Son,
    and by God the Holy Spirit,
    holy, holy, Three in One.

2 By His will He sanctifieth,
    by the Spirit's power within;
    by the loving hand that chasteneth,
    fruits of righteousness to win;
    by His truth, and by His promise,
    by His word, His gift unpriced,
    by His blood, and by our union
    With the risen life of Christ.

3 Holiness by faith in Jesus.
    Not by effort of thine own,
    sin's dominion crushed and broken,
    by the power of grace alone;
    God's own holiness within thee,
    His own beauty on thy brow,
    this shall be thy pilgrim brightness,
    this thy blessed portion now.

4 He will sanctify thee wholly;
    body, spirit, soul shall be
    blameless till thy Saviour's coming
    in His glorious majesty:
    He hath perfected for ever
    those whom He hath sanctified;
    spotless, glorious and holy
    is the Church, His chosen Bride.

574   Bianco da Siena
tr./arr.: R F Littledale (1833-1890)

1 Come down, O love divine,
    seek Thou this soul of mine
    and visit it with Thine own ardour
     glowing;
    O Comforter, draw near,
    within my heart appear,
    and kindle it, Thy holy flame
     bestowing.

2 O let it freely burn,
    till earthly passions turn
    to dust and ashes in its heat consuming,
    and let Thy glorious light
    shine ever on my sight,
    and clothe me round, the while my path
     illuming.

3 Let holy charity
    mine outward vesture be,
    and lowliness become mine inner
     clothing;
    true lowliness of heart,
    which takes the humbler part,
    and o'er its own shortcomings weeps
     with loathing.

4 And so the yearning strong,
    with which the soul will long,
    shall far outpass the power of human
     telling;
    for none can guess its grace,
    till he become the place
    wherein the Holy Spirit makes His
     dwelling.

575 Charles Wesley (1707-88)

1 Come, Jesus, Lord, with holy fire!
  Come, and my quickened heart inspire,
  cleansed in Thy precious blood.
  Now to my soul Thyself reveal.
  Thy mighty working let me feel,
  since I am born of God,
  since I am born of God,

2 Let nothing now my heart divide;
  since with Thee I am crucified,
  and live to God in Thee.
  Dead to the world and all its toys,
  its idle pomp, and fading joys,
  Jesus my glory be!
  Jesus my glory be!

3 Me with a quenchless thirst inspire,
  a longing infinite desire,
  and fill my craving heart.
  Less than Thyself, oh, do not give,
  in might Thyself within me live,
  come, all Thou hast and art!
  come, all Thou hast and art!

4 My will be swallowed up in Thee,
  light in Thy light still may I see,
  in Thine unclouded face;
  called the full strength of trust to prove,
  let all my quickened heart be love,
  my spotless life be praise,
  my spotless life be praise,

576 Charles Wesley (1707-88)

1 Come, O Thou Traveller unknown,
  whom still I hold, but cannot see!
  My company before is gone,
  and I am left alone with Thee;
  with Thee all night I mean to stay,
  and wrestle till the break of day.

2 I need not tell Thee who I am,
  my misery and sin declare;
  Thyself hast called me by my name;
  look on Thy hands, and read it there:
  but who, I ask Thee, who art Thou?
  Tell me Thy name, and tell me now.

3 In vain Thou strugglest to get free;
  I never will unloose my hold!
  Art Thou the Man that died for me?
  The secret of Thy love unfold:
  wrestling, I will not let Thee go,
  till I Thy name, Thy nature know.

4 Yield to me now; for I am weak,
  but confident in self-despair;
  speak to my heart, in blessings speak,
  be conquered by my instant prayer;
  speak, or Thou never hence shalt move,
  and tell me if Thy name is Love.

5 'Tis love! 'tis love! Thou diedst for
      me!
  I hear Thy whisper in my heart;
  the morning breaks, the shadows flee,
  pure, universal Love Thou art;
  to me, to all, Thy mercies move:
  Thy nature and Thy name is Love.

6 I know Thee, Saviour, who Thou
      art,
  Jesus, the feeble sinner's Friend;
  nor wilt Thou with the night depart,
  but stay and love me to the end;
  Thy mercies never shall remove:
  Thy nature and Thy name is Love.

577 R Hudson Pope © Scripture Gift Mission

Cleanse me from my sin, Lord,
put Thy power within, Lord,
take me as I am, Lord,
and make me all Thine own.
Keep me day by day, Lord,
underneath Thy sway, Lord,
make my heart Thy palace,
and Thy royal throne.

578 Charles Wesley (1707-88)

1 Come, Saviour Jesus, from above,
assist me with Thy heavenly grace,
empty my heart of earthly love,
and for Thyself prepare the place.

2 Oh, let Thy sacred presence fill,
and set my longing spirit free
to have, henceforth, no other will,
but day and night to follow Thee.

3 While in this region here below,
no other good will I pursue;
I bid this world of noise and show,
with all its glittering snares, adieu.

4 Wealth, honour, pleasure, and what else
this short-enduring world can give,
tempt as ye will, my soul repels,
to Christ alone resolved to live.

5 Henceforth let no profane delight
divide this consecrated soul;
possess it Thou, who hast the right,
as Lord and Master of the whole.

6 Thee would I love, and Thee alone,
with pure delight and inward bliss;
to know Thou tak'st me for Thine
own;
oh, what a happiness is this!

579 C Fry (1837-1882)

1 Come, Thou burning Spirit, come!
Lo! we stretch our hands to Thee,
from the Father to the Son,
let us now Thy glory see.

Come, oh come, Great Spirit, come!
Let the mighty deed be done,
satisfy our souls' desire,
see us waiting for the fire,
waiting, waiting,
see us waiting for the fire.

2 On the altar now we lay
soul and body, mind and will;
all the evil passions slay,
come and every corner fill.

3 Now the sacrifice we make,
though as dear as a right eye,
for our blessed Saviour's sake,
who for us did bleed and die.

4 Now, by faith, the gift I claim,
bought for me by blood Divine;
through the all-prevailing Name,
all the promises are mine.

580
Dave Fellingham
© 1983 Kingsway's Thankyou Music

Create in me a clean heart, O God,
and renew a right spirit in me.
Create in me a clean heart, O God,
and renew a right spirit in me.
Wash me, cleanse me, purify me,
make my heart as white as snow.
Create in me a clean heart, O God,
and renew a right spirit in me.

581
James Rowe (d. 1933) © The Rodeheaver Co./
Word Music/Admin. by Copycare

1 Earthly pleasures vainly call me,
   I would be like Jesus;
   nothing worldly shall enthral me,
   I would be like Jesus.

   Be like Jesus, this my song,
   in the home and in the throng;
   be like Jesus, all day long!
   I would be like Jesus.

2 He has broken every fetter,
   I would be like Jesus;
   that my soul may serve Him better,
   I would be like Jesus.

3 All the way from earth to glory,
   I would be like Jesus;
   telling o'er and o'er the story,
   I would be like Jesus.

4 That in heaven He may meet me,
   I would be like Jesus;
   that His words, "Well done", may greet
      me
   I would be like Jesus.

582
Lelia N Morris (1862-1929) © Unidentified

1 For a fresh anointing, Lord, for service
   come we now in Jesus' precious name;
   for the blessed pentecostal fullness,
   every heart with heavenly love aflame.

   Send a new touch of fire on our
   *   souls, Lord.*
   Send it now, Lord. Send it now, Lord.
   Touch our lips today with the living
   *   coals.*
   Send a new touch of fire on our souls.

2 Make us free to tell the gospel story;
   liberty in service may we have,
   showing forth the Saviour's grace and
      glory,
   telling of His wondrous power to save.

3 Bringing all we have in consecration
   as a living sacrifice for Thee;
   trusting for an uttermost salvation,
   Jesus' precious blood our only plea.

4 Let the great Refiner throughly purge us,
   purify our hearts like as by fire;
   while for all the sanctifying fullness
   here our waiting, longing hearts aspire.

583
tr. Frances Bevan (1827-1909)

1 God in heaven hath a treasure,
   riches none may count or tell;
   hath a deep eternal pleasure,
   Christ, the Son, He loveth well.
   God hath here on earth a treasure,
   none but He its price may know,
   deep unfathomable pleasure,
   Christ revealed in saints below.

2 God, in tongues of fire descending,
  chosen vessels thus to fill,
  with the treasure never ending,
  ever spent, unfailing still.
  God's own hand the vessel filling
  from the glory far above,
  longing hearts for ever stilling
  with the riches of His love.

3 Thus though worn, and tried, and
    tempted,
  glorious calling, saint, is thine;
  let the Lord but find thee emptied,
  living branch in Christ the Vine!
  Vessels of the world's despising,
  vessels weak, and poor, and base,
  bearing wealth God's heart is prizing
  glory from Christ's blessed face.

4 Oh to be but emptier, lowlier,
  mean, unnoticed, and unknown,
  and to God a vessel holier,
  filled with Christ and Christ alone!
  Naught of earth to cloud the glory
  naught of self the light to dim,
  telling forth His wondrous story,
  emptied, to be filled with Him.

584 © Colin N Peckham

1 I come, my God, for cleansing, free
  from sin's defiling stains,
  I see, oh God, I weep to see
  the sinfulness corrupting me
  which in my heart remains.

2 I hate my envy and my pride,
  my failure and my sin,
  to think that all these things could hide
  within, where blood had been applied,
  and stay concealed therein.

3 Oh, let me not side-step the cross
  in this my crisis hour,
  excuse so subtly selfish dross,
  and gain my life when death seems
    loss,
  and miss Your path, Your power.

4 I come, Lord Jesus, hear my cry,
  oh cleanse my heart today,
  I come to Calvary to die,
  and with Your death identify,
  this is the only way.

5 I come, I trust, and now I see
  the power of Jesus' blood;
  grace channels in His purity,
  and in Him I find liberty
  and rest and joy in God.

585 Thomas Chisholm (1866-1960)
  © Lillenas Publishing Co./Admin. by Copycare

1 I have one deep, supreme desire,
  that I may be like Jesus.
  To this I fervently aspire,
  that I may be like Jesus.
  I want my heart His throne to be,
  so that a watching world may see
  His likeness shining forth in me.
  I want to be like Jesus.

2 He spent His life in doing good;
  I want to be like Jesus.
  In lowly paths of service trod;
  I want to be like Jesus.
  He sympathised with hearts distressed,
  He spoke the words that cheered and
    blessed,
  He welcomed sinners to His breast.
  I want to be like Jesus.

3 A holy, harmless life He led;
I want to be like Jesus.
The Father's will, His drink and bread;
I want to be like Jesus.
And when at last He comes to die,
"Forgive them, Father," hear Him cry
for those who taunt and crucify.
I want to be like Jesus.

4 O perfect life of Christ, my Lord!
I want to be like Jesus.
My recompense and my reward,
that I may be like Jesus.
His Spirit fill my hungering soul,
His power all my life control.
My deepest prayer, my highest goal,
that I may be like Jesus.

586 vv1, 2, 5 Nicolause Ludwig von Zinzendorf;
vv3, 4 Johann Nitschmann; tr. John Wesley

1 I thirst, Thou wounded Lamb of God,
to wash me in Thy cleansing blood;
to dwell within Thy wounds; then pain
is sweet, and life or death is gain.

2 Take my poor heart, and let it be
for ever closed to all but Thee;
seal Thou my breast, and let me wear
that pledge of love for ever there.

3 How blest are they who still abide
close sheltered in Thy bleeding side!
Who life and strength from thence
derive,
and by Thee move, and in Thee live.

4 What are our works but sin and death,
till Thou Thy quickening Spirit breathe?
Thou givest the power, Thy grace doth
move:
O wondrous grace! O boundless love!

5 Ah, Lord, enlarge our scanty thought
to know the wonders Thou hast
wrought;
unloose our stammering tongues to tell
Thy love immense, unsearchable.

587 George Jackson (1866-93)

1 I want, dear Lord, a heart that's true
and clean;
a sunlit heart, with not a cloud between;
a heart like Thine, a heart divine, a
heart as white as snow;
on me, dear Lord, a heart like this
bestow.

2 I want, dear Lord, a love that feels for
all;
a deep, strong love that answers every
call;
a love like Thine, a love divine, a love
for high and low;
on me, dear Lord, a love like this
bestow.

3 I want, dear Lord, a soul on fire for
Thee;
a soul baptised with heavenly energy,
a willing mind, a ready hand, to do
whate'er I know,
to spread Thy light wherever I may go.

4 I want, dear Lord, a faith that looks to
Thee
to cheer the way when naught but clouds
I see;
a faith sublime, a faith divine, a faith
that will not fail
to trust in Thee and over sin prevail.

5   I want, dear Lord, a hope steadfast and
        sure,
     a hope that holds to things that will
        endure;
     a hope in heaven, a hope in Thee, a
        hope that's bright and clear,
     dispelling doubt and conquering every
        fear.

588   Terry Butler
          © 1991 Mercy/Vineyard Publishing/Music
          Services/Admin. by Copycare

It is the cry of my heart to follow You,
it is the cry of my heart to be close to
   You;
it is the cry of my heart to follow
all of the days of my life.

1   Teach me Your holy ways, O Lord,
     so I can walk in Your truth;
     teach me Your holy ways, O Lord,
     and make me wholly devoted to You.
     Oh, oh, oh, ...

2   Open my eyes so I can see
     the wonderful things that you do,
     open my heart up more and more
     and make it wholly devoted to you.
     Oh, oh, oh, ...

All of the days of my life;
all of the days of my life.

589   E H Stokes (1815-1895)

1   Hover o'er me, Holy Spirit;
     bathe my trembling heart and brow;
     fill me with Thy hallowed presence.
     Come, oh, come and fill me now.

Fill me now, fill me now,
Jesus come and fill me now.
Fill me with Thy hallowed presence,
come, oh, come and fill me now.

2   Thou canst fill me, gracious Spirit,
     though I cannot tell Thee how.
     But I need Thee, greatly need Thee;
     come, oh, come and fill me now.

3   I am weakness, full of weakness.
     At Thy sacred feet I bow;
     blest, divine, eternal Spirit,
     fill with love, and fill me now.

4   Cleanse and comfort, bless and save me;
     bathe, oh, bathe my heart and brow.
     Thou art comforting and saving;
     Thou art sweetly filling now.

590   Joseph L Lyne
          © Unidentified

1   Let me come closer to Thee, Lord
        Jesus,
     oh, closer day by day!
     Let me lean harder on Thee, Lord
        Jesus,
     yes, harder all the way.

2   Let me show forth Thy beauty, Lord
        Jesus,
     like the sunshine on the hills;
     oh, let my lips pour forth Thy sweetness
     in joyous, sparkling rills!

3   Yes, like a fountain, precious Lord
        Jesus,
     make me and let me be;
     keep me and use me daily, Lord Jesus,
     for Thee, for only Thee.

4 In all my heart and will, Lord Jesus,
   be altogether King!
   Make me a loyal subject, Lord Jesus,
   to Thee in everything.

5 Thirsting and hungering for Thee,
   Lord Jesus,
   with blessed hunger here,
   looking for home on Zion's mountain,
   no thirst, no hunger there.

591 Albert Orsborn
© Salvationist Publishing & Supplies/Admin.
by Copycare

Let the beauty of Jesus be seen in me,
all His wondrous compassion and purity:
oh, Thou Spirit divine,
all my nature refine,
till the beauty of Jesus be seen in me.

592 Charles Wesley (1707-88)

1 Lord, I believe a rest remains
   to all Thy people known;
   a rest where pure enjoyment reigns,
   and Thou art loved alone.

2 A rest where all our soul's desire
   is fixed on things above;
   where fear and sin and grief expire,
   cast out by perfect love.

3 Oh that I now the rest might know,
   believe, and enter in;
   now, Saviour, now the power bestow,
   and let me cease from sin.

4 Remove this hardness from my heart,
   this unbelief remove:
   to me the rest of faith impart,
   the Sabbath of Thy love.

5 I would be Thine, Thou knowest I
   would,
   and have Thee all my own;
   Thee, O my all-sufficient Good,
   I want, and Thee alone.

593 J Nicholson (1828-78)

1 Lord Jesus, I long to be perfectly whole,
   I want You for ever to live in my soul:
   break down every idol, cast out every
   foe:
   now wash me, and I shall be whiter
   than snow.
        *Whiter than snow, yes whiter than
        snow;*
        *now wash me and I shall be whiter
        than snow*

2 Lord Jesus, let nothing unholy remain,
   apply Your own blood and extract
   every stain;
   to get this blest cleansing I all things
   forego:
   now wash me, and I shall be whiter
   than snow.

3 Lord Jesus, look down from Your
   throne in the skies,
   and help me to make a complete
   sacrifice;
   I give up myself and whatever I know:
   now wash me, and I shall be whiter
   than snow.

4 Lord Jesus, for this I most humbly
entreat:
I wait, blessed Lord, at Your crucified
feet;
by faith for my cleansing I see Your
blood flow:
now wash me, and I shall be whiter
than snow.

5 Lord Jesus, You see that I patiently
wait;
come now, and within me a clean heart
create:
to those who have sought You , You
never said, No:
now wash me, and I shall be whiter than
snow.

3 Come, Almighty to deliver!
let us all Thy grace receive;
suddenly return, and never,
never more Thy temples leave.
Thee we would be always blessing,
serve Thee as Thy hosts above,
pray, and praise Thee without ceasing,
glory in Thy perfect love.

4 Finish, then, Thy new creation!
pure and spotless let us be:
let us see Thy great salvation,
perfectly restored in Thee!
Changed from glory into glory,
till in heaven we take our place,
till we cast our crowns before Thee,
lost in wonder, love, and praise.

594 Charles Wesley (1707-88)

1 Love Divine, all loves excelling,
joy of heaven, to earth come down!
Fix in us Thy humble dwelling,
all Thy faithful mercies crown.
Jesus! Thou art all compassion,
pure, unbounded love Thou art;
visit us with Thy salvation,
enter every trembling heart.

2 Breathe, oh, breathe Thy loving Spirit
into every troubled breast!
Let us all in Thee inherit,
let us find Thy promised rest;
take away the love of sinning,
Alpha and Omega be;
end of faith, as its beginning,
set our hearts at liberty.

595 E H Hopkins (1818-1901)

1 My Saviour, Thou hast offered rest:
oh! give it, then, to me;
the rest of ceasing from myself,
to find my all in Thee.
This cruel self, oh, how it strives,
and works within my breast,
to come between Thee and my soul,
and keep me back from rest!

2 How many subtle forms it takes
of seeming verity,
as if it were not safe to rest
and venture all on Thee.
O Lord, I seek a holy rest,
a victory over sin!
I seek that Thou alone shouldst reign
o'er all, without, within.

3 In Thy strong hand I lay me down,
so shall the work be done:
for who can work so wondrously
as Thou, Almighty One!
Work on then, Lord, till on my soul
eternal light shall break,
and, in Thy likeness perfected,
I, satisfied, shall wake.

596 Catherine Booth-Clibborn
© Salvationist Publishing & Supplies/Admin.
by Copycare

1 O Lamb of God! Thou wonderful
sin-bearer,
hard after Thee my soul doth follow on;
as pants the hart for streams in desert
dreary,
so pants my soul for Thee, O Thou
life-giving One.

*At Thy feet I fall, yield Thee up my
all,
to suffer, live, or die for my Lord
crucified.*

2 I mourn, I mourn the sin that drove
Thee from me,
and blackest darkness brought into
my soul;
now I renounce the accursed thing
that hindered,
and come once more to Thee, to be
made fully whole.

3 Descend the heavens, Thou whom
my soul adoreth!
Exchange Thy throne for my poor
longing heart;
for Thee, for Thee I watch as for the
morning;
no rest or peace is mine from my
Saviour apart.

4 Come, Holy Ghost, Thy mighty aid
bestowing,
destroy the works of sin, the self,
the pride;
burn, burn in me, my idols overthrowing,
prepare my heart for Him, for my
Lord crucified!

597 Keith Green
© BMG Songs Inc./Birdwing Music/EMI
Christian Music Publishing/Admin. by Copycare

1 O Lord, You're beautiful,
Your face is all I seek;
for when Your eyes are on this child,
Your grace abounds to me.

2 O Lord, please light the fire
that once burned bright and clear;
replace the lamp of my first love
that burns with holy fear!

I want to take Your word and shine it
all around,
but first help me just to live it Lord!
And when I'm doing well,
help me to never seek a crown,
for my reward is giving glory to You.

3 O Lord, You're beautiful,
Your face is all I seek;
for when Your eyes are on this child,
Your grace abounds to me.

598 M D James (1810-83)

1 My spirit, soul, and body,
Jesus, I give to Thee,
a consecrated offering,
Thine evermore to be.

My all is on the altar,
Lord, I am all Thine own;
oh, may my faith ne'er falter!
Lord, keep me Thine alone.

2 O Jesus, mighty Saviour,
   I trust in Thy great name;
   I look for Thy salvation,
   Thy promise now I claim.

3 Now, Lord, I yield my members,
   from sin's dominion free,
   for warfare and for triumph,
   as weapons unto Thee.

4 I'm Thine, O blessed Jesus,
   washed in Thy precious blood,
   sealed by Thy Holy Spirit,
   a sacrifice to God.

599 T O Chisholm (1866-1960) © Unidentified

1 O to be like Thee, blessed Redeemer,
   this is my constant longing and prayer;
   gladly I'll forfeit all of earth's treasures,
   Jesus, Thy perfect likeness to wear.

   O to be like Thee,
   O to be like Thee,
   blessed Redeemer, pure as Thou art;
   come in Thy sweetness,
   come in Thy fullness:
   stamp Thine own image deep on my
   heart.

2 O to be like Thee, full of compassion,
   loving, forgiving, tender and kind,
   helping the helpless, cheering the
   fainting,
   seeking the wandering sinner to find.

3 O to be like Thee, lowly in spirit,
   holy and harmless, patient and brave;
   meekly enduring cruel reproaches,
   willing to suffer, others to save.

4 O to be like Thee, Lord, I am coming,
   now to receive the anointing divine,
   all that I am and have I am bringing,
   Lord, from this moment all shall be
   Thine.

5 O to be like Thee, while I am pleading,
   pour out Thy Spirit, fill with Thy love,
   make me a temple meet for Thy
   dwelling,
   fit me for life and heaven above.

600 Charles Wesley (1707-88)

1 Oh for a heart to praise my God,
   a heart from sin set free,
   a heart that always feels the blood
   so freely shed for me;

2 A heart resigned, submissive, meek,
   my great Redeemer's throne,
   where only Christ is heard to speak,
   where Jesus reigns alone!

3 A humble, lowly, contrite heart,
   believing, true, and clean,
   which neither life nor death can part
   from Him that dwells within:

4 A heart in every thought renewed,
   and filled with love divine,
   perfect, and right, and pure, and good,
   a copy, Lord, of Thine!

5 Thy nature, gracious Lord, impart;
   come quickly from above;
   write Thy new name upon my heart,
   Thy new, best name of Love.

601 J H Watson
© Unidentified

1 Oh, for a life to please my God,
   in every little thing,
   a holy life, that day by day
   to Him will glory bring!

2 A life lived only unto Him,
   no double aim in view,
   the outcome of a Christ-like heart,
   by God made pure and new.

3 A life which Jesus guides alone,
   o'er which He has control!
   A life which others seeing, say
   that Jesus owns the whole.

4 Jesus, complete Thy work in me,
   the work Thou hast begun:
   each day may I grow more like Thee,
   until my race is run.

602 Walter G Smith
© Unidentified

1 One thing I of the Lord desire,
   for all my path hath miry been:
   be it by water or by fire,
   oh, make me clean, oh, make me
   clean!

   So wash me, Thou, without within,
   or purge with fire, if that must be;
   no matter how, if only sin
   die out in me, die out in me.

2 I watch to shun the miry way,
   and staunch the springs of guilty
     thought;
   but, watch and struggle as I may,
   pure I am not, pure I am not.

3 If clearer vision Thou impart,
   grateful and glad my soul shall be,
   but yet to have a purer heart
   is more to me, is more to me.

4 Yea, only as this heart is clean
   may larger vision yet be mine,
   for mirrored in the depths are seen
   the things divine, the things divine.

603 Brian Doerksen
© 1990 Mercy/Vineyard Publishing/Music
Services/Admin. by Copycare

1 Purify my heart,
   let me be as gold and precious silver;
   purify my heart,
   let me be as gold, pure gold.

   Refiner's fire,
   my heart's one desire is to be holy,
   set apart for you, Lord;
   I choose to be holy,
   set apart for you, my Master,
   ready to do your will.

2 Purify my heart,
   cleanse me from within and make me
     holy;
   purify my heart,
   cleanse me from my sin, deep within.

604 F Bottome (1823-94)

1 Search me, O God! my actions try,
   and let my life appear,
   as seen by Thine all-searching eye,
   to mine my ways make clear.

2 Search all my sense, and know my
      heart,
   who only canst make known,
   and let the deep, the hidden part
   to me be fully shown.

3 Throw light into the darkened cells
   where passion reigns within;
   quicken my conscience till it feels
   the loathsomeness of sin.

4 Search all my thoughts, the secret
      springs,
   the motives that control;
   the chambers where polluted things
   hold empire o'er the soul.

5 Search, till Thy fiery glance has cast
   its holy light through all,
   and I by grace am brought at last
   before Thy face to fall.

6 Thus prostrate I shall learn of Thee
   what now I feebly prove,
   that God alone in Christ can be
   unutterable love.

9.3   CONSECRATION AND HOLINESS
Dedication

605   Mary D James (1810-1883)

1 All for Jesus! all for Jesus!
   All my being's ransomed powers;
   all my thoughts and words and doings,
   all my days and all my hours.

2 Let my hands perform His bidding,
   let my feet run in His ways,
   let mine eyes see Jesus only,
   let my lips speak forth His praise.

3 Since my eyes were fixed on Jesus,
   I've lost sight of all beside;
   so enchained my spirit's vision,
   looking at the Crucified.

4 Oh, what wonder! how amazing!
   Jesus, glorious King of kings,
   deigns to call me His beloved,
   lets me rest beneath His wings.

*(Words to be sung at end of each verse
when using tune 605b: vs 1-3 All for Jesus, all for
Jesus + last line of each verse (repeat) v4
Hallelujah! hallelujah! Resting now beneath
His wings (repeat))*

606   © Noel Grant

1 Above thine own ambitions here,
   another voice is sounding clear;
   it is the call of God to thee,
   "Oh, leave thine all and follow Me."

   *Go through with God, thy vows to pay,
   thy life upon the altar lay;
   the Holy Ghost will do the rest,
   and bring to thee God's very best!*

2 The call of God, it is so clear,
   but friendships call, and home is dear;
   ah, lonely was the path He trod;
   then wilt thou not go through with God?

3 So soon Eternal Morn shall dawn,
   how fast the night is hastening on;
   so soon His lovely face to see,
   how sad to empty-handed be!

4 The price is high, severe the test,
   for those who would enjoy God's best;
   surrender all, then take the road,
   with those who will go through with
      God.

607 Judson W Van De Venter
© Harper Collins Religious/Admin. by
Copycare

1 All to Jesus I surrender,
all to Him I freely give;
I will ever love and trust Him,
in His presence daily live.

I surrender all,
I surrender all,
all to Thee, my blessed Saviour,
I surrender all.

2 All to Jesus I surrender,
humbly at His feet I bow;
worldly pleasures all forsaken,
take me, Jesus, take me now.

3 All to Jesus I surrender,
make me, Saviour, wholly Thine;
let me feel the Holy Spirit,
truly know that Thou art mine.

4 All to Jesus I surrender,
Lord, I give myself to Thee;
fill me with Thy love and power,
let Thy blessing fall on me.

5 All to Jesus I surrender,
now I feel the sacred flame;
oh, the joy of full salvation!
Glory, glory to His name!

608 W J Govan (d. 1901)

1 God is for us! Thou hast given,
in Thy love, the gift unpriced,
Thine own Son, Thy well-beloved,
Thou hast given us the Christ!
We are for Thee, at Thy service,
yielding all that Thou dost claim,
heeding not the worldling's scorning,
jealous only for Thy name.

2 Thou art with us, Thou almighty,
through the darkness, through the
strife,
binding up the broken hearted,
crowning with eternal life.
We are with Thee in Thy warfare,
heart and sword be all Thine own:
we are with Thee in Thy triumph,
joy that earth has never known!

3 Thou art in us, in Thy temple,
so our hearts in silence thrill
while we wait to hear the whisper
of the blessed Master's will.
We are in Thee, in the Holiest,
here our prayers and praise ascend;
in Thy secret place abiding,
till the battle din shall end.

609 Ken Chant © 1974 Scripture in Song, a
division of integrity Music/Adm. by
Kingsway's Thankyou Music

Fill my eyes, O my God, with a vision of
the cross,
fill my heart with love for Jesus the
Nazarene,
fill my mouth with Thy praise, let me sing
through endless days, take my will, let my
life be wholly Thine.

610 A A Pollard (1862-1934)
© Harper Collins Religious/Admin. by
Copycare

1 Have Thine own way, Lord, have
Thine own way;
Thou art the potter, I am the clay;
mould me and make me after Thy will,
while I am waiting, yielded and still.

2 Have Thine own way, Lord, have
  Thine own way;
  search me and try me, Master, today.
  Whiter than snow, Lord, wash me just
  now,
  as in Thy presence humbly I bow.

3 Have Thine own way, Lord, have
  Thine own way;
  wounded and weary, help me, I pray.
  Power, all power, surely is Thine;
  touch me and heal me, Saviour divine.

4 Have Thine own way, Lord, have
  Thine own way;
  hold o'er my being absolute sway;
  fill with Thy Spirit till all shall see
  Christ only, always, living in me.

611 George Bennard © The Rodeheaver Co./Word
Music/Admin. by Copycare

Have Thy way, Lord, have Thy way!
This with all my heart I say;
I'll obey Thee, come what may;
Dear Lord, have Thy way!

612 Matt Redman
© 1994 Kingsway's Thankyou Music

1 I will offer up my life in spirit and truth,
  pouring out the oil of love as my
  worship to you.
  In surrender I must give my every part;
  Lord, receive the sacrifice of a broken
  heart.

  Jesus, what can I give,
  what can I bring to so faithful a
  friend,
  to so loving a king?
  Saviour, what can be said,
  what can be sung as a praise of your
  name
  for the things you have done?
  Oh, my words could not tell,
  not even in part,
  of the debt of love that is owed
  by this thankful heart.
  { *What can I give, what can I bring,* }
  { *what can I sing as an offering, Lord?* }

2 You deserve my every breath for you've
  paid the great cost,
  giving up your life to death, even death
  on a cross.
  You took all my shame away, there
  defeated my sin,
  opened up the gates of heaven and have
  beckoned me in.

613 Francis Jane van Alstyne (1820-1915)
(Fanny J Crosby)

1 I am Thine, O Lord; I have heard Thy
  voice,
  and it told Thy love to me;
  but I long to rise in the arms of faith
  and be closer drawn to Thee.

  Draw me nearer, nearer, blessed Lord,
  to the cross where Thou hast died;
  draw me nearer, nearer, nearer,
  blessed Lord,
  to Thy precious, bleeding side.

2 Consecrate me now to Thy service,
    Lord,
  by the power of grace divine;
  let my soul look up with a steadfast
    hope,
  and my will be lost in Thine.

3 Oh, the pure delight of a single hour
  that before Thy throne I spend,
  when I kneel in prayer, and with Thee,
    my God,
  I commune as friend with friend.

4 There are depths of love that I cannot
    know
  till I cross the narrow sea;
  there are heights of joy that I may not
    reach
  till I rest in peace with Thee.

614 Charles Edward Mudie (1818-90)

1 I lift my heart to Thee,
  Saviour divine;
  for Thou art all to me,
  and I am Thine.
  Is there on earth a closer bond than this,
  that my Beloved's mine, and I am His?

2 Thine am I by all ties;
  but chiefly Thine,
  that through Thy sacrifice
  Thou, Lord, art mine.
  By Thine own cords of love so sweetly
    wound
  around me, I to Thee am closely bound.

3 To Thee, Thou bleeding Lamb,
  I all things owe;
  all that I have and am,
  and all I know.
  All that I have is now no longer mine,
  and I am not my own; Lord, I am Thine.

4 How can I, Lord, withhold
  life's brightest hour
  from Thee, or gathered gold,
  or any power?
  Why should I keep one precious thing
    from Thee,
  when Thou hast given Thine own dear
    Self for me?

615 Frances Ridley Havergal (1836-79)

1 In full and glad surrender,
  I give myself to Thee,
  Thine utterly and only
  and evermore to be.

2 O Son of God, who lovest me,
  I will be Thine alone;
  and all I have and am, Lord,
  shall henceforth be Thine own!

3 Reign over me, Lord Jesus,
  O make my heart Thy throne;
  it shall be Thine, dear Saviour,
  it shall be Thine alone.

4 O come and reign, Lord Jesus,
  rule over everything!
  and keep me always loyal
  and true to Thee, my King.

616 G Railton (1849-1913)

1 Jesus, my Saviour King,
  I will be Thine!
  Only to Thee I cling;
  I will be Thine!
  Mine not the worldling's gain,
  mine not his pleasures vain!
  Man's honours I disdain,
  I will be Thine!

2 Let others seek their own,
I will be Thine!
I'll live for Thee alone!
I will be Thine!
Riches and earthly fame,
each mean or selfish aim,
forever I disclaim,
I will be Thine!

3 Whate'er Thou wilt I'll do;
I will be Thine!
Gladly I'll suffer too;
I will be Thine!
Only possess my heart,
bid sin and fear depart.
Oh, let us never part!
I will be Thine!

And whilst Thou shalt smile upon me,
God of wisdom, love, and might,
foes may hate, and friends disown me:
show Thy face and all is bright.

3 Man may trouble and distress me,
'twill but drive me to Thy breast;
life with trials hard may press me,
heaven will bring me sweeter rest.
Oh! 'tis not in grief to harm me,
while Thy love is left to me;
oh! 'twere not in joy to charm me,
were that joy unmixed with Thee.

618 Dave Bryant
© 1978 Kingsway's Thankyou Music

Jesus take me as I am,
I can come no other way.
Take me deeper into You,
make my flesh life melt away.
Make me like a precious stone,
crystal clear and finely honed.
Life of Jesus shining through,
giving glory back to You.

617 Henry Francis Lyte (1793-1847)

1 Jesus, I my cross have taken,
all to leave and follow Thee,
destitute, despised, forsaken,
Thou from hence, my all shalt be.
Perish every fond ambition,
all I've sought, and hoped and known:
yet how rich is my condition!
God and heaven are still my own.

I will follow Thee, my Saviour,
Thou hast shed Thy blood for me;
and though all men should forsake
Thee,
by Thy grace I will follow Thee.

2 Let the world despise and leave me:
they have left my Saviour too -
human hearts and looks deceive me:
Thou art not, like them, untrue.

619 Jenny Evelyn Hussey (1874-1958)
© 1921 Renewed 1949 Hope Publishing/
Admin. by Copycare

1 King of my life I crown Thee now,
Thine shall the glory be;
lest I forget Thy thorn-crowned brow,
lead me to Calvary.

Lest I forget Gethsemane,
lest I forget Thine agony,
lest I forget Thy love for me,
lead me to Calvary.

2 Show me the tomb where Thou wast laid,
   tenderly mourned and wept:
   angels in robes of light arrayed,
   guarded Thee whilst Thou slept.

3 Let me, like Mary, through the gloom,
   come with a gift to Thee;
   show to me now the empty tomb,
   lead me to Calvary.

4 May I be willing, Lord, to bear
   daily my cross for Thee;
   even Thy cup of grief to share,
   Thou hast borne all for me.

5 Fill me, O Lord, with Thy desire
   for all who know not Thee;
   then touch my lips with holy fire,
   to speak of Calvary.

620 Mrs. C.H. Norris (1862-1929)
© Harper Collins Religious/Admin. by Copycare

1 My stubborn will at last hath yielded,
   I would be Thine and Thine alone;
   and this the prayer my lips are bringing,
   Lord, let in me Thy will be done.

   Sweet will of God, still fold me closer,
   till I am wholly lost in Thee;
   sweet will of God, still fold me closer,
   till I am wholly lost in Thee.

2 I'm tired of sin, footsore and weary,
   the darksome path hath dreary grown,
   but now a light has risen to cheer me!
   I find in Thee my Star, my Sun.

3 Thy precious will, O conquering Saviour,
   doth now embrace and compass me;
   all discords hushed, my peace a river,
   my soul, a prisoned bird set free.

4 Shut in with Thee, O Lord, for ever,
   my wayward feet no more to roam;
   what power from Thee my soul can sever?
   The centre of God's will my home.

621 Sylvanus Dryden Phelps (1816-95)

1 Saviour, Thy dying love
   Thou gavest me,
   nor should I aught withhold,
   my Lord, from Thee;
   in love my soul would bow,
   my heart fulfil its vow,
   some offering bring Thee now,
   something for Thee.

2 At the blest mercy-seat
   pleading for me,
   my feeble faith looks up,
   Jesus, to Thee:
   help me the cross to bear,
   Thy wondrous love declare,
   some song to raise, or prayer,
   something for Thee.

3 Give me a faithful heart,
   likeness to Thee,
   that each departing day
   henceforth may see
   some work of love begun,
   some deed of kindness done,
   some wanderer sought and won,
   something for Thee.

4 All that I am and have,
   Thy gifts so free,
   in joy, in grief, through life,
   O Lord, for Thee.
   And when Thy face I see,
   my ransomed soul shall be,
   through all eternity,
   something for Thee.

622 © Unidentified

1 Lord, I make a full surrender,
   all I have I yield to Thee;
   for Thy love so great and tender
   asks the gift of me.

2 Lord, I bring my whole affection,
   claim it, take it for Thine own,
   safely kept by Thy protection,
   fixed on Thee alone.

3 Lord, my will I here present Thee,
   gladly now no longer mine:
   let no evil thing prevent me
   blending it with Thine.

4 Lord, my life I lay before Thee,
   hear, this hour, the sacred vow!
   All Thine own I now restore Thee,
   Thine for ever now.

5 Glory, glory, hallelujah!
   I have given my all to God;
   and I now have full salvation,
   through the precious blood.

(Repeat last two lines of each verse)

623 Frances Ridley Havergal (1836-79)

1 Take my life and let it be
   consecrated, Lord, to Thee;
   take my moments and my days,
   let them flow in ceaseless praise.

2 Take my hands, and let them move
   at the impulse of Thy love;
   take my feet, and let them be
   swift and beautiful for Thee.

3 Take my voice, and let me sing
   always, only, for my King;
   take my lips, and let them be
   filled with messages from Thee.

4 Take my silver and my gold,
   not a mite would I withhold;
   take my intellect, and use
   every power as Thou shalt choose.

5 Take my will, and make it Thine!
   It shall be no longer mine;
   take my heart, it is Thine own,
   it shall be Thy royal throne.

6 Take my love; my Lord, I pour
   at Thy feet its treasure-store!
   Take myself, and I will be
   ever, only, all for Thee!

624 Frances Ridley Havergal (1836-79)

1 Thy life was given for me,
   Thy blood, O Lord, was shed,
   that I might ransomed be,
   and quickened from the dead:
   Thy life, Thy life was given for me;
   what have I given for Thee?

2 Thy Father's home of light,
  Thy rainbow-circled throne,
  were left for earthly night,
  for wanderings sad and lone;
  yea, all, yea, all was left for me;
  have I left aught for Thee?

3 Thou, Lord, hast borne for me
  more than my tongue can tell
  of bitterest agony,
  to rescue me from hell;
  Thou sufferedst all for me, for me;
  what have I borne for Thee?

4 Oh, let my life be given,
  my years for Thee be spent;
  world-fetters all be riven,
  and joy with suffering blent.
  To Thee, to Thee my all I bring,
  my Saviour and my King!

  (Repeat last two lines of each verse)

625 Homer W Grime
© Unidentified

1 What shall I give Thee, Master?
  Thou who did'st die for me.
  Shall I give less of what I possess,
  or shall I give all to Thee?

  Jesus, my Lord and Saviour,
  Thou hast given all for me;
  Thou did'st leave Thy home above
  to die on Calvary.
  What shall I give Thee, Master?
  Thou hast given all for me;
  Not just a part or half of my heart,
  I will give all to Thee.

2 What shall I give Thee, Master?
  Thou hast redeemed my soul;
  my gift is small but it is my all
  surrendered to Thy control.

3 What shall I give Thee, Master?
  Giver of gifts divine!
  I will not hold time, talents or gold
  for everything shall be Thine.

**9.4   CONSECRATION AND
       HOLINESS:**
       Appropriation

626 T Ryder © Unidentified

1 Buried with Christ, and raised with
    Him too;
  what is there left for me to do?
  Simply to cease from struggling and
    strife,
  simply to walk in newness of life.
  Glory be to God.

2 Risen with Christ, my glorious Head,
  holiness now the pathway I tread,
  beautiful thought, while walking therein;
  He that is dead is freed from sin.
  Glory be to God.

3 Living with Christ, who dieth no more,
  following Christ, who goeth before;
  I am from bondage utterly freed,
  reckoning self as dead indeed.
  Glory be to God.

4 Living for Christ, my members I yield,
  servants to God, for evermore sealed,
  not under law, I'm now under grace,
  sin is dethroned and Christ takes its
    place.
  Glory be to God.

5 Growing in Christ; no more shall be
  named
  things of which now I'm truly ashamed,
  fruit unto holiness will I bear,
  life evermore, the end I shall share.
  Glory be to God.

627 Charles Wesley (1707-88)

1 Jesus, Thine all-victorious love
  shed in my soul abroad;
  then shall my heart no longer rove,
  rooted and fixed in God,
  rooted and fixed in God.

2 Oh, that in me the sacred fire
  might now begin to glow,
  burn up the dross of base desire
  and make the mountains flow,
  and make the mountains flow!

3 Oh, that it now from heaven might
  fall,
  and all my sins consume!
  Come, Holy Ghost, for Thee I call;
  Spirit of burning, come,
  Spirit of burning, come!

4 Refining fire, go through my heart,
  illuminate my soul;
  scatter Thy life through every part,
  and sanctify the whole,
  and sanctify the whole.

5 My steadfast soul, from falling free,
  shall then no longer move;
  while Christ is all the world to me,
  and all my heart is love,
  and all my heart is love.

628 G M Irons (1855-1928)
© Unidentified

1 Drawn to the Cross which Thou hast
  blest,
  with healing gifts for souls distressed,
  to find in Thee my life, my rest,
  Christ crucified, I come.

2 Weary of selfishness and pride,
  false pleasures gone, vain hopes denied,
  deep in Thy wounds my shame to hide,
  Christ crucified, I come.

3 Wash me, and take away each stain,
  let nothing of my sin remain;
  for cleansing, though it be through pain,
  Christ crucified, I come.

4 A life of labour, prayers and love,
  which shall my heart's conversion prove,
  till to a glorious rest above,
  Christ crucified, I come.

5 To share with Thee Thy life divine,
  Thy righteousness, Thy likeness mine,
  since Thou hast made my nature Thine,
  Christ crucified, I come.

6 To be what Thou woulds't have me be,
  accepted, sanctified in Thee,
  through what Thy grace shall work in me,
  Christ crucified, I come.

629 H H Booth (1862-1926)

1 From every stain made clean,
  from every sin set free;
  oh, blessed Lord, this is the gift
  that Thou hast promised me.
  And pressing through the past
  of failure, fault, and fear,
  before Thy cross my all I cast,
  and dare to leave it there.

2 From Thee I would not hide
my sin because of fear
what men may think; I hate my pride,
and as I am appear.
Just as I am, O Lord,
not what I'm thought to be;
just as I am, a struggling soul
for life and liberty.

3 While in Thy light I stand,
my heart, I seem to see,
has failed to take from Thine own hand
the gifts it offers me.
O Lord, Thy plenteous grace,
Thy wisdom and Thy power,
I here proclaim before Thy face,
can keep me every hour.

4 Upon the altar here
I lay my treasure down;
I only want to have Thee near,
King of my heart to crown.
The fire doth surely burn
my every selfish claim;
and while from them to Thee I turn,
I trust in Thy great name.

5 A heart by blood made clean,
in every wish and thought;
a heart that by God's power has been
into subjection brought;
to walk, to weep, to sing,
within the light of heaven;
this is the blessing, Saviour, King,
that Thou to me hast given!

630   W MacDonald (1820-1901)

1 I am coming to the cross,
I am poor and weak and blind;
I am counting all but dross;
I shall full salvation find.

I am trusting, Lord, in Thee,
blessed Lamb of Calvary;
humbly at Thy cross I bow:
Jesus saves me, saves me now.

2 Long my heart has sighed for Thee,
long has evil reigned within;
Jesus sweetly speaks to me:
"I will cleanse you from all sin."

3 Here I give my all to Thee,
friends and time and earthly store,
soul and body, Thine to be,
wholly Thine for evermore.

4 In the promises I trust,
now I know the blood applied;
I am prostrate in the dust,
I with Christ am crucified.

5 Jesus comes! He fills my soul!
Perfected in Him I am:
I am every whit made whole:
Glory, glory to the Lamb!

631   A B Simpson (1843-1919)

1 I clasp the hand of Love divine,
I claim the gracious promise mine,
and add to His my countersign,
I take, He undertakes.

I take Thee, blessed Lord,
I give myself to Thee,
and Thou, according to Thy word,
dost undertake for me.

2 I take salvation full and free,
through Him who gave His life for me,
He undertakes my All to be,
I take, He undertakes.

3 I take Him as my holiness,
  my spirit's spotless heavenly dress,
  I take the Lord my Righteousness,
  I take, He undertakes.

4 I take the promised Holy Ghost,
  I take the power of Pentecost,
  to fill me to the uttermost,
  I take, He undertakes.

5 I take Him for this mortal frame,
  I take my healing through His name,
  and all His risen life I claim,
  I take, He undertakes.

6 I simply take Him at His word,
  I praise Him that my prayer is heard,
  and claim my answer from the Lord,
  I take, He undertakes.

632 Herbert H Booth (1862-1926)

1 Lord, through the blood of the Lamb
    that was slain,
  cleansing for me, cleansing for me;
  from all the guilt of my sins now I claim
  cleansing from Thee, cleansing from
    Thee.
  Sinful and black though the past may
    have been,
  many the crushing defeats I have seen,
  yet on Thy promise, O Lord, now I lean,
  cleansing for me, cleansing for me.

2 From all the sins over which I have wept,
  cleansing for me, cleansing for me.
  Far, far away, by the blood-current
    swept,
  cleansing for me, cleansing for me.

Jesus, Thy promise I dare to believe,
and as I come Thou dost now me receive,
that over sin I may never more grieve,
cleansing for me, cleansing for me.

3 From all the doubts that have filled
    me with gloom,
  cleansing for me, cleansing for me.
  From all the fears that would point me
    to doom,
  cleansing for me, cleansing for me.
  Jesus, although I may not understand,
  in childlike faith now I put forth my
    hand,
  and through Thy word and Thy grace
    I shall stand,
  cleansed by Thee, cleansed by Thee.

4 From all the care of what men think or
    say,
  cleansing for me, cleansing for me.
  From ever fearing to speak, sing, or pray,
  cleansing for me, cleansing for me.
  Lord, in Thy love and Thy power make
    me strong,
  that all may know that to Thee I belong;
  when I am tempted, let this be my song:
  cleansing for me, cleansing for me.

633 © Colin N Peckham

1 Never later than this day
  now, my God, Thy power display.
  Now, oh cleanse by Jesus' blood,
  set me free to live for God.
  Vain the worldling's fleeting joys,
  vain his pomp, his power, his poise.
  Lord, I come again to Thee,
  Christ my present Saviour be.

2   Now my longing soul, Lord, fill,
    now restore to do Thy will,
    desperate, Lord, I fall on Thee,
    now my God, deliver me.
    Perish every vain desire,
    burn with pure, celestial fire,
    Holy Ghost Thy promise prove,
    fill me now with perfect love.

3   On Thy Word my stand I take,
    Thou dost cleanse for Jesus sake!
    Thou the mighty work must do,
    to Thy promises be true.
    Now the blood doth sanctify,
    now with Christ I gladly die,
    now the Holy Ghost doth purge,
    now, through all, His life doth surge.

4   Lord, the wonder of this hour,
    God hath come in mighty power,
    sinful fetters broken lie,
    God by grace hath brought me nigh.
    What redemption, Lord, I find!
    God possessing heart and mind.
    Thou, oh Lord, dost set me free,
    all my life I yield to Thee.

634   H E Govan (1866-1932)
          © The Faith Mission

1   O Father of Jesus, exalted on high,
    in sense of our need would we humbly
       draw nigh,
    low down in Thy presence ourselves
       would abase,
    and open our hearts to the inflow of
       grace.

    *Here find Thy rest, Saviour most
       blest!*
    *By Thy Holy Spirit, come, dwell in
       each breast!*

2   Our Father in heaven, by Thy Spirit,
       we pray,
    come, inwardly strengthen Thy
       servants to day!
    Let Christ, in His love, make our hearts
       His abode,
    that we may be filled with the fullness
       of God!

3   Thy love, in its length and its breadth
       and its height,
    its infinite depth and its measureless
       might,
    how feebly we know, and how poorly
       display!
    Oh, shed it abroad in us fully to-day!

4   Our prayer it is large, and our quest it
       is deep,
    yet surely Thy promise of grace Thou
       wilt keep.
    Exceeding abundantly, past all we pray,
    our need Thou canst meet if we trust
       and obey.

635   Phoebe Palmer (1807-1887)

1   Oh, now I see the cleansing wave,
    the fountain deep and wide;
    Jesus, my Lord, mighty to save,
    points to His wounded side.

    The cleansing stream I see, I see!
    I plunge, and oh, it cleanseth me!
    Oh, praise the Lord! it cleanseth me.
    It cleanseth me, yes, cleanseth me.

2   I see the new creation rise;
    I hear the speaking blood!
    It speaks! polluted nature dies!
    Sinks 'neath the cleansing flood.

3 I rise to walk in heaven's own light,
above the world and sin,
with heart made pure and garments
white,
and Christ enthroned within.

4 Amazing grace! 'tis heaven below
to feel the blood applied;
and Jesus, only Jesus know,
my Jesus crucified.

636 H E Govan (1866-1932)
© The Faith Mission

1 Saviour, my sin-stained soul
longs to be fully whole
and all Thy great salvation see.
Haste I to Calvary's flow
that washes white as snow,
Thy blood, so freely shed for me.

2 Long have I vainly tried
to stem back nature's tide
that, surging up, defiles my days.
Foul, helpless, all undone,
hope in myself is none:
yet bring me forth to sing Thy praise!

3 Lord, I Thy word believe
that I in Thee shall live
if I but truly die with Thee.
Make Thou me pure in heart,
grant me the better part
secured by Thine own blood for me.

4 Henceforth Thy life is mine
and I am wholly Thine,
my members under Thy control;
kept every day and hour,
held by Thy mighty power,
Thine while eternal ages roll.

637 Frances Ridley Havergal (1836-79)

1 I am trusting Thee, Lord Jesus,
trusting only Thee!
Trusting Thee for full salvation,
great and free.

2 I am trusting Thee for pardon,
at Thy feet I bow;
for Thy grace and tender mercy,
trusting now.

3 I am trusting Thee for cleansing,
in the crimson flood;
trusting Thee to make me holy,
by Thy blood.

4 I am trusting Thee to guide me,
Thou alone shalt lead;
every day and hour supplying
all my need.

5 I am trusting Thee for power,
Thine can never fail;
words which Thou Thyself shalt give
me,
must prevail.

6 I am trusting Thee, Lord Jesus,
never let me fall!
I am trusting Thee for ever,
and for all.

638 Mrs Louisa M R Stead (1852-1917)

1 'Tis so sweet to trust in Jesus,
just to take Him at His word,
just to rest upon His promise,
just to know, "Thus saith the Lord."

Jesus, Jesus, how I trust Him;
how I've proved Him o'er and o'er,
Jesus, Jesus, precious Jesus!
O for grace to trust Him more.

2 O how sweet to trust in Jesus,
   just to trust His cleansing blood;
   just in simple faith to plunge me,
   'neath the healing, cleansing flood.

3 Yes, 'tis sweet to trust in Jesus,
   just from sin and self to cease;
   just from Jesus simply taking
   life and rest and joy and peace.

4 I'm so glad I learned to trust Thee,
   precious Jesus, Saviour, Friend;
   and I know that Thou art with me,
   wilt be with me to the end.

639 H B Beagle
© Unidentified

1 Wash me, O Lamb of God,
   wash me from sin!
   By Thine atoning blood,
   oh, make me clean!
   Purge me from every stain,
   let me Thine image gain,
   in love and mercy reign
   o'er all within.

2 Wash me, O Lamb of God,
   wash me from sin!
   I long to be like Thee,
   all pure within.
   Now let the crimson tide,
   shed from Thy wounded side,
   be to my heart applied,
   and make me clean.

3 Wash me, O Lamb of God,
   wash me from sin!
   I will not, cannot, rest
   till pure within.
   All human skill is vain,
   but Thou canst cleanse each stain
   till not a spot remain,
   made wholly clean.

4 Wash me, O Lamb of God,
   wash me from sin!
   By faith Thy cleansing blood
   now makes me clean.
   So near art Thou to me,
   so sweet my rest in Thee,
   oh, blessed purity,
   saved, saved from sin!

5 Wash me, O Lamb of God,
   wash me from sin!
   Thou, while I trust in Thee,
   wilt keep me clean.
   Each day to Thee I bring
   heart, life, yea, everything;
   saved, while to Thee I cling,
   saved from all sin!

640 Charles Wesley (1707-88)

1 When shall Thy love constrain
   and draw me to Thy breast?
   When shall my soul return again
   to her eternal rest?

2 To rescue me from woe
   Thou didst with all things part,
   didst lead a suffering life below
   to win my worthless heart.

3 Thy condescending grace
   to me did freely move;
   it calls me now to seek Thy face,
   and stoops to ask my love.

4 And can I yet delay,
my little all to give,
to tear my soul from earth away
for Jesus to receive?

5 Nay, but I yield, I yield!
I can hold out no more!
I sink, by dying love compelled,
and own Thee conqueror.

6 My own desire be this -
Thy love alone to know;
to seek and taste no other bliss,
no other good below!

9.5 CONSECRATION AND HOLINESS
Exultation

641 Gary Garrett © 1980 Scripture in Song a division of Integrity Music/Admin. by Kingsway's Thankyou Music

There is none holy as the Lord,
there is none beside Thee;
neither is there any rock like our God,
there is none holy as the Lord.

642 Eliza Edmunds Hewitt (1851-1920)

1 Abundant salvation through Jesus I
know;
rich streams of refreshing from Calvary
flow;
believing His word, with rejoicing I see
the fountain of blessing is flowing for
me!
flowing for me, for me;
the fountain of blessing is flowing for
me.

2 Alive evermore, He's a Saviour
indeed,
His fullness surpassing my uttermost
need;
His bounty is royal, exceeding my plea;
the fountain of blessing is flowing for
me!

3 There's strength in temptation, the
victory to gain;
there's sunshine in darkness and
comfort in pain;
this plenteous redemption in Jesus
is free;
the fountain of blessing is flowing for
me!

4 The brightening waves of the river of
peace
and joy, fresh and sparkling, find
happy increase:
all honour and glory, dear Saviour to
Thee!
the fountain of blessing is flowing for
me!

643 F Bottome (1823-1894)

1 Beneath the glorious throne above,
the crystal fountain springing,
a river full of life and love,
is joy and gladness bringing.

O fount of cleansing! flowing free,
that fount is open wide to me,
to me, to me, 'tis open wide to me.

2 Through all my soul its waters flow,
through all my nature stealing;
and deep within my heart I know
the consciousness of healing.

3 The barren wastes are fruitful lands,
the desert blooms with roses;
and He, the glory of all lands,
His lovely face discloses.

4 My sun no more goes down by day,
my moon no more is waning;
my feet run swift the shining way,
the heavenly portals gaining.

644 Freda Hanbury Allen (b. 1926)
© Unidentified

1 From the heart whose cup o'erfloweth,
from the crowned life,
from the souls made more than
   conquerors
in the midst of strife,
rises one glad "Hallelujah"
to the King of love,
as a fragrance sweet ascending
to His throne above.

   Praise to Thee who hast redeemed us,
   O all-glorious King!
   Now and through the endless ages
   shall Thy praises ring,
   shall Thy praises ring,
   shall Thy praises ring.
   Now and through the endless ages
   shall Thy praises ring.

2 Praise for all the full deliverance
of Thy wondrous Cross,
where to death our life we yielded,
that most blessed loss.
Praise for that deep, boundless ocean
of the life in Thee,
and the anointing of Thy Spirit
which hath set us free.

3 Praise for all Thy grace untasted
lying yet before,
and the things past understanding
Thou hast kept in store.
Praise for life within the Holiest
even now begun,
for the radiance pure and holy
of the unsetting Sun.

4 But past all the bliss Thou sheddest
on the yielded heart,
we would praise Thee and adore Thee,
Lord, for what Thou art.
Evermore in lowly worship
bending at Thy feet,
till within the gates of glory
face to face we meet.

645 F Bottome (1823-94)

1 Full Salvation! full Salvation!
lo! the fountain opened wide
streams through every land and nation
from the Saviour's wounded side.
Full Salvation! Full Salvation!
Full Salvation! Full Salvation!
streams an endless crimson tide.

2 Oh, the glorious revelation!
see the cleansing current flow,
washing stains of condemnation
whiter than the driven snow!
Full Salvation!
oh! the rapturous bliss to know!

3 Love's resistless current sweeping
all the regions deep within;
thought and wish and senses keeping
now, and every instant, clean.
Full Salvation!
from the guilt and power of sin.

4 Life immortal, heaven descending,
lo! my heart the Spirit's shrine!
God and man in oneness blending,
oh, what fellowship is mine!
Full Salvation!
raised in Christ to life divine!

5 Care and doubting, gloomy sorrow,
fear and grief are mine no more;
faith knows naught of dark tomorrow
for my Saviour goes before.
Full Salvation!
full and free for evermore.

646 Eugene M Bartlett
© 1967 Albert E Brumley & Sons/Integrated
Copyright Group/Admin. by Copycare

1 I heard an old, old story,
how a Saviour came from glory,
how He gave His life on Calvary
to save a wretch like me.
I heard about His groaning,
of His precious blood's atoning.
Then I repented of my sins and won
the victory.

Oh, victory in Jesus, my Saviour,
forever!
He sought me and bought me with
His redeeming blood.
He loved me ere I knew Him,
and all my love is due Him.
He plunged me to victory beneath
the cleansing flood.

2 I heard about His healing,
of His cleansing power revealing,
how He made the lame to walk again
and caused the blind to see.
And then I cried, "Dear Jesus,
come and heal my broken spirit;"
and somehow Jesus came and brought
to me the victory.

3 I heard about a mansion
He has built for me in glory,
and I heard about the streets of gold
beyond the crystal sea;
about the angels singing,
and the old redemption story.
And some sweet day I'll sing up there
the song of victory.

647 J Parker
© Unidentified

1 I'm more than conqueror through His
blood,
Jesus saves me now;
I rest beneath the shield of God,
Jesus saves me now;
I go a kingdom to obtain,
I shall through Him the victory gain,
Jesus saves me now.

2 Before the battle lines are spread,
before the boasting foe is dead,
I win the fight though not begun,
I'll trust and shout, still marching on,
Jesus saves me now.

3 I'll ask no more that I may see,
His promise is enough for me,
though foes be strong and walls be high,
I'll shout, He gives the victory,
Jesus saves me now.

4 Why should I ask a sign from God?
Can I not trust the precious blood?
Strong in His word I meet the foe,
and shouting, win without a blow,
Jesus saves me now.

5 Should Satan come like 'whelming
    waves,
  ere trials crush, my Father saves,
  He hides me till the storm is past,
  for me He tempers every blast,
  Jesus saves me now.

648   Frances Ridley Havergal (1836-79)

1 Live out Thy life within me,
  O Jesus, King of kings!
  Be Thou Thyself the answer
  to all my questionings.
  Live out Thy life within me,
  in all things have Thy way!
  I, the transparent medium,
  Thy glory to display.

2 The temple has been yielded
  and purified of sin;
  let Thy shekinah glory
  now flash forth from within.
  And all the earth keep silence,
  the body henceforth be
  Thy silent, docile servant,
  moved only as by Thee.

3 Its members every moment
  held subject to Thy call,
  ready to have Thee use them,
  or not be used at all.
  Held without restless longing,
  or strain or stress or fret,
  or chafings at Thy dealings,
  or thoughts of vain regret.

4 Kept restful, calm, and pliant,
  from bond and bias free,
  permitting Thee to settle
  when Thou hast need of me.

Live out Thy life within me,
O Jesus, King of kings!
Be Thou the glorious answer
to all my questionings.

649   F A Blackmer (1855-1930) © Unidentified

1 Once I thought I walked with Jesus,
  yet such changeful feelings had:
  sometimes trusting, sometimes
  doubting,
  sometimes joyful, sometimes sad.

    Oh, what peace my Saviour gives,
    peace I never knew before!
    How my way has brighter grown,
    since I learned to trust Him more.

2 For He called me closer to Him,
  bade my doubting, fearing cease
  and, when I had fully yielded,
  filled my soul with perfect peace.

3 Now I'm trusting every moment,
  nothing less can be enough;
  and my Saviour bears me gently,
  o'er the places once so rough.

4 Day by day my soul He's keeping,
  by His wondrous power within;
  and my heart is full of singing
  to my Saviour from all sin.

650   Haldor Lillenas
© Lillenas Publishing Co./Admin. by Copycare

1 Once I was bound by sin's galling
    fetters;
  chained like a slave, I struggled in vain.
  But I received a glorious freedom
  when Jesus broke my fetters in twain.

*Glorious freedom! Wonderful
    freedom!
No more in chains of sin I repine!
Jesus, the glorious emancipator!
Now and forever He shall be mine.*

2 Freedom from all the carnal affections;
    freedom from envy, hatred, and strife;
    freedom from vain and worldly
      ambitions;
    freedom from all that saddened my life.

3 Freedom from pride and all sinful
      follies;
    freedom from love and glitter of gold;
    freedom from evil temper and anger,
    glorious freedom, rapture untold!

4 Freedom from fear with all of its
      torments,
    freedom from care with all of its pain;
    freedom in Christ, my blessed
      Redeemer,
    He who has rent my fetters in twain.

651 Lelia N Morris (1862-1929)
    © Nazarene Publishing/Admin. by Copycare

1 The Saviour has come in His mighty
      power
    and spoken peace to my soul,
    and all of my life from that very hour
    I've yielded to His control,
    I've yielded to His control.

    *Wonderful, wonderful,
    marvellous and wonderful,
    what He has done for my soul!
    the half has never been told;
    oh, it is wonderful,
    it is marvellous and wonderful,
    what Jesus has done for this soul of
      mine!
    the half has never been told!*

2 From glory to glory He leads me on,
    from grace to grace every day,
    and brighter and brighter the glory
      dawns
    while pressing my homeward way,
    while pressing my homeward way.

3 If fellowship here with my Lord can be
    so inexpressibly sweet,
    O what will it be when His face we see,
    when round the white throne we meet,
    when round the white throne we meet.

652 W A Ogden (1841-77)

1 'Tis the grandest theme through the
      ages rung;
    'tis the grandest theme for a mortal
      tongue,
    'tis the grandest theme that the world
      e'er sung,
    our God is able to deliver thee.

    *He is able to deliver thee!
    He is able to deliver thee!
    Though by sin oppressed,
    go to Him for rest;
    our God is able to deliver thee.*

2 'Tis the grandest theme in the earth or
      main,
    'tis the grandest theme for a mortal
      strain,
    'tis the grandest theme, tell the world
      again,
    our God is able to deliver thee.

3 'Tis the grandest theme, let the tidings
      roll,
    to the guilty heart, to the sinful soul,
    look to God in faith, He will make
      thee whole,
    our God is able to deliver thee.

10   REVIVAL

653 James L. Black (1856-1938)
© Hope Publishing/Admin. by Copycare

1   God is here, and that to bless us
    with the Spirit's quickening power;
    see, the cloud already bending,
    waits to drop the grateful shower.

    Let it come, O Lord, we pray Thee,
    let the shower of blessing fall;
    we are waiting, we are waiting,
    oh, revive the hearts of all.

2   God is here! We feel His presence
    in this consecrated place:
    but we need the soul refreshing
    of His free, unbounded grace.

3   God is here! Oh, then, believing,
    bring to Him our one desire,
    that His love may now be kindled,
    till its flame each heart inspire.

4   Saviour, grant the prayer we offer,
    while in simple faith we bow!
    From the windows of Thy mercy
    pour us out a blessing now.

654 Jennie Garnett
Copyright Control

1   Here in Thy name we are gathered,
    come and revive us, O Lord;
    "There shall be showers of blessing,"
    Thou hast declared in Thy Word.

    Oh, graciously hear us,
    graciously hear us, we pray;
    pour from Thy windows upon us
    showers of blessing to-day.

2   Oh! that the showers of blessing
    now on our souls may descend,
    while at the footstool of mercy
    pleading Thy promise we bend.

3   "There shall be showers of blessing,"
    promise that never can fail;
    Thou wilt regard our petition;
    surely our faith will prevail.

4   Showers of blessing, we need them,
    showers of blessing from Thee;
    showers of blessing, oh, grant them!
    Thine all the glory shall be.

655 Francis Jane van Alstyne (1820-1915)
(Fanny J Crosby)

1   Here from the world we turn,
    Jesus to seek;
    here may His loving voice
    graciously speak!
    Jesus, our dearest friend,
    while at Thy feet we bend
    oh, let Thy smile descend!
    'Tis Thee we seek.

2   Come, Holy Comforter,
    presence divine,
    now in our longing hearts
    gloriously shine!
    Oh, for Thy mighty power!
    Oh, for a blessed shower,
    filling this hallowed hour
    with joy divine!

3 Saviour, Thy work revive!
   Here may we see
   those who are dead in sin
   quickened by Thee;
   come, to our heart's delight,
   make every burden light,
   cheer Thou our waiting sight,
   we long for Thee.

656 Elizabeth Codner (1824-1919)

1 Lord, I hear of showers of blessing
   Thou art scattering full and free,
   showers the thirsty land refreshing,
   let some drops descend on me,
   even me, even me,
   let some drops descend on me.

2 Pass me not, O God, my Father,
   sinful though my heart may be!
   Thou might'st leave me, but the rather
   let Thy mercy light on me,
   even me, even me,
   let Thy mercy light on me.

3 Pass me not, O tender Saviour!
   Let me love and cling to Thee.
   I am longing for Thy favour;
   whilst Thou'rt calling, oh, call me,
   even me, even me,
   whilst Thou'rt calling, oh call me.

4 Pass me not, O mighty Spirit!
   Thou canst make the blind to see:
   witnesser of Jesus' merit,
   speak the word of power to me,
   even me, even me,
   speak the word of power to me.

5 Love of God, so pure and changeless,
   blood of Christ, so rich and free;
   grace of God, so rich and boundless,
   magnify it all in me,
   even me, even me,
   magnify it all in me.

657 Elizabeth A P Head (1850-1936)
        © Unidentified

1 Oh! Breath of Life, come sweeping
      through us,
   revive Thy Church with life and power;
   oh! Breath of Life, come, cleanse,
      renew us,
   and fit Thy Church to meet this hour.

2 Oh! Wind of God, come bend us,
      break us,
   till humbly we confess our need;
   then in Thy tenderness remake us,
   revive, restore; for this we plead.

3 Oh! Breath of Love, come breathe
      within us,
   renewing thought and will and heart;
   come, Love of Christ, afresh to win us,
   revive Thy Church in every part.

4 Revive us, Lord! Is zeal abating
   while harvest fields are vast and white?
   Revive us, Lord, the world is waiting,
   equip Thy Church to spread the light.

658 Graham Kendrick
        © 1987 Make Way Music

1 O Lord, the clouds are gathering,
      the fire of judgement burns.
   How we have fallen!
   O Lord, You stand appalled to see
   Your laws of love so scorned
   and lives so broken.

MEN	Have mercy, Lord,
WOMEN	have mercy, lord.
MEN	Forgive us, Lord,
WOMEN	forgive us, Lord.
ALL	Restore us, Lord;
	revive Your church again.
MEN	Let justice flow,
WOMEN	let justice flow,
MEN	like rivers,
WOMEN	like rivers;
ALL	and righteousness like a
	never-failing stream.

2   O Lord, over the nations now, where
      is the dove of peace?
    Her wings are broken,
    O Lord, while precious children
      starve, the tools of war increase,
    their bread is stolen.

3   O Lord, dark powers are poised to
      flood our streets with hate and fear.
    We must awaken!
    O Lord, let love reclaim the lives that
      sin would sweep away,
    and let Your kingdom come!

4   Yet, O Lord, Your glorious Cross shall
      tower triumphant in this land,
    evil confounding;
    through the fire, Your suffering church
      display the glories of her Christ,
    praises resounding.

*(After last chorus sing) a never
failing stream.*

659 Graham Kendrick
        © 1981 Kingsway's Thankyou Music

1   Restore, O Lord, the honour of Your
      name!

In works of sovereign power come
   shake the earth again,
that men may see,
and come with reverent fear to the
   Living God,
whose Kingdom shall outlast the years.

2   Restore, O Lord, in all the earth Your
      fame,
    and in our time revive the Church
      that bears Your name,
    and in Your anger,
    Lord, remember mercy, O Living God,
    whose mercy shall outlast the years.

3   Bend us, O Lord, where we are hard
      and cold,
    in Your refiner's fire;
    come purify the gold:
    though suffering comes,
    and evil crouches near, still our Living
      God
    is reigning, He is reigning here.

660 Francis Jane van Alstyne (1820-1915)
        (Fanny J Crosby)

1   Revive Thy work, O Lord!
    Thy mighty arm make bare!
    Speak with the voice that wakes the
      dead,
    and make Thy people hear!

    Revive Thy work, O Lord;
    give Pentecostal showers;
    be Thine the glory, Thine alone!
    The blessing, Lord, be ours.

2   Revive Thy work, O Lord!
    Disturb this sleep of death;
    quicken the smouldering embers now
    by Thine almighty breath.

3 Revive Thy work, O Lord!
Create soul-thirst for Thee;
and hungering for the bread of life,
oh, may our spirits be!

4 Revive Thy work, O Lord!
And bless to all Thy word!
Oh, may its pure and sacred truth
in living faith be heard!

5 Revive Thy work, O Lord!
Exalt Thy precious name:
and by the Holy Ghost, our love
for Thee and Thine inflame.

661 J Edwin Orr
© Maranatha! Music/Admin. by Copycare

1 Search me, O God, and know my heart
today;
try me, O Lord, and know my thoughts
I pray:
see if there be some wicked way in me,
cleanse me from every sin and set me
free.

2 I praise Thee, Lord, for cleansing me
from sin;
fulfil Thy word, and make me pure
within;
fill me with fire, where once I burned
with shame,
grant my desire to magnify Thy name.

3 Lord, take my life, and make it wholly
Thine;
fill my poor heart with Thy great love
divine;
take all my will, my passion, self and
pride;
I now surrender: Lord, in me abide.

4 O Holy Ghost, revival comes from Thee;
send a revival, start the work in me:
Thy word declares Thou wilt supply
our need;
for blessing now, O Lord, I humbly
plead.

662 Charles Wesley (1707-88)

1 See how great a flame aspires,
kindled by a spark of grace!
Jesus' love the nations fires,
sets the kingdoms on a blaze.
To bring fire on earth He came;
kindled in some hearts it is;
O that all might catch the flame,
all partake the glorious bliss!

2 When He first the work begun,
small and feeble was His day;
now the word doth swiftly run,
now it wins its widening way;
more and more it spreads and grows
ever mighty to prevail;
sin's strongholds it now o'erthrows,
shakes the trembling gates of hell.

3 Sons of God, your Saviour praise!
He the door hath opened wide;
He hath given the word of grace,
Jesus' word is glorified;
Jesus, mighty to redeem,
He alone the work hath wrought;
worthy is the work of Him,
Him who spake a world from nought.

4   Saw ye not the cloud arise,
    little as a human hand?
    Now it spreads along the skies,
    hangs o'er all the thirsty land:
    lo! the promise of a shower
    drops already from above;
    but the Lord will shortly pour
    all the Spirit of His love!

663   Graham Kendrick
          © 1987 Make Way Music

1   Lord, the light of Your love is shining,
    in the midst of the darkness, shining:
    Jesus, Light of the world, shine upon us;
    set us free by the truth You now bring
      us -
    shine on me, shine on me.

    Shine, Jesus, shine,
    fill this land with the Father's glory;
    blaze, Spirit, blaze,
    set our hearts on fire.
    Flow river, flow,
    flood the nations with grace and
      mercy;
    send forth Your word, Lord, and let
      there be light!

2   Lord, I come to Your awesome
      presence,
    from the shadows into Your radiance;
    by Your blood I may enter Your
      brightness:
    search me, try me, consume all my
      darkness;
    shine on me, shine on me.

3   As we gaze on Your kingly brightness
    so our faces display Your likeness,
    ever changing from glory to glory:
    mirrored here, may our lives tell Your
      story;
    shine on me, shine on me.

664   © Unidentified

Send it this way, Lord, humbly we pray!
A mighty revival, send it this way!
Remove every hindrance, my spirit set
      free,
that I in revival Thy channel may be.

Coming this way, yes, coming this way,
a mighty revival is coming this way!
Keep on believing, trust and obey;
a mighty revival is coming this way.

665   © Colin N Peckham

1   Send the flood-tides of Thy blessing!
    Pour exhaustless draughts of grace;
    in the spate of heavenly glory
    oh, my God, spare me a place.
    Come around us, o'er us, on us,
    fill our souls with holy fire,
    come in glory, stand among us!
    Oh my soul, to God aspire!

2   Cleanse! Thou mighty flood-tide -
      cleanse me
    purer than the driven snow!
    Oh the precious blood doth reach me,
    His blest cleansing now I know!
    God is here in matchless splendour,
    gone the glory of earth's sun,
    blinded by the vision glorious,
    Lord in me, Thy will be done.

3 Hallelujah! Glory! Glory!
God in majesty doth sweep,
gushing forth a mighty torrent,
o'er land and sea His power doth leap.
Oh Thou victor - ride in triumph!
Blood-bought riches Thou must claim,
on till we with hosts of glory
swell fore'er Thy mighty fame!

666 D W Whittle (1840-1901)

1 There shall be showers of blessing:
this is the promise of love;
there shall be seasons refreshing,
sent from the Saviour above.

   Showers of blessing,
   showers of blessing we need;
   mercy drops round us are falling,
   but for the showers we plead.

2 There shall be showers of blessing,
precious reviving again;
over the hills and the valleys,
sound of abundance of rain.

3 There shall be showers of blessing:
Send them upon us, O Lord!
Grant to us now a refreshing;
come, and now honour Thy Word.

4 There shall be showers of blessing,
oh, that to-day they might fall,
now, as to God we're confessing,
now as on Jesus we call!

5 There shall be showers of blessing,
if we but trust and obey;
there shall be seasons refreshing,
if we let God have His way.

667 W. Leslie © Unidentified

1 Under the burdens of guilt and care,
many a spirit is grieving,
who in the joy of the Lord might
share,
life everlasting receiving.

   Life! life! eternal life!
   Jesus alone is the Giver!
   Life! life! abundant life!
   Glory to Jesus for ever!

2 Burdened one, why will you longer bear
sorrows from which He releases?
Open your heart, and, rejoicing, share
life more abundant in Jesus!

3 Leaving the mountain, the streamlet
grows,
flooding the vale with a river;
so, from the hill of the Cross, there flows
life more abundant for ever.

4 Oh, for the floods on the thirsty land!
Oh, for a mighty revival!
Oh, for a sanctified fearless band,
ready to hail its arrival!

668 H E Govan (1866-1932)
© The Faith Mission

1 Visit us, Lord, with revival!
Stricken with coldness and death,
where is our hope of survival
save in Thy life-giving breath?

   Lord, send us revival!
   Let it begin now in me!
   Gladly dethroning each rival,
   yield I my heart unto Thee.

2 The world, in its proud exultation,
   lust of the flesh and the eye,
   bent on the soul's desecration,
   God and His people defy.

3 Turning aside into byways,
   letting their ardour grow cold,
   many are leaving the highways
   trod by our fathers of old.

4 Oh, for the breath of the Spirit!
   Oh, for the might of His sword,
   leading us on to inherit
   all that in Jesus is stored!

5 Surely 'tis time for revival;
   surely soon dawneth the day;
   soon shall we hail its arrival,
   chasing the shadows away!

669 Psalm 126 (Scottish Psalter)

1 When Sion's bondage God turned back,
   as men that dreamed were we.
   Then filled with laughter was our mouth,
   our tongue with melody.

2 They 'mong the heathen said, The Lord
   great things for them hath wrought.
   The Lord hath done great things for us,
   whence joy to us is brought.

3 As streams of water in the south,
   our bondage, Lord, recall.
   Who sow in tears, a reaping time
   of joy enjoy they shall.

4 That man who, bearing precious seed,
   in going forth doth mourn,
   He doubtless, bringing back his sheaves,
   rejoicing shall return.

670 H Tee © Singspiration Music/Brentwood Benson Music Publishing Inc./Admin. by Copycare

1 They were gathered in an upper
     chamber,
   as commanded by the risen Lord,
   and the promise of the Father
   there they sought with one accord,
   when the Holy Ghost from heaven
     descended
   like a rushing wind and tongues of fire:
   so dear Lord, we seek Thy blessing,
   come with glory now our hearts
   inspire.

   Let the fire fall, let the fire fall,
   let the fire from heaven fall;
   we are waiting and expecting,
   now in faith, dear Lord, we call;
   let the fire fall, let the fire fall,
   on Thy promise we depend;
   from the glory of Thy presence
   let the Pentecostal fire descend.

2 As Elijah we would raise the altar
   for our testimony clear and true,
   Christ the Saviour, loving Healer,
   coming Lord, Baptizer too,
   ever flowing grace and full salvation,
   for a ruined race Thy love has planned;
   for this blessed revelation,
   for Thy written word we dare to stand.

3 'Tis the covenanted promise given
   to as many as the Lord shall call,
   to the fathers and their children,
   to Thy people, one and all;
   so rejoicing in Thy word unfailing,
   we draw nigh in faith Thy power to
     know -
   come, O come, Thou burning Spirit,
   set our hearts with heavenly fire
   aglow.

4 With a living coal from off Thy altar
touch our lips to swell Thy wondrous
   praise,
to extol Thee, bless, adore Thee,
and our songs of worship raise;
let the cloud of glory now descending
fill our hearts with holy ecstasy,
come in all Thy glorious fullness,
blessed Holy Spirit, have Thy way.

11   CHRISTIAN SERVICE

671 Graham Kendrick
         © 1993 Make Way Music

1 Beauty for brokenness,
hope for despair,
Lord, in your suffering world,
this is our prayer:
bread for the children,
justice, joy, peace,
sunrise to sunset
your kingdom increase.

2 Shelter for fragile lives,
cures for their ills,
work for the craftsmen,
trade for their skills;
land for the dispossessed,
rights for the weak,
voices to plead the cause
of those who can't speak.
   God of the poor,
   Friend of the weak,
   give us compassion we pray;
   melt our cold hearts,
   let tears fall like rain,
   come change our love from a spark to
      a flame

3 Refuge from cruel wars,
havens from fear,
cities for sanctuary,
freedoms to share;
peace to the killing fields,
scorched earth to green,
Christ for the bitterness,
His cross for the pain.
God of the poor ...

4 Rest for the ravaged earth,
oceans and streams,
plundered and poisoned,
our future, our dreams.
Lord, end our madness,
carelessness, greed,
make us content with
the things that we need.
God of the poor ...

5 Lighten our darkness,
breathe on this flame
until your justice burns
brightly again;
until the nations
learn of your ways,
seek your salvation
and bring you their praise.
God of the poor ...

672 Frank Houghton (1894-1972)
         © OMF International

1 Facing a task unfinished,
that drives us to our knees,
a need that, undiminished,
rebukes our slothful ease.
We who rejoice to know Thee,
renew before Thy throne
the solemn pledge we owe Thee,
to go and make Thee known.

2 Where other lords beside Thee
hold their unhindered sway,
where forces that defied Thee
defy Thee still today,
with none to heed their crying
for life, and love, and light,
unnumbered souls are dying,
and pass into the night.

3 We bear the torch that, flaming,
fell from the hands of those
who gave their lives, proclaiming
that Jesus died and rose.
Ours is the same commission,
the same glad message ours,
fired by the same ambition,
to Thee we yield our powers.

4 O Father who sustained them,
O Spirit who inspired,
Saviour, whose love constrained them
to toil with zeal untired.
From cowardice defend us,
from lethargy awake!
Forth on Thine errands send us
to labour for Thy sake.

673 James McGranahan (1840-1907)

1 Far, far away in heathen darkness
dwelling,
millions of souls for ever may be lost;
who, who will go, salvation's story
telling,
looking to Jesus, counting not the cost?

"All power is given unto Me!
All power is given unto Me!
Go ye into all the world and preach
the gospel;
and, lo, I am with you alway."

2 See o'er the world, wide open doors
inviting:
soldiers of Christ, arise and enter in!
Christians, awake! your forces all
uniting,
send forth the gospel, break the chains
of sin.

3 "Why will ye die?" the voice of God is
calling;
"Why will ye die?" re-echo in His
Name:
Jesus hath died to save from death
appalling;
life and salvation, therefore, go
proclaim.

4 God speed the day when those of
every nation,
"Glory to God!" triumphantly shall sing;
ransomed, redeemed, rejoicing in
salvation,
shout, "Hallelujah, for the Lord is King!"

674 Edward Henry Bickersteth (1825-1906)

1 "For My sake and the gospel's, go
and tell redemption's story";
His heralds answer, "Be it so,
and Thine, Lord, all the glory!"
They preach His birth, His life, His
Cross,
the love of His atonement,
for whom they count the world but loss,
His Easter, His enthronement.

2 Hark, hark, the trump of jubilee
  proclaims to every nation,
  from pole to pole, by land and sea,
  glad tidings of salvation.
  As nearer draws the day of doom,
  while still the battle rages,
  the heavenly day-spring, through the
    gloom,
  breaks on the night of ages.

3 Still on and on the anthems spread
  of hallelujah voices,
  in concert with the holy dead
  the warrior church rejoices;
  their snow-white robes are washed in
    blood,
  their golden harps are ringing;
  earth and the paradise of God
  one triumph song are singing.

4 He comes, whose advent trumpet
    drowns
  the last of time's evangels;
  Emmanuel crowned with many crowns,
  the Lord of saints and angels:
  O Life, Light, Love, the great I AM,
  triune, who changest never;
  the throne of God and of the Lamb
  is Thine, and Thine for ever!

675 Unidentified
tr. Frances Bevan (1827-1909)

1 From the brightness of the glory,
  "Go ye forth," He said:
  "Heal the sick and cleanse the lepers,
  raise the dead.

2 "Freely give I thee the treasure,
  freely give the same;
  take no store of gold or silver
  take my Name.

3 "Thou art fitted for the journey,
  how so long it be:
  Thou shalt come, unworn, unwearied,
  back to Me.

4 "Thou shalt tell Me in the glory
  all that thou hast done,
  setting forth alone, returning
  not alone.

5 "Thou shalt bring the ransomed with
    thee,
  they with songs shall come
  as the golden sheaves of harvest,
  gathered home."

676 Horatius Bonar (1808-89)

1 Go, labour on, spend, and be spent,
  thy joy to do the Father's will;
  it is the way the Master went,
  should not the servant tread it still?

2 Go, labour on; 'tis not for nought,
  thy earthly loss is heavenly gain;
  men heed thee, love thee, praise thee not,
  the Master praises, what are men?

3 Men die in darkness at your side,
  without a hope to cheer the tomb:
  take up the torch, and wave it wide,
  the torch that lights time's thickest
    gloom.

4 Toil on, and in thy toil rejoice,
  for toil comes rest, for exile home;
  soon shalt thou hear the Bridegroom's
    voice,
  the midnight peal, "Behold, I come!"

677 John W Peterson
© John Peterson Company/Admin. by Copycare

1 Give me a vision, Lord, I plead,
   vision of souls and a world in need:
   loved ones and friends, the one next
        door,
   then let me see there are millions more.

   Give me a vision,
   heart-stirring vision,
   open my eyes, Lord, today;
   show me the sighing,
   doomed and the dying,
   give me a vision, I pray.

2 Give me a vision, Lord divine,
   kindle with fire this cold heart of mine;
   may with unselfishness it burn,
   fill me with love and a deep concern.

3 Give me a vision, Lord divine,
   so charged with power that it shall shine
   out to the lost in deepest night,
   wandering alone in their sad, sad plight.

4 Give me a vision, Lord divine,
   without a limit or boundary line;
   help me to see a world in sin,
   not just the field I am working in.

678 Charles Wesley (1707-88)

1 Give me the faith that can remove
   and sink the mountain to a plain:
   give me the child-like praying love
   which longs to build Thy house again:
   Thy love let it my heart o'erpower,
   and all my yearning soul devour!

2 I would the precious time redeem,
   and longer live for this alone,
   to spend and to be spent for them
   who have not yet my Saviour known;
   and turn them to a pardoning God,
   and quench the brands in Jesus' blood.

3 My talents, gifts, and graces, Lord,
   into Thy blessed hands receive;
   and let me live to preach Thy word;
   and let me to Thy glory live;
   my every sacred moment spend
   in publishing the sinners' friend.

4 Enlarge, inflame, and fill my heart
   with boundless charity divine!
   So shall I all my strength exert,
   and love them with a zeal like Thine;
   and lead them to Thy open side,
   the sheep for whom their Shepherd died.

679 J E Seddon (1915-83)
© Mrs M Seddon/Jubilate Hymns

1 Go forth and tell! O Church of God,
        awake!
   God's saving news to all the nations
        take:
   proclaim Christ Jesus, Saviour, Lord
        and King,
   that all the world His worthy praise may
        sing.

2 Go forth and tell! God's love embraces
        all;
   He will in grace respond to all who call:
   how shall they call if they have never
        heard
   the gracious invitation of His word?

3 Go forth and tell! men still in darkness lie;
in wealth or want, in sin they live and die:
give us, O Lord, concern of heart and mind,
a love like Yours which cares for all mankind.

4 Go forth and tell! the doors are open wide:
share God's good gifts - let no one be denied;
live out your life as Christ your Lord shall choose,
Your ransomed powers for His sole glory use.

5 Go forth and tell! O church of God, arise!
Go in the strength which Christ your Lord supplies;
go till all nations His great name adore
and serve Him, Lord and King for evermore.

680 Carol Owens
© 1972 Bud John Songs/EMI Christian Publishing/Admin. by Copycare

1 God forgave my sin in Jesus' name;
I've been born again in Jesus' name,
and in Jesus' name I come to you
to share His love as He told me to.

He said:
"Freely, freely you have received,
freely, freely give;
go in My name and because you believe,
others will know that I live."

2 All power is given in Jesus' name
in earth and heaven in Jesus' name;
and in Jesus' name I come to you
to share His power as He told me to.

681 Alexcenah Thomas (b. 19th c)

1 Hark! 'tis the Shepherd's voice I hear,
out in the desert dark and drear,
calling the lambs who've gone astray,
far from the Shepherd's fold away.

Bring them in, bring them in,
bring them in from the fields of sin;
bring them in, bring them in,
bring the wandering ones to Jesus.

2 Who'll go and help this Shepherd kind,
help Him the wandering lambs to find?
Who'll bring the lost ones to the fold,
where they'll be sheltered from the cold?

3 Out in the desert hear their cry;
out on the mountains wild and high;
hark! 'tis the Master speaks to thee,
"Go, find My lambs, where'er they be."

682 George Bennard
© The Rodeheaver Co./Word Music/Admin. by Copycare

1 Hear the Lord of harvest sweetly calling,
"Who will go and work for Me to-day?
Who will bring to Me the lost and dying?
Who will point them to the narrow way?"

Speak, my Lord, speak to me,
Speak, and I'll be quick to answer
Thee;
Speak, my Lord, speak to me,
Speak, and I will answer, "Lord,
send me."

2 When the coal of fire touched the
   prophet,
   making him as pure, as pure can be,
   when the voice of God said, "Who'll go
   for us?"
   then he answered, "Here I am, send me."

3 Millions now in sin and shame are
   dying;
   listen to their sad and bitter cry;
   hasten, brother, hasten to the rescue;
   quickly answer, "Master, here am I."

4 Soon the time for reaping will be over;
   soon we'll gather for the harvest-home;
   may the Lord of harvest smile upon us,
   may we hear His blessed, "Child, well
   done!"

683   Mary Bazeley
         © Unidentified

1 Help me to hear, as Jesus heard,
   cries of the lost and lonely;
   help me to live, as Jesus lived,
   having one purpose only;
   help me to see, as Jesus saw,
   multitudes faint and dying;
   help me to pray, to give, to go,
   but always on Him relying!

2 Help me to love, as Jesus loved,
   all of my heart outpouring;
   help me to feel, as Jesus felt,
   always the cost ignoring.
   Help me to do, as Jesus did,
   spend myself without measure,
   finding in Him a full reward,
   since He is my only treasure.

3 Help me to seek, as Jesus sought,
   hearts that are cold and dreary;
   help me to bring, as Jesus brought,
   comfort to all the weary;
   living to manifest His grace,
   telling the old, old story,
   kept in His fellowship divine,
   yes, all the way home to glory!

684   Chris Bowater
         © 1981 Sovereign Lifestyle Music

Here I am, wholly available:
as for me, I will serve the Lord.

1 The fields are white unto harvest
   but oh, the labourers are so few;
   so Lord I give myself to help the
   reaping,
   to gather precious souls unto You.

2 The time is right in the nation
   for works of power and authority;
   God's looking for a people who are
   willing
   to be counted in His glorious victory.

3 As salt are we ready to savour,
   in darkness are we ready to be light?
   God's seeking out a very special people
   to manifest His truth and His might.

685 M E Maxwell
© Harper Collins Religious/Admin. by Copycare

1 How I praise Thee, precious Saviour,
that Thy love laid hold of me!
Thou hast saved, and cleansed, and
filled me,
that I may Thy channel be.

Channels only, blessed Master,
yet, with all Thy wondrous power
flowing through us, Thou canst use us
every day and every hour.

2 Emptied that Thou shouldest fill me,
a clean vessel in Thine hand,
with no power but as Thou givest,
graciously, with each command.

3 Witnessing Thy power to save me,
setting free from self and sin;
Thou who bought'st me to possess me,
in Thy fullness, Lord, come in.

4 Just a channel full of blessing,
to the thirsty hearts around;
to tell out Thy full salvation,
all Thy loving message sound.

5 Jesus, fill now with Thy Spirit
hearts that full surrender know,
that the streams of living water
from our inner man may flow.

686 © Timothy Dudley Smith

1 "How shall they hear," who have not
heard
news of a Lord who loved and came;
nor known His reconciling word,
nor learned to trust the Saviour's name?

2 "To all the world," to every place,
neighbours and friends and far-off lands,
preach the good news of saving grace;
go while the great commission stands.

3 "Whom shall I send?" Who hears the
call,
constant in prayer, through toil and pain,
telling of one who died for all,
to bring a lost world home again?

4 "Lord, here am I:" Your fire impart
to this poor cold self-centred soul;
touch but my lips, my hands, my heart,
and make a world for Christ my goal.

5 Spirit of love, within us move:
Spirit of truth, in power come down!
So shall they hear and find and prove
Christ is their life, their joy, their crown.

687 Chris Rolinson
© 1988 Kingsway's Thankyou Music

1 I want to serve You, Lord, in total
abandonment,
I want to yield my heart to You;
I want to give my life in all surrender,
I want to live for You alone.

2 I want to give my all in total
abandonment,
releasing all within my grasp;
I want to live my life in all its fullness,
I want to worship Christ alone.

3 I want to come to You in total
abandonment,
Lord, will You set my heart ablaze?
I want to love You with all my soul
and strength,
I want to give You all my days.

688 E.W. Blandy (b. 19th c.)

1 I can hear my Saviour calling,
   I can hear my Saviour calling,
   I can hear my Saviour calling,
   "Take thy cross and follow, follow Me!"

   Where He leads me I will follow,
   where He leads me I will follow,
   where He leads me I will follow,
   I'll go with Him, with Him all the way.

2 Though He lead through fiery trials,
   though He lead through fiery trials,
   though He lead through fiery trials,
   I'll go with Him, with Him, all the way.

3 He will give me grace and glory,
   He will give me grace and glory,
   He will give me grace and glory,
   and go with me, with me all the way.

689 J H Watson
        © Unidentified

1 I'm the property of Jesus,
   Satan has no right to me;
   for, to free me from his bondage,
   Jesus died on Calvary.

   Oh, I love, I love my Master,
   and I will not go out free.
   I am His today, for ever,
   His for all eternity.

2 I'm the property of Jesus;
   I no longer am my own;
   all my heart to Him is yielded,
   and He sits upon the throne.

3 I'm the property of Jesus;
   oh, what joy the knowledge brings!
   I belong to Christ the Saviour,
   Christ, who is the King of kings.

690 Sue Rinaldi/Steve Bassett © Word's Spirit of
        Praise Music/Admin. by Copycare

1 I'm yours, and I'm willing to stand,
   I'm yours, I am at your command;
   I'm yours, I want you to know
   that I will do anything for you.

2 I'm yours, I'm a soldier for you,
   I'm yours, show me what I can do;
   I'm yours, I want you to know
   that I will do anything for you.

   I want to work for you, my Lord,
   I want to make a difference in this
      world.
   I want to work for you, my Lord,
   I want to make a difference in this
      world.

3 I'm yours, and I'm willing to stand,
   I'm yours, I am at your command;
   I'm yours, I want you to know
   that I will do anything for you.

   I'm yours!

691 H G Smyth © Salvationist Publishing &
        Supplies/Admin. by Copycare

1 Is your life a channel of blessing?
   Is the love of God flowing through you?
   Are you telling the lost of the Saviour?
   Are you ready His service to do?

Make me a channel of blessing today,
make me a channel of blessing, I pray:
my life possessing, my service
 blessing,
make me a channel of blessing today.

2 Is your life a channel of blessing?
 Are you burdened for those that are lost?
 Have you urged upon those who are
  straying,
 the Saviour who died on the cross?

3 Is your life a channel of blessing?
 Is it daily telling for Him?
 Have you spoken the word of salvation
 To those who are dying in sin?

4 We cannot be channels of blessing
 if our lives are not free from all sin;
 we will barriers be and a hindrance
 to those we are trying to win.

692   Mary Brown v1/Charles E Prior vs 2 & 3 (d. 1927)

1 It may not be on the mountain's height,
 or over the stormy sea;
 it may not be at the battle's front
 my Lord will have need of me;
 but if by a still, small voice He calls
 to paths that I do not know,
 I'll answer, "Dear Lord, with my hand
  in Thine,
 I'll go where You want me to go."

 I'll go where You want me to go,
  dear Lord,
 over mountain, or plain, or sea;
 I'll say what You want me to say,
  dear Lord,
 I'll be what You want me to be.

2 Perhaps today there are loving words
 which Jesus would have me speak;
 there may be now in the paths of sin
 some wanderer whom I should seek;
 O Saviour, if Thou wilt be my guide,
 though dark and rugged the way,
 my voice shall echo the message sweet,
 I'll say what You want me to say.

3 There's surely somewhere a lowly
  place,
 in earth's harvest fields so wide,
 where I may labour through life's short
  day
 for Jesus the crucified.
 So trusting my all to Thy tender care,
 and knowing Thou lovest me,
 I'll do Thy will with a heart sincere,
 I'll be what You want me to be.

693   C F Alexander (1818-95)

1 Jesus calls us; o'er the tumult
 of our life's wild restless sea,
 day by day His sweet voice soundeth
 saying, "Christian, follow Me!"

2 As of old, apostles heard it
 by the Galilean lake,
 turned from home and toil and kindred,
 leaving all for His dear sake.

3 Jesus calls us from the worship
 of the vain world's golden store,
 from each idol that would keep us
 saying, "Christian, love Me more."

4 In our joys and in our sorrows,
 days of toil and hours of ease,
 still He calls, in cares and pleasures,
 "Christian, love Me more than these."

5   Jesus calls us! By Thy mercies,
     Saviour, may we hear Thy call,
     give our hearts to Thy obedience,
     serve and love Thee best of all.

694   Frances Ridley Havergal (1836-79)

1   Lord, speak to me, that I may speak
     in living echoes of Thy tone;
     as Thou hast sought, so let me seek
     Thy erring children lost and lone.

2   Oh, lead me, Lord, that I may lead
     the wandering and the wavering feet;
     oh, feed me, Lord, that I may feed
     Thy hungering ones with manna sweet.

3   Oh, strengthen me, that, while I stand
     firm on the Rock and strong in Thee,
     I may stretch out a loving hand
     to wrestlers with the troubled sea.

4   Oh, teach me, Lord, that I may teach
     the precious things Thou dost impart,
     and wing my words that they may reach
     the hidden depths of many a heart.

5   Oh, give Thine own sweet rest to me,
     that I may speak with soothing power
     a word in season, as from Thee,
     to weary ones in needful hour.

6   Oh, fill me with Thy fullness, Lord,
     until my very heart o'erflow
     in kindling thought and glowing word,
     Thy love to tell, Thy praise to show.

7   Oh, use me, Lord, use even me,
     just as Thou wilt, and when and where;
     until Thy blessed face I see,
     Thy rest, Thy joy, Thy glory share.

695   George Matheson (1842-1906)

1   Make me a captive, Lord,
     and then I shall be free;
     force me to render up my sword,
     and I shall conqueror be.
     I sink in life's alarms
     when by myself I stand;
     imprison me within Thine arms,
     and strong shall be my hand.

2   My heart is weak and poor
     until its master find;
     it has no spring of action sure,
     it varies with the wind.
     It cannot freely move,
     till Thou hast wrought its chain;
     enslave it with Thy matchless love,
     and deathless it shall reign.

3   My power is faint and low
     till I have learned to serve;
     it wants the needed fire to glow,
     it wants the breeze to nerve;
     it cannot drive the world,
     until itself be driven;
     its flag can only be unfurled
     when Thou shalt breathe from heaven.

4   My will is not my own
     till Thou hast made it Thine;
     if it would reach a monarch's throne
     it must its crown resign;
     it only stands unbent,
     amid the clashing strife,
     when on Thy bosom it has leant
     and found in Thee its life.

696 E C W Boulton
Copyright Control

1 Move me, dear Lord, and others I shall
move
to do Thy will;
mould Thou this life into a vessel fair
Thyself to fill;
no charm with which to draw do I
possess,
in Thee I find the secret of success.

2 O touch these yielded lips and through
them pour
Thy living thought;
I would not give to hungry souls the
words
that man hath taught;
shall they who seek the bread a stone
receive?
It is God's Word alone that can relieve.

3 How wonderful a channel thus to be,
to those forlorn,
a messenger of peace and joy and hope,
to them that mourn;
O grant that I Thy risen life may share,
the virtue of Thy name to others bear.

4 Under the anointing daily let me live,
a priest and king;
relying not on fleshly energy
Thy smile to win;
a simple soul in contact with my Lord,
in whom all fullness is forever stored.

5 O teach me, Lord, henceforth with Thee
to walk
in union deep;
whilst tending other souls not to neglect
my own to keep;
a separated soul unto the One
whose grace and love for me so much
hath done.

697 C C Luther
© Harper Collins Religious/Admin. by Copycare

1 Must I go and empty-handed,
Thus my dear Redeemer meet?
Not one day of service give Him,
Lay no trophy at His feet?

Must I go and empty-handed,
Must I meet my Saviour so?
Not one soul with which to greet Him,
Must I empty-handed go?

2 Not at death I shrink or falter,
for my Saviour saves me now;
but to meet Him empty-handed,
thought of that now clouds my brow.

3 Oh, the years of sinning wasted!
Could I but recall them now
I would give them to my Saviour;
to His will I gladly bow.

4 Oh, ye saints, arouse, be earnest!
Up and work while yet 'tis day;
ere the night of death o'ertake you,
strive for souls while yet you may.

698 J E Bode (1816-74)

1 O Jesus, I have promised
to serve Thee to the end;
be Thou for ever near me,
my Master and my Friend.
I shall not fear the battle
if Thou art by my side,
nor wander from the pathway
if Thou wilt be my Guide.

2 O let me feel Thee near me;
   the world is ever near;
   I see the sights that dazzle,
   the tempting sounds I hear;
   my foes are ever near me,
   around me and within;
   but, Jesus, draw Thou nearer,
   and shield my soul from sin.

3 O let me hear Thee speaking
   in accents clear and still,
   above the storms of passion,
   the murmurs of self-will;
   O speak to reassure me,
   to hasten or control;
   O speak, and make me listen,
   Thou guardian of my soul.

4 O Jesus, Thou hast promised,
   to all who follow Thee,
   that where Thou art in glory
   there shall Thy servant be;
   and, Jesus, I have promised
   to serve Thee to the end;
   O give me grace to follow
   my Master and my friend.

5 O let me see Thy foot-marks,
   and in them plant mine own;
   my hope to follow duly
   is in Thy strength alone;
   O guide me, call me, draw me,
   uphold me to the end;
   and then in heaven receive me,
   my Saviour and my friend!

699 Charles Wesley (1707-88)

1 O Thou who camest from above,
   the pure celestial fire to impart,
   kindle a flame of sacred love
   on the mean altar of my heart.

2 There let it for Thy glory burn
   with inextinguishable blaze;
   and trembling to its source return,
   in humble prayer and fervent praise.

3 Jesus, confirm my heart's desire
   to work, and speak, and think for Thee;
   still let me guard the holy fire,
   and still stir up Thy gift in me.

4 Ready for all Thy perfect will,
   my acts of faith and love repeat,
   till death Thy endless mercies seal
   and make the sacrifice complete.

700 © Unidentified

Lord crucified, give me a heart like Thine!
Teach me to love the souls of dying men,
and keep my heart in closest touch with
      Thee,
and give me love, pure Calvary love,
to bring the lost to Thee!

701 E E Rexford © Unidentified

1 Oh, where are the reapers that gather in
   the sheaves of the good from the fields
   of sin?
   With sickles of truth must the work be
   done,
   and no one may rest till the harvest
   home.

   Where are the reapers? Oh, who will
   *   come?*
   And share in the glory of the harvest
   *   home?*
   Oh, who will help us to gather in
   The sheaves of good from the fields of
   *   sin?*

2 Go out in the by-ways and search them
   all:
   the wheat may be there, though the
   weeds are tall;
   then search in the highway, and pass
   none by,
   but gather from all for the home on high.

3 The fields are all ripening, and far and
   wide
   the world is awaiting the harvest tide;
   but reapers are few, and the work is
   great,
   and much will be lost should the
   harvest wait.

4
   So come with your sickles, ye sons of
   men,
   and gather together the golden grain;
   toil on till the Lord of the harvest come,
   then share in the joy of the harvest
   home.

702 F Kirkland
© Unidentified

1 Out in the darkness,
   shadowed by sin,
   souls are in bondage,
   souls we would win.
   How can we win them?
   How show the way?
   Love never faileth,
   love is the way;
   love never faileth,
   love is the way.

2 Think how the Master
   came from above,
   suffered on Calvary,
   breathing out love;
   think how He loves us,

e'en when we stray.
We must love others,
love is the way;
we must love others,
love is His way.

3 See, they are waiting,
   looking at you,
   furtively watching
   all that you do:
   seeming so careless,
   hardened and lost.
   Love never faileth,
   count not the cost;
   love never faileth,
   count not the cost.

4 Love never faileth,
   love is pure gold;
   love is what Jesus
   came to unfold;
   make us more loving,
   Master, we pray,
   help us remember
   love is Thy way;
   help us remember
   love is Thy way.

703 Francis Jane van Alstyne (1820-1915)
(Fanny J Crosby)

1 Rescue the perishing, care for the
   dying,
   snatch them in pity from sin and the
   grave:
   weep o'er the erring one, lift up the
   fallen,
   tell them of Jesus, the mighty to save.

Rescue the perishing, care for the
dying;
Jesus is merciful, Jesus will save.

2 Though they are slighting Him, still
He is waiting,
waiting the penitent child to receive.
Plead with them earnestly, plead with
them gently:
He will forgive if they only believe.

3 Down in the human heart, crushed
by the tempter,
feelings lie buried that grace can restore:
touched by a loving hand, wakened by
kindness,
chords that were broken will vibrate
once more.

4 Rescue the perishing, duty demands it!
Strength for thy labour the Lord will
provide;
back to the narrow way patiently win
them;
tell the poor wanderer a Saviour has
died.

704 Elisha A Hoffman (1839-1929) © Unidentified

1 Send me forth, oh, blessed Master,
where are souls in sorrow bowed;
send me forth to homes of want and
homes of care;
and with joy I will obey the call,
and in Thy blessed name
I will take the blessed light of the
gospel there.

Call me forth...to active service,
and my prompt response shall be,
"Here am I! send me."
I am ready to report for orders,
Master, summon me,
and I'll go on any errand of love for
Thee.

2 There are lives that may be brightened
by a word of hope and cheer,
there are souls with whom life's
blessings I should share,
there are hearts that may be lightened
of the burdens which they bear;
let me take the blessed hope of the
gospel there.

3 There is work within the vineyard,
there is service to be done,
there's a message of salvation to declare;
send me forth to tell the story to the
hearts of sinful men;
let me take the blessed Christ of the
gospel there.

4 Oh, I would not be an idler in the
vineyard of the Lord;
with the Christ the vineyard labour I
would share;
into hearts that know not Jesus I
would speak the saving word;
let me take the blessed joy of the
gospel there.

705 A B Simpson (1843-1919)

1 Send the gospel of salvation,
to a world of dying men;
tell it out to every nation,
'til the Lord shall come again.

Go and tell them, go and tell
them,
Jesus died for sinful men.
Go and tell them, go and tell
them,
He is coming, He is coming,
He is coming back again.

2 'Tis the church's great commission,
   'tis the Master's last command;
   Christ has died for every creature,
   tell it out in every land.

3 Christ is gathering out a people
   to His name from every race;
   haste to give the invitation
   ere shall end the day of grace.

4 Give the gospel as a witness
   to a world of sinful men;
   till the Bride shall be completed,
   and the Lord shall come again.

706 Margaret E Clarkson
© Singspiration Music/Brentwood Benson
Music Publishing Inc./Admin. by Copycare

1 So send I you to labour unrewarded,
   to serve unpaid, unloved, unsought,
   unknown,
      to bear rebuke, to suffer scorn and
      scoffing,
   so send I you, to toil for Me alone.

2 So send I you to bind the bruised
   and broken,
      o'er wandering souls to work, to
      weep, to wake,
   to bear the burdens of a world aweary,
   so send I you, to suffer for My sake.

3 So send I you to loneliness and
   longing,
   with heart a-hungering for the
   loved and known,
   forsaking home and kindred,
   friend and dear one,
   so send I you, to know My love alone.

4 So send I you to leave your life's
   ambition,
   to die to dear desire, self-will resign,
   to labour long
   and love where men revile you,
   so send I you,
   to lose your life in Mine.

5 So send I you to hearts made hard
   by hatred,
   to eyes made blind because they
   will not see,
   to spend, though it be blood,
   to spend and spare not,
   so send I you, to taste of Calvary.

   "As the Father hath sent Me,
   so send I you."

707 Knowles Shaw (1834-78)

1 Sowing in the morning, sowing
   seeds of kindness,
   sowing in the noon-tide and the
   dewy eves;
   waiting for the harvest and the
   time of reaping,
   we shall come rejoicing, bringing
   in the sheaves.

Bringing in the sheaves,
bringing in the sheaves,
we shall come rejoicing,
bringing in the sheaves.
Bringing in the sheaves,
bringing in the sheaves,
we shall come rejoicing,
bringing in the sheaves.

2 Sowing in the sunshine, sowing
     in the shadows,
   fearing neither clouds nor winter's
     chilling breeze;
   by and by the harvest and the
     labour ended,
   we shall come rejoicing, bringing
     in the sheaves.

3 Go, then, ever weeping, sowing
     for the Master,
   though the loss sustained our
     spirit often grieves;
   when our weeping's over, He will
     bid us welcome,
   we shall come rejoicing, bringing
     in the sheaves.

708   Katherine O Barker © Unidentified

1 Speak just a word for Jesus,
   tell how He died for you,
   often repeat the story,
   wonderful, glad and true!

   Speak just a word,
   ever to Him be true;
   speak just a word,
   tell what He's doing for you!

2 Speak just a word for Jesus,
   tell how He helps you live,
   tell of the strength and comfort
   which He will freely give!

3 Speak just a word for Jesus,
   do not for others wait;
   gladly proclaim the message
   ere it shall be too late!

4 Speak just a word for Jesus,
   why should you doubt or fear?
   Surely His love will bless it;
   some one will gladly hear.

5 Speak just a word for Jesus,
   tell of His love for men!
   Some one distressed may listen,
   willing to trust Him then.

709   Charles Gabriel (1858-1932)
© Word Music (UK)/The Rodeheaver Co/
Admin. by Copycare

1 There's a call comes ringing o'er
     the restless wave,
   send the light! send the light!
   There are souls to rescue, there
     are souls to save,
   send the light! send the light!

   Send the light, the blessed
     gospel light.
   Let it shine from shore to shore!
   Send the light! and let its
     radiant beams
   light the world for evermore.

2 We have heard the Macedonian
     call today,
   and a golden offering at the cross
     we lay.

3 Let us pray that grace may
     everywhere abound,
   and a Christ-like spirit
     everywhere be found.

4 Let us not grow weary in the work
   of love,
  let us gather jewels for a crown
   above.

710 E Yale © The Rodeheaver/Word Music/Admin.
by Copycare

1 There's a work for Jesus,
  ready at your hand,
  'tis a task the Master
  just for you has planned.
  Haste to do His bidding,
  yield Him service true;
  there's a work for Jesus
  none but you can do.

> *Work for Jesus, day by day,*
> *serve Him ever, falter never,*
>   *Christ obey.*
> *Yield Him service, loyal, true;*
> *there's a work for Jesus none*
>   *but you can do.*

2 There's a work for Jesus,
  humble though it be,
  'tis the very service
  He would ask of thee.
  Go where fields are whitened,
  and the labourers few;
  there's a work for Jesus
  none but you can do.

3 There's a work for Jesus,
  precious souls to bring,
  tell them of His mercies,
  tell them of your King.
  Faint not, grow not weary,
  He will strength renew;
  there's a work for Jesus
  none but you can do.

711 Anon
© Unidentified

1 Thou hast snapped my fetters;
  Thou hast made me free.
  Liberty and gladness I have found
   in Thee,
  liberty from bondage, from my
   weary load,
  Satan's slave no longer, now a
   child of God!

> *I am Thine Lord Jesus, ever*
>   *Thine, Thine I am,*
> *and my heart is singing,*
>   *"Glory to the Lamb."*

2 Living in the sunshine, shining
  in Thy light,
  fighting as Thy soldier, mighty in
   Thy might;
  going on Thy mission,
  pointing men to Thee,
  telling of the Saviour who can
  set them free.

3 Such the life, Lord Jesus, I would
   ever live,
  such the grateful tribute I would
   ever give;
  witnessing for Thee, Lord,
  everywhere I go,
  of the Blood that cleanseth,
  washing white as snow.

4 And when life is ended, when
  the victory's won,
  when I hear from Thee, Lord, the
   glad words, "Well done",
  with what joy and rapture shall I
   sing of Thee,
  who from sin's dark chains didst
   set my spirit free!

712 H E Govan (1866-1932)
© The Faith Mission

1 We have answered the summons
   and joined in the fight;
we are soldiers in battle for God
   and the right;
with our Captain to lead us we
   fear not the foe,
for His strength is sufficient to
carry us through.

We shall win! we shall win!
We shall win! we shall win!
We will trust! We will pray!
And battle for the Lord our King.

2 Though the night may be dark
   and the fight may be long,
yet the tumult of warfare shall
   change into song
when the strongholds of darkness
   and evil shall fall,
and our Lord shall be conqueror
   and reign over all.

3 See the millions that stray from
   the way of the Lord,
caring nought for His wrath and
   defying His word,
casting scorn on our Saviour,
   despising His blood!
Will you not, then, enlist in the
battle for God?

4 Come and join in the fight!
There are foes you must meet;
there are rebels and scoffers to
   bring to His feet;
there is work for you all, and
your strength is secure;
there's a crown for the victor,
and victory is sure.

713 Colin Sterne (1862-1926)

1 We've a story to tell to the nations,
that shall turn their hearts to the
   right;
a story of truth and sweetness,
a story of peace and light,
a story of peace and light:

   For the darkness shall turn to
     dawning,
   and the dawning to noon-day
     bright,
   and Christ's great kingdom
     shall come on earth,
   the kingdom of love and light.

2 We've a song to be sung to the
   nations,
that shall lift their hearts to the
   Lord;
a song that shall conquer evil,
and shatter the spear and sword,
and shatter the spear and sword:

3 We've a message to give to the
   nations,
that the Lord who reigneth above
hath sent us His Son to save us,
and show us that God is love,
and show us that God is love:

4 We've a Saviour to show to the
   nations,
who the path of sorrow has trod,
that all of the world's great
   peoples,
might come to the truth of God,
might come to the truth of God:

714 © Colin N. Peckham

1 "Whom shall I send?" the prophet
    heard
   when he, enraptured, saw the
    Lord;
   He rose and went, his spirit stirred,
   "Whom shall I send today?"

   "Whom shall I send?" O hear the cry!
   "Whom shall I send?" from sky to sky!
   "Whom shall I send to bring men nigh?
   Whom shall I send, Whom shall I send,
   Whom shall I send today?"

2 Do the bright youth no longer
    care?
   Do they not see the treasures rare?
   Where are they then, O where,
    O where?
   "Whom shall I send today?"

3 Following far they hear no call!
   Sleeping so sound while millions
    fall!
   Do they not care at all, at all?
   "Whom shall I send today?"

4 "Whom shall I send?" O who will
    go?
   Who then will preach with a voice
    of woe?
   Who will be sped by love's strong
    bow?
   "May I send you today?"

   Lord of the harvest, here am I,
   I can no more resist Thy cry -
   cost what it may: to live or die.
   Send me, dear Lord, today.

715 Danny Daniels/Randy Rigby
© 1982 Mercy/Vineyard Publishing/Music
Services/Admin. by Copycare

You are the Vine, we are the branches,
keep us abiding in You.
You are the Vine, we are the branches,
keep us abiding in You.
Then we'll grow in Your love,
then we'll go in Your name,
that the world will surely know
that You have power to heal and to save.
You are the Vine, we are the branches,
keep us abiding in You.

716 E M Govan (1898-1983)
© The Faith Mission

1 You ask me why I see no charm nor
    glory
   in this world's pleasures or its
    wealth and fame?
   And why I love that Galilean story
   of One who died upon a cross of
    shame?
   It is because my soul hath known
    her sinning,
   the grief and darkness of that cry
    "undone,"
   and at that Cross has found a new
    beginning,
   life through the death of that dear
    dying One.

2 You ask me why I find no rest nor
    gladness
   in paths where selfish ease would
    while my hours?
   And why I toil where hearts in
    bitter sadness
   lie crushed beneath sin's fierce
    o'erwhelming powers?

It is because I know life's thread
is slender,
but one short hour, one little stretch
of road.
Then yearns my heart with love
divinely tender,
to seek the lost and bring them
home to God.

3   You ask me why what gifts I
have, what graces
are poured an offering at His holy
feet,
and why I brave the cold
contemptuous faces
of those who love this world and
find it sweet?
It is because I see a distant
morning
when stand God's sons around
His jasper throne;
I see bright crowns those holy
brows adorning,
and I, too, long to hear my
Lord's "Well done."

717   Priscilia Owens (1829-1907)

1   We have heard the joyful sound,
Jesus saves;
spread the gladness all around,
Jesus saves;
bear the news to every land,
climb the steeps and cross the
waves,
onward, 'tis our Lord's command,
Jesus saves.

2   Waft it on the rolling tide,
tell to sinners far and wide,
sing, ye islands of the sea,
echo back, ye ocean caves,
earth shall keep her jubilee,
Jesus saves.

3   Sing above the battle's strife,
by His death and endless life,
sing it softly through the gloom,
when the heart for mercy craves,
sing in triumph o'er the tomb,
Jesus saves.

4   Give the winds a mighty voice,
let the nations now rejoice,
shout salvation full and free,
highest hills and deepest caves,
this our song of victory,
Jesus saves.

718   John Chisum and George Searcy © 1993
Integrity's Praise! Music/Adm. by Kingsway's
Thankyou Music

Our heart, our desire,
is to see the nations worship,
our cry, our prayer,
is to sing Your praise to the ends of the
earth;
that with one mighty voice
every tribe and tongue rejoices,
our heart, our desire,
is to see the nations worship You.

Heavenly Father, Your mercy showers
down upon Your people,
every race upon this earth;
may your Spirit pierce the darkness,
may it break the chains of death upon us,
let us rise in honest worship,
to declare Your matchless worth.

12   CHILDREN

719 Philip P Bliss (1838-76)

1 Standing by a purpose true,
heeding God's command,
honour them the faithful few
all hail to Daniel's band.
 Dare to be a Daniel!
 Dare to stand alone!
 Dare to have a purpose firm!
 Dare to make it known.

2 Many mighty men are lost,
daring not to stand,
who for God had been a host
by joining Daniel's band.

3 Many giants, great and small,
stalking through the land,
headlong to the earth would fall,
if met by Daniel's band.

4 Hold the gospel banner high!
On to victory grand!
Satan and his host defy,
and shout for Daniel's band!

720 Karen Lafferty
© 1981 Maranatha! Music/Admin. by Copycare

Don't build your house on the sandy land,
don't build it too near the shore.
Well, it might look kind of nice,
but you'll have to build it twice,
oh, you'll have to build your house once
 more.
You better build your house upon a rock,
make a good foundation on a solid spot.
Oh, storms may come and go,
but the peace of God you will know.
 { *Rock of ages cleft for me,* }
 { *let me hide myself in Thee.* }

721 Mrs H S Lehman
© Singspiration Music/Brentwood Benson
Music Publishing Inc./Admin. by Copycare

1 Do you know that you've
 been born again?
 Do you know that you've
 been born again?
 Does the Spirit dwell within,
 bearing witness that you've been
 cleansed from ev'ry sin and stain?
 Are you ready if the Lord should come,
 or today your soul should claim?
 Can you face eternal years free from
 doubt and dread and fears?
 Do you know, know, know, that
 you've been born again?

2 Yes, I know that I've been born again.
 Yes, I know that I've been born again.
 For the Spirit dwells within, bearing
 witness that I've been
 cleansed from ev'ry sin and stain;
 I am ready if the Lord should come,
 or today my soul should claim;
 I can face eternal years free from
 doubt and dread and fears.
 Yes, I know, know, know, that I've
 been born again!

722 Frances Towle Rath
© 1974 Child Evangelism Fellowship

Did you ever talk to God above?
Tell Him that you need a friend to
 love.
Pray in Jesus' name believing that
 God answers prayer.
Have you told Him all your cares
 and woes?
Ev'ry tiny little fear He knows.
You can know He'll always hear
 and He will answer prayer.

You can whisper in a crowd to Him.
You can cry when you're alone to Him.
You don't have to pray out loud to Him;
He knows your thoughts.
On a lofty mountain peak He's there.
In a meadow by a stream, He's there.
Anywhere on earth you go, He's
been there from the start.
Find the answer in His Word; it's true.
You'll be strong because He walks
with you.
By His faithfulness He'll change
you too.
God answers prayer.

723 Mrs W. B. Liggett
© 1947, 1975 Child Evangelism Fellowship Press

Faith is just believing what God says He
will do;
He will never fail us; His promises
are true.
If we but receive Him, His children we
become; Faith is just
believing this wondrous thing is done.

724 Philip Paul Bliss (1838-76)

1 I am so glad that our Father in heaven
tells of His love in the Book He has
given:
wonderful things in the Bible I see:
this is the dearest, that Jesus loves me.

I am so glad that Jesus loves me,
Jesus loves me, Jesus loves me.
I am so glad that Jesus loves me,
Jesus loves even me.

2 Jesus loves me and I know I love Him;
love brought Him down my lost soul
to redeem,
yes, it was love made Him die on the
tree;
oh, I am certain that Jesus loves me!

3 In this assurance I find sweetest rest,
trusting in Jesus I know I am blest;
Satan, dismayed, from my soul now
doth flee,
when I just tell him that Jesus loves me.

4 Oh, if there's only one song I can sing,
when in His beauty I see the great King,
this shall my song in eternity be,
"Oh, what a wonder that Jesus loves
me!"

725 Vern Stromberg
© Unidentified

1 I have a precious Book, it's the
Word of God.
It's the only Book that God has giv'n.
As I read, God speaks to me,
I see Christ and Calvary.
The wonderful Word of God.

2 Forever it will stand as the ages roll,
It's the living and eternal Word.
It's my guiding light each day,
and without it I would stray;
The Wonderful Word of God.

3 Dear Lord may I each day read
Thy precious Word.
May I love it and obey it too.
May I grow to be like Thee.
May my friends see Christ in me.
In Jesus' Name, Amen.

726 Anna Bartlett Warner (1820-1915)

1 Jesus loves me! this I know,
   for the Bible tells me so;
   little ones to Him belong;
   they are weak, but He is strong.

   Yes, Jesus loves me!
   Yes, Jesus loves me!
   Yes, Jesus loves me!
   The Bible tells me so!

2 Jesus loves me! He who died
   Heaven's gates to open wide:
   He will wash away my sin,
   let His little child come in.

3 Jesus loves me! He will stay
   close beside me all the way:
   if I love Him, when I die
   He will take me home on high.

727 © Unidentified

1 Mirrors hanging in their place
   show the dirt upon my face.
   God's Word shows me that within
   I am deeply stained with sin.

   I love the Bible, I love the Bible,
   I love the Bible, it is the Word of God.

2 Milk is good for babies small
   and for grown-ups, great and tall.
   Milk is likened to God's Word,
   helps me grow to please the Lord.

3 After dark we take a light,
   making daylight out of night.
   If we read God's Word each day,
   it will guide us on our way.

4 Satan is my enemy
   but he runs away from me,
   if I use the Spirit's sword.
   Great and mighty is God's Word.

728 Larry Mayfield
        © 1974 Child Evangelism Fellowship Press

1 Don't be afraid, Jesus is watching you.
   In the dark night, He is protecting you.
   Talk to the Lord, ask Him to make
      you brave;
   Jesus will hear when you pray.

   Jesus is caring for you;
   Jesus is helping you too.
   Jesus is always there keeping you
   for He loves you;
   Jesus is caring for you;
   Jesus is helping you too.
   Jesus is with you whatever you do.

2 You're not alone, Jesus is there
      with you.
   He can't be seen, but He is there, it's true.
   He is your friend, He'll keep you in
      His care.
   He goes with you ev'rywhere.

729 Mike and Ruth Green
        © 1977 Majesty Music Inc.

1 Obedience is the very best way to show
      that you believe.
   Doing exactly as the Lord commands,
      doing it happily.
   Action is the key, do it immediately, joy
      you will receive.
   Obedience is the very best way to show
      that you believe.
   O-B-E-D-I-E-N-C-E.
   Obedience is the very best way to show
      that you believe.

2   We want to live pure, we want to live
     clean, we want to do our best.
  Sweetly submitting to authority, leaving
    to God the rest.
  Walking in the light, keeping our
  attitude right, on the narrow way.
  For if we believe the Word we receive,
    we always will obey.
  O-B-E-D-I-E-N-C-E.
  Obedience is the very best way to show
    that you believe.

730   Albert Midlane (1825-1909)

1   There's a Friend for little children
  above the bright blue sky,
  a Friend that never changes,
  whose love will never die:
  unlike our friends by nature,
  who change with changing years,
  this Friend is always worthy
  the precious name He bears.

2   There's a rest for little children
  above the bright blue sky,
  who love the blessed Saviour,
  and to His Father cry:
  a rest from every trouble,
  from sin and danger free;
  there every little pilgrim
  shall rest eternally.

3   There's a home for little children
  above the bright blue sky,
  where Jesus reigns in glory,
  a home of peace and joy:
  no home on earth is like it,
  or can with it compare,
  for every one is happy,
  nor can be happier there.

4   There's a crown for little children
  above the bright blue sky,
  and all who look to Jesus
  shall wear it by and by:
  a crown of brightest glory,
  which He shall sure bestow
  on all who love the Saviour,
  and walk with Him below.

5   There's a song for little children
  above the bright blue sky,
  and a harp of sweetest music
  for their hymn of victory;
  and all above is treasured
  and found in Christ alone;
  O come, dear little children,
  that all may be your own!

731   John Nixon
© 1978 European Child Evangelism
Fellowship

Oh, who can please the Holy One,
  who can God's ten commands obey?
Besides me you shall have no god,
nor turn to images to pray.
God's Holy Name, use not in vain,
and keep for Him the Sabbath day.
Honour your parents, you shall not kill,
you shall not commit adultery.
You shall not steal, you shall not lie,
nor covet life your neighbour's way.
We all have failed to keep this law,
but God in love has made a way;
that sinful man could be forgiven,
the Christ who lives for us did die.
Trust Jesus to forgive your sins,
  then by His power God's law obey.

732 Jemima Luke (1813-1906)

1 I think when I read that sweet
   story of old,
   when Jesus was here among men,
   how He called little children as lambs
      to His fold,
   I should like to have been with Him then.
   I wish that His hands had been placed
      on my head,
   That His arms had been thrown around
      me,
   and that I might have seen His kind look
      when He said,
   "Let little children come unto Me."

2 Yet still to His footstool in prayer I may
      go,
   and ask for a share of His love;
   and, if I now earnestly seek Him below,
   I shall see Him and hear Him above
   in that beautiful place He has gone to
      prepare
   for all who are washed and forgiven;
   and many dear children are gathering
      there,
   for of such is the kingdom of heaven.

3 But thousands and thousands who
      wander and fall
   never heard of that heavenly home;
   I should like them to know there is room
      for them all,
   and that Jesus has bid them to come.
   I long for the joy of that glorious day,
   the fairest and brightest and best,
   when the dear little children of every
      clime,
   shall crowd to His arms and be blest.

SCRIPTURE INDEX

Reference	Songs			
Heb. 13:15	46			
James 1:2	459			
James 2:5	13			
James 2:19	109 481			
James 4:8	553			
James 4:9	554			
James 4:14	312			
1 Pet. 1:6	450			
1 Pet. 1:8	32 492			
1 Pet. 1:10-12	249			
1 Pet. 1:15	567 671			
1 Pet. 1:15-16	564			
1 Pet. 1:18-19	276 646			
1 Pet. 1:19-20	174			
1 Pet. 1:25	248			
1 Pet. 2:2	727			
1 Pet. 2:6	255 258			
1 Pet. 2:7	502			
1 Pet. 2:9	381			
1 Pet. 2:11	486			
1 Pet. 2:24-25	157 189 191 586 681			
1 Pet. 4:12	450 451			
1 Pet. 5:4	232 483			
1 Pet. 5:7	35 469 529 532			
2 Pet. 1:4	250			
2 Pet. 1:17	111			
2 Pet. 1:19	53			
2 Pet. 1:21	247 725			
2 Pet. 3:8	70			
2 Pet. 3:18	411 601			

Reference	Songs		
1 Jn. 1:5-7	83		
1 Jn. 1:7	36 277 339 360 531 600 603		
1 Jn. 1:7-9	169 636		
1 Jn. 1:9	323 324 329		
1 Jn. 2:1	169		
1 Jn. 2:8	399		
1 Jn. 2:15	363 581		
1 Jn. 3:1	282		
1 Jn. 3:2	599		
1 Jn. 3:5	54		
1 Jn. 3:6	344		
1 Jn. 3:8	157		
1 Jn. 4:4	215		
1 Jn. 4:7	594		
1 Jn. 4:10	283 303 625		
1 Jn. 4:14	159		
1 Jn. 4:19	18 32 507		
1 Jn. 5:4-5	471		
1 Jn. 5:21	519		
Jude 21	498		
Jude 25	115		
Rev. 1:5	207 216 219 629		
Rev. 1:6	111		
Rev. 1:7	227		
Rev. 1:8	9 68		
Rev. 1:13	64		
Rev. 1:14-18	199		
Rev. 1:18	117 594		
Rev. 3:7	150		
Rev. 3:20	301 303 309 568		
Rev. 3:21	483		
Rev. 4:8	82		

Reference	Songs			
Rev. 4:6	376			
Rev. 4:8	9 77			
Rev. 4:10	228			
Rev. 4:10-11	87			
Rev. 4:11	124 125 131			
Rev. 5:8	541			
Rev. 5:9	36 45 191 296 360 542 718			
Rev. 5:11-13	27 86 89 90 94 111 125 129 130 131 198 214 233			
Rev. 7:9, 14	479			
Rev. 7:9-12	52			
Rev. 7:14	229			
Rev. 11:15	117 159 230			
Rev. 12:10-11	157			
Rev. 12:11	323			
Rev. 14:3	355			
Rev. 14:13	542			
Rev. 14:15	223			
Rev. 17:14	1 215 217 218			
Rev. 19:1	7 81			
Rev. 19:6-7	14			
Rev. 19:12	90 228			
Rev. 19:12, 16	217 218			
Rev. 19:12-15	88			
Rev. 19:16	1 10			
Rev. 20:11-15	325			
Rev. 21:2	257			
Rev. 21:4	229 538			
Rev. 21:22-26	537			
Rev. 22:4	163 222 534			
Rev. 22:12	232			
Rev. 22:16	53			
Rev. 22:17	236			

TOPICAL INDEX

INDEX OF FIRST LINES

(Some refrains included in italics)

Songs Of Victory

METRICAL PSALMS

COPYRIGHT ADDRESSES

African Evangelical Fellowship
6 Station Approach,
Borough Green,
Sevenoaks,
Kent, TN15 8AD

Carlin Music Corporation
Iron Bridge House,
3 Bridge Approach,
Chalk Farm,
London, NW1 8BD

Kay Chance
Glaubenszentrum
3353 Bad Gandershelm,
Germany

Chatto & Windus
Random House UK Ltd.,
20 Vauxhall Bridge Road,
London SW1V 2SA, UK

Chester Music Limited
8/9 Frith Street,
London W1V 5TZ

Child Evangelism Fellowship
c/o The Harry Fox Agency Inc.
711 Third Avenue,
8th Floor, New York,
NY10017, U.S.A.

Child Evangelism Fellowship (Europe)
Kilchzimmer, CH4438,
Langenbruck ,
Switzerland.

Copycare
P.O Box 77 Hailsham,
East Sussex BN27 3EF UK

Daybreak Music Limited
Silverdale Road,
Eastbourne,
East Sussex, BN20 7AB, UK.

Timothy Dudley-Smith
9 Ashlands, Ford,
Salisbury, Wilts.
SP4 6DY, UK

Empire Music Limited
c/o Polygram Music Publishing Limited,
Bond House,
347-353 Chiswick High Rd.
London, W4 4HS

The Faith Mission
Govan House,
2 Drum Street,
Edinburgh, EH17 8QG, UK

Gabriel Music
66 Melbourne Way,
Bush Hill Park,
Enfield,
Middlesex, EN1 1XQ UK

Wild Goose Resource Group
Iona Community,
840 Govan Road,
Glasgow, G51 3UU, UK

Gospel Publishing House
1445 Boonville Avenue,
Springfield,
MS 65802 USA

Evangelist Noel Grant
"Hebron"
581 Belfast Road,
Bangor,
Co. Down, BT19 1UD, UK

William V Higham
58 King George V Drive,
Heath,
Cardiff,
South Glamorgan, CF4 4EF, UK

P Horrobin
Ellel Grange, Ellel,
Nr. Lancaster,
LA2 0HN, UK

Japan Evangelistic Band
275 London Road,
North End,
Portsmouth, PO2 9HE, UK

Jubilate Hymns
4 Thorn Park Road,
Chelston,
Torquay,
Devon, TQ2 6RX

Kingsway's Thank You Music
P.O. Box 75,
Eastbourne,
East Sussex BN23 6NW UK

G Leavers
1 Haws Hill,
Carnforth,
Lancashire LA5 9DD, UK

Makeway Music
P.O. Box 263,
Croydon, CR9 5AP, U.K.

Majesty Music Inc.
P.O. Box 6524,
Greenville, SC 29606 U.S.A.

MCA Music Limited
77 Fulham Palace Road,
London, W6

Music Sales Limited.
8-9 Frith Street,
London, W1V 5TZ

OMF International
Station Approach,
Borough Green,
Sevenoaks,
Kent. TH15 8BG

Colin N Peckham
c/o The Faith Mission,
Bible College,
2 Drum Street,
Edinburgh EH17 8QG

Colin M Peckham
c/o Carrubbers Christian Centre,
65 High Street,
Edinburgh, EH1 1SR, UK

Restoration Music Limited
P.O. Box 356,
Leighton Buzzard,
Beds. LU7 8WP, UK.

Scripture Gift Mission
Radstock House,
3 Eccleston Street,
London, SW1W 9LZ, UK

Scripture Union
207-209 Queensway,
Blecthley,
Milton Keynes, MK2 2EB. UK

Sovereign Lifestyle Music
P.O. Box 356,
Leighton Buzzard,
Beds, LU7 8WP, UK

Young Life
Spring Cottage,
Spring Road,
Leeds, LS6 1AD